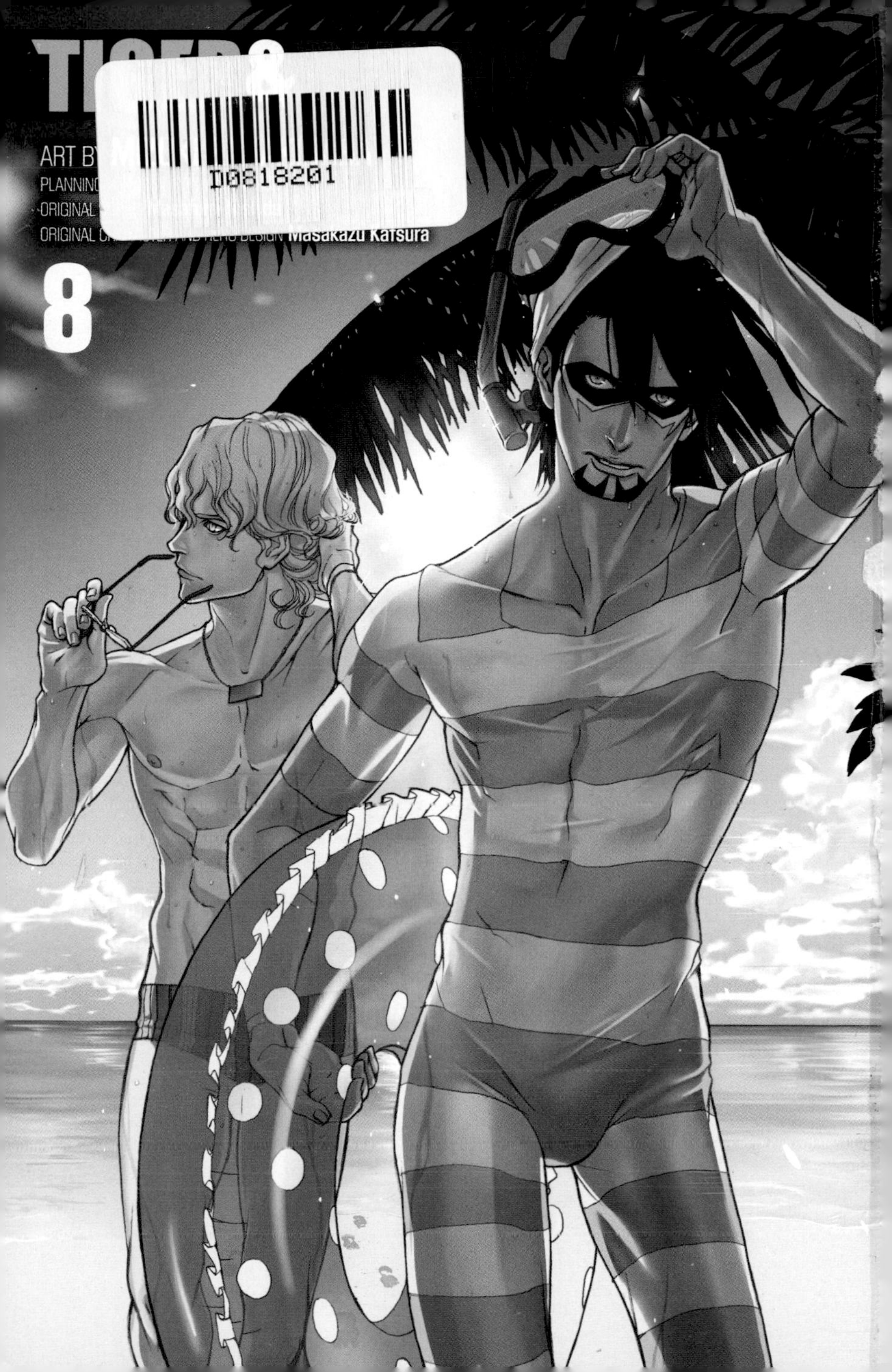
ART BY
PLANNING
ORIGINAL
ORIGINAL CHARACTER AND HERO DESIGN Masakazu Katsura
8

宝

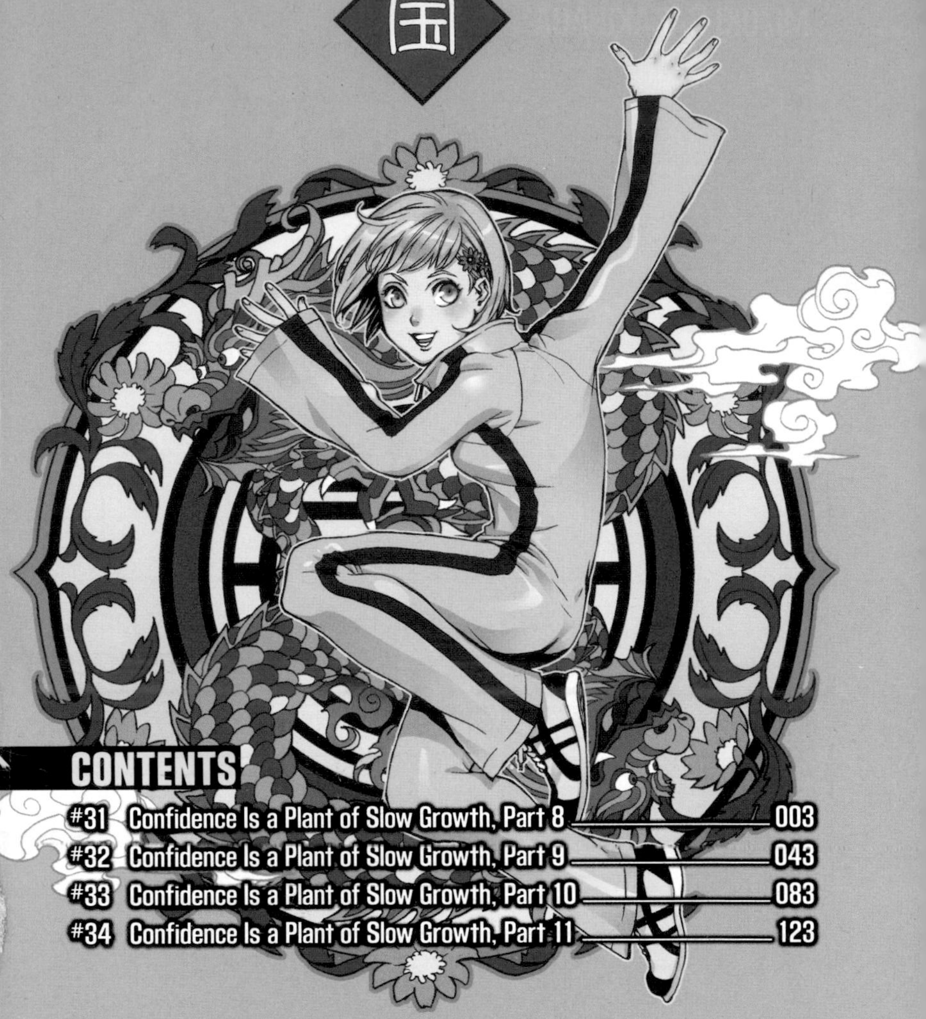

CONTENTS

鈴

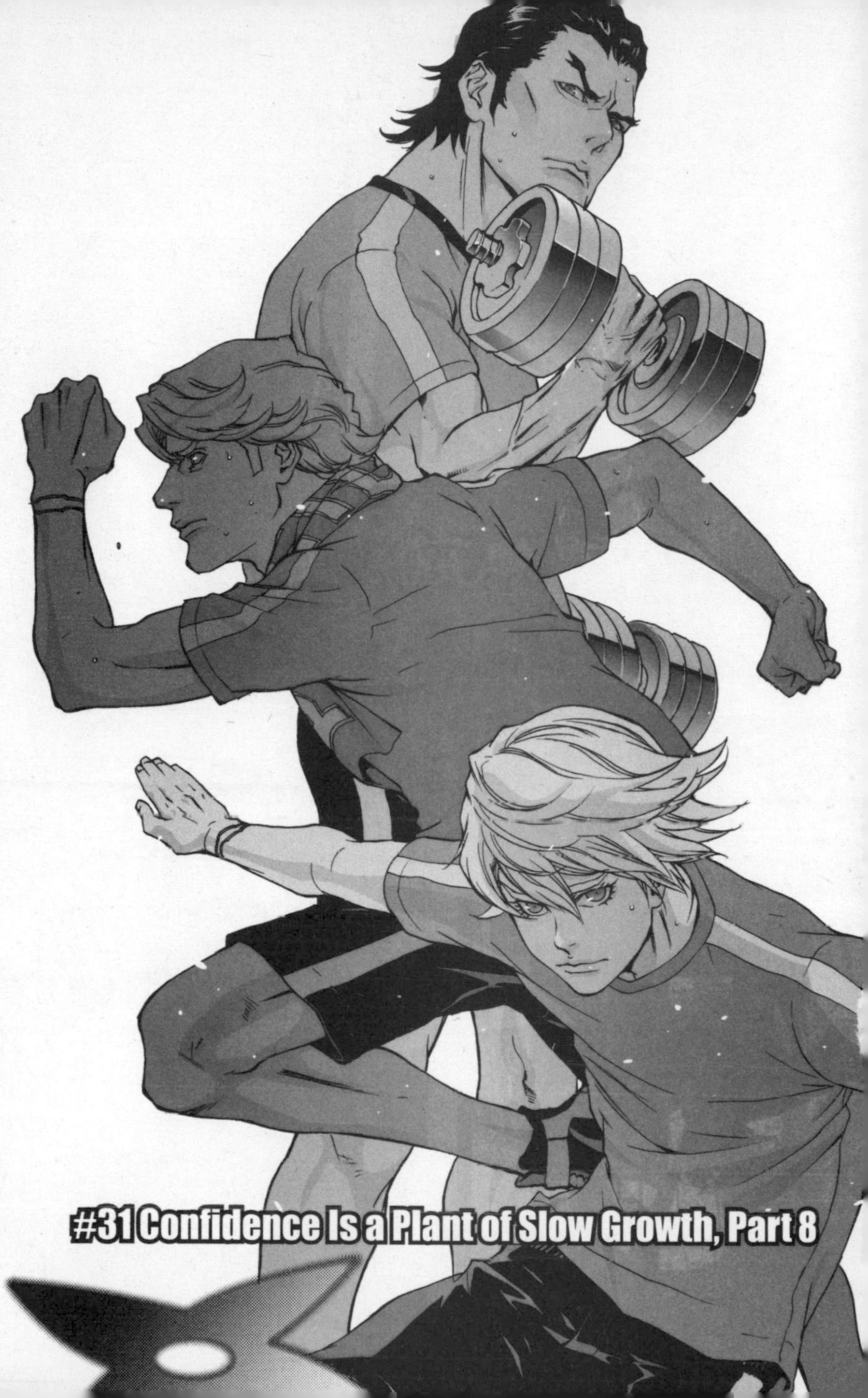
#31 Confidence Is a Plant of Slow Growth, Part 8

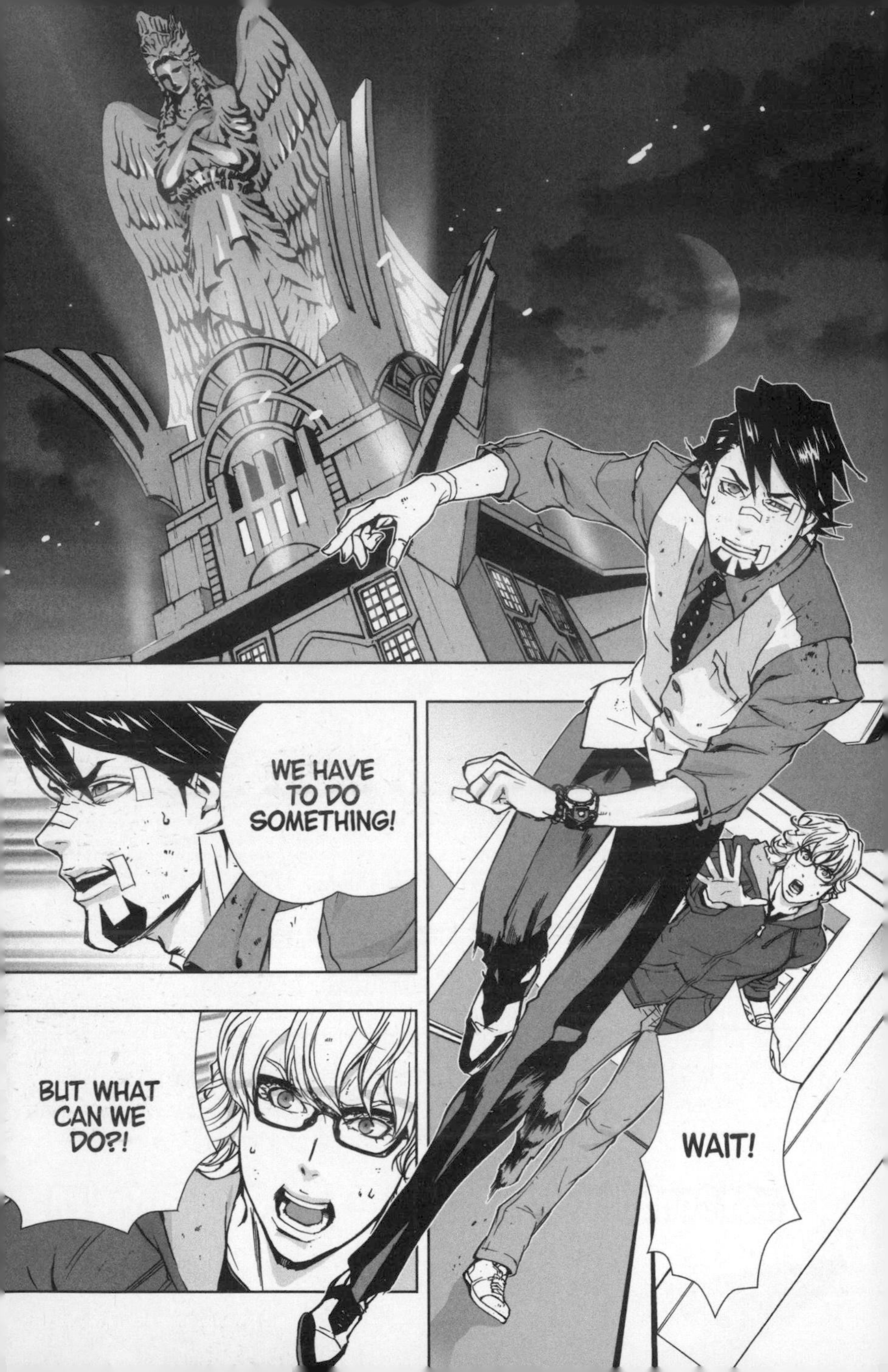
WAIT!
WE HAVE TO DO SOMETHING!
BUT WHAT CAN WE DO?!

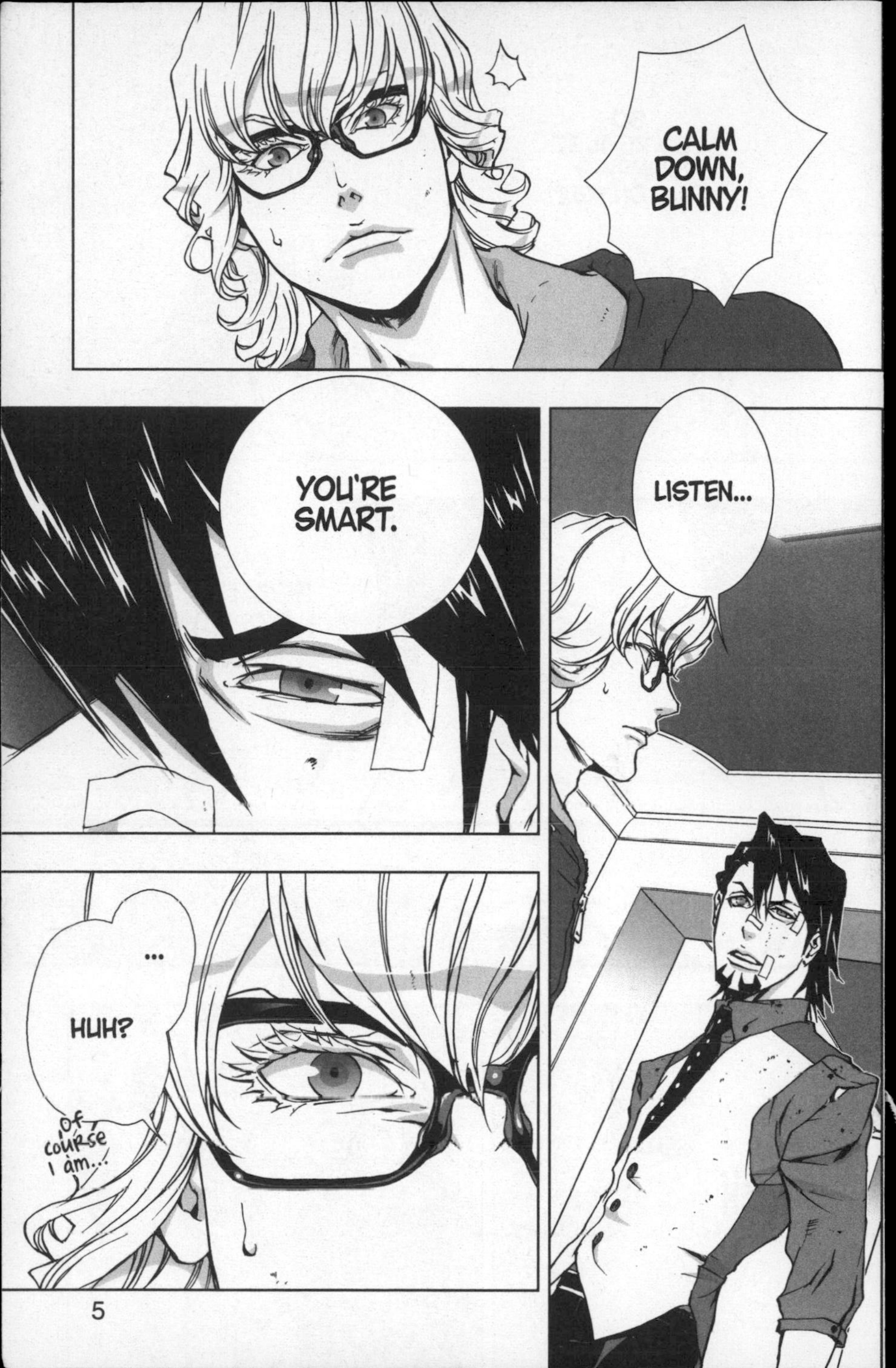
CALM DOWN, BUNNY!
LISTEN...
YOU'RE SMART.
... HUH?
Of course I am...

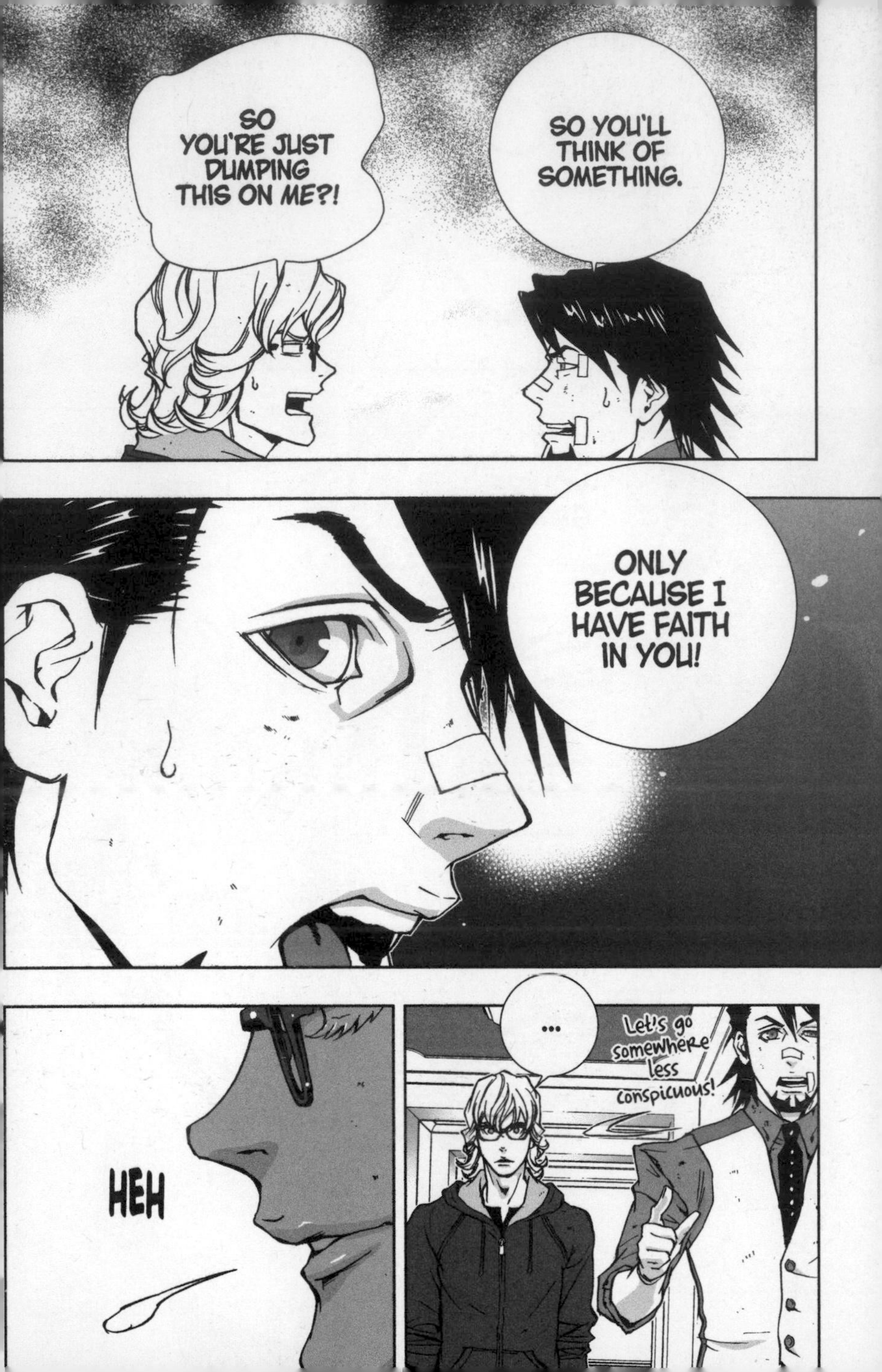
SO YOU'LL THINK OF SOMETHING.
SO YOU'RE JUST DUMPING THIS ON ME?!
ONLY BECAUSE I HAVE FAITH IN YOU!
...
Let's go somewhere less conspicuous!
HEH

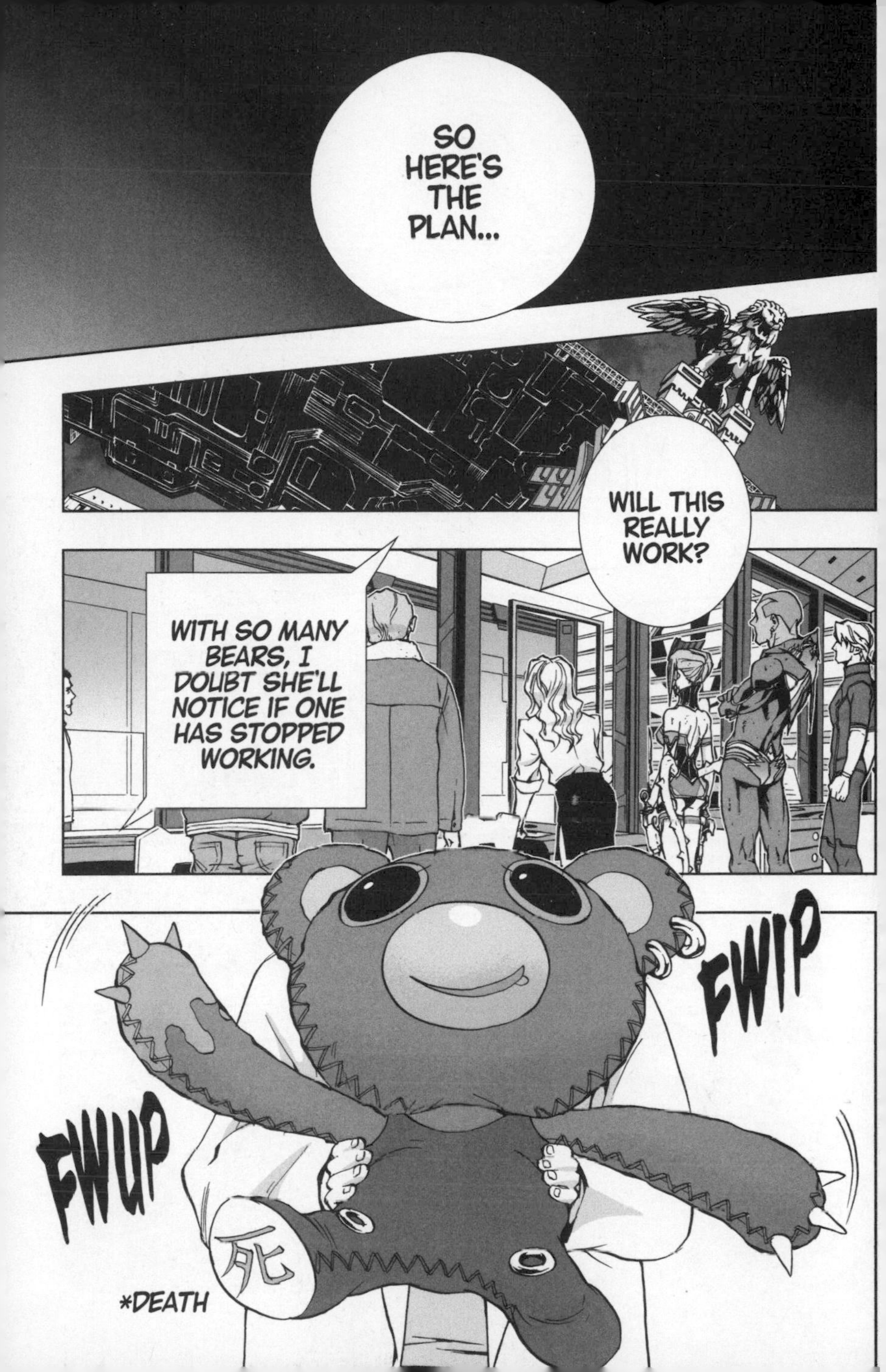
SO HERE'S THE PLAN...
WILL THIS REALLY WORK?
WITH SO MANY BEARS, I DOUBT SHE'LL NOTICE IF ONE HAS STOPPED WORKING.
FWIP
FWUP
死
*DEATH

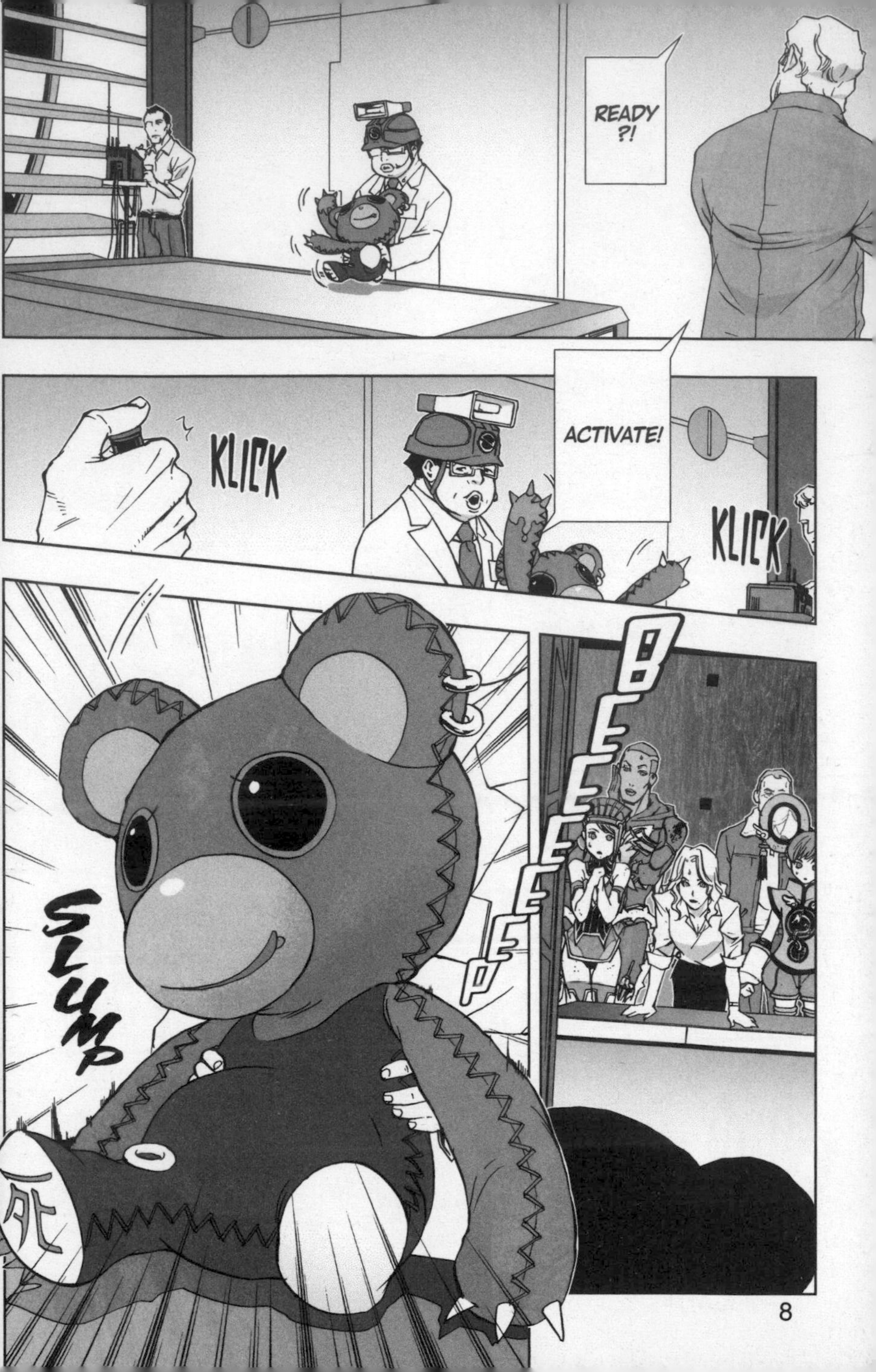
READY ?!
ACTIVATE!
KLICK
KLICK
BEEEEEEEP
SLUMP

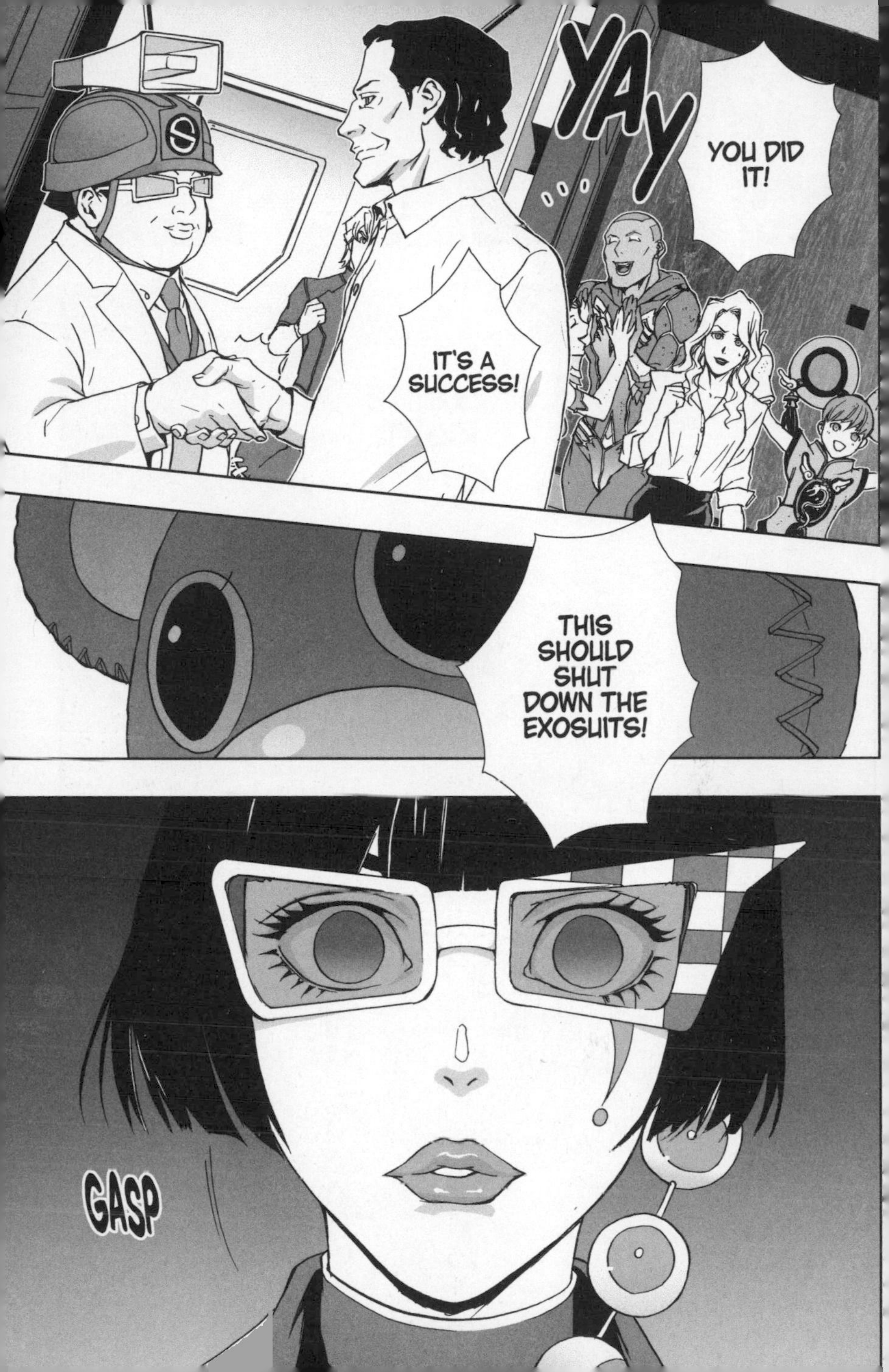
YAY
YOU DID IT!
IT'S A SUCCESS!
THIS SHOULD SHUT DOWN THE EXOSUITS!
GASP

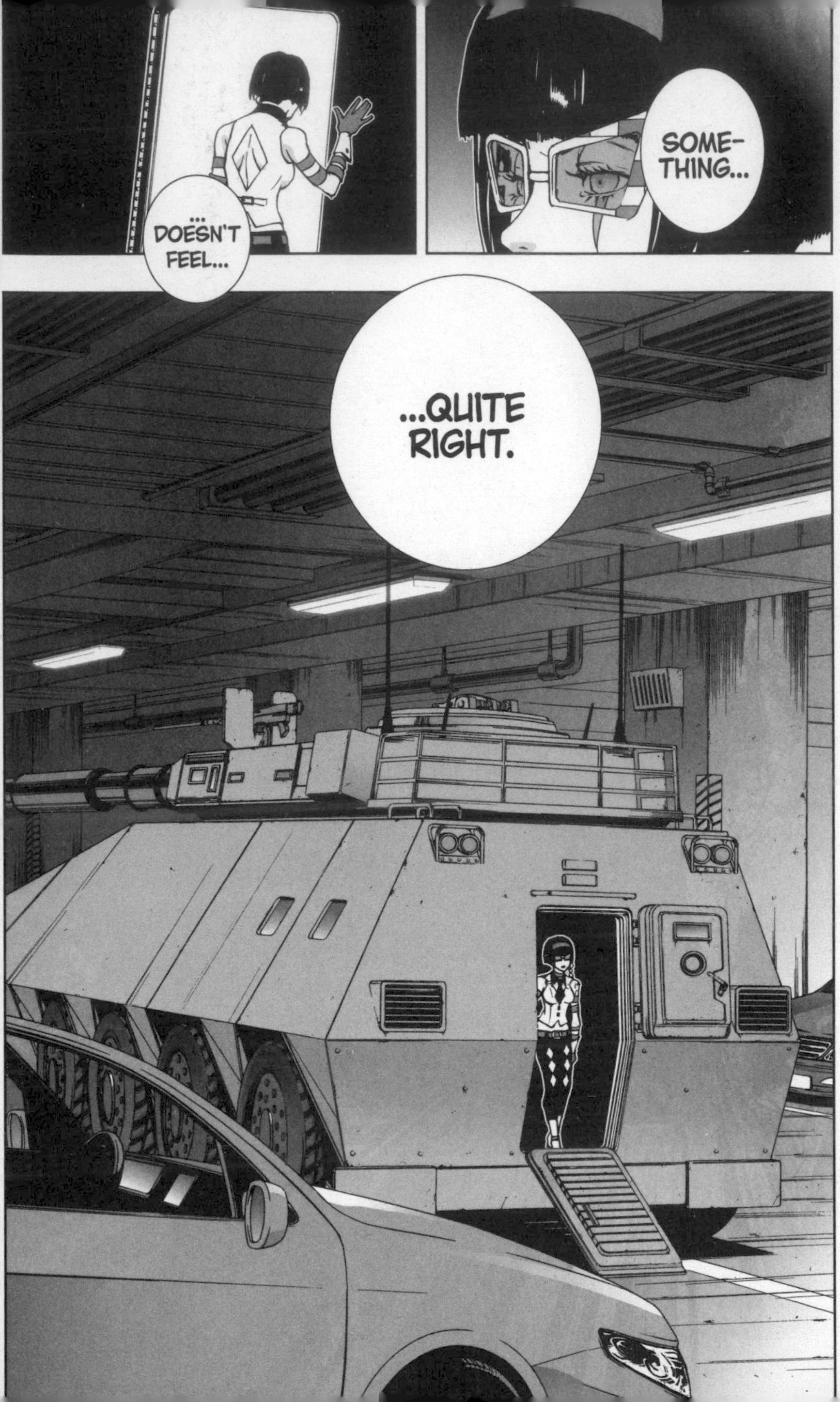
SOME-THING...
...DOESN'T FEEL...
...QUITE RIGHT.

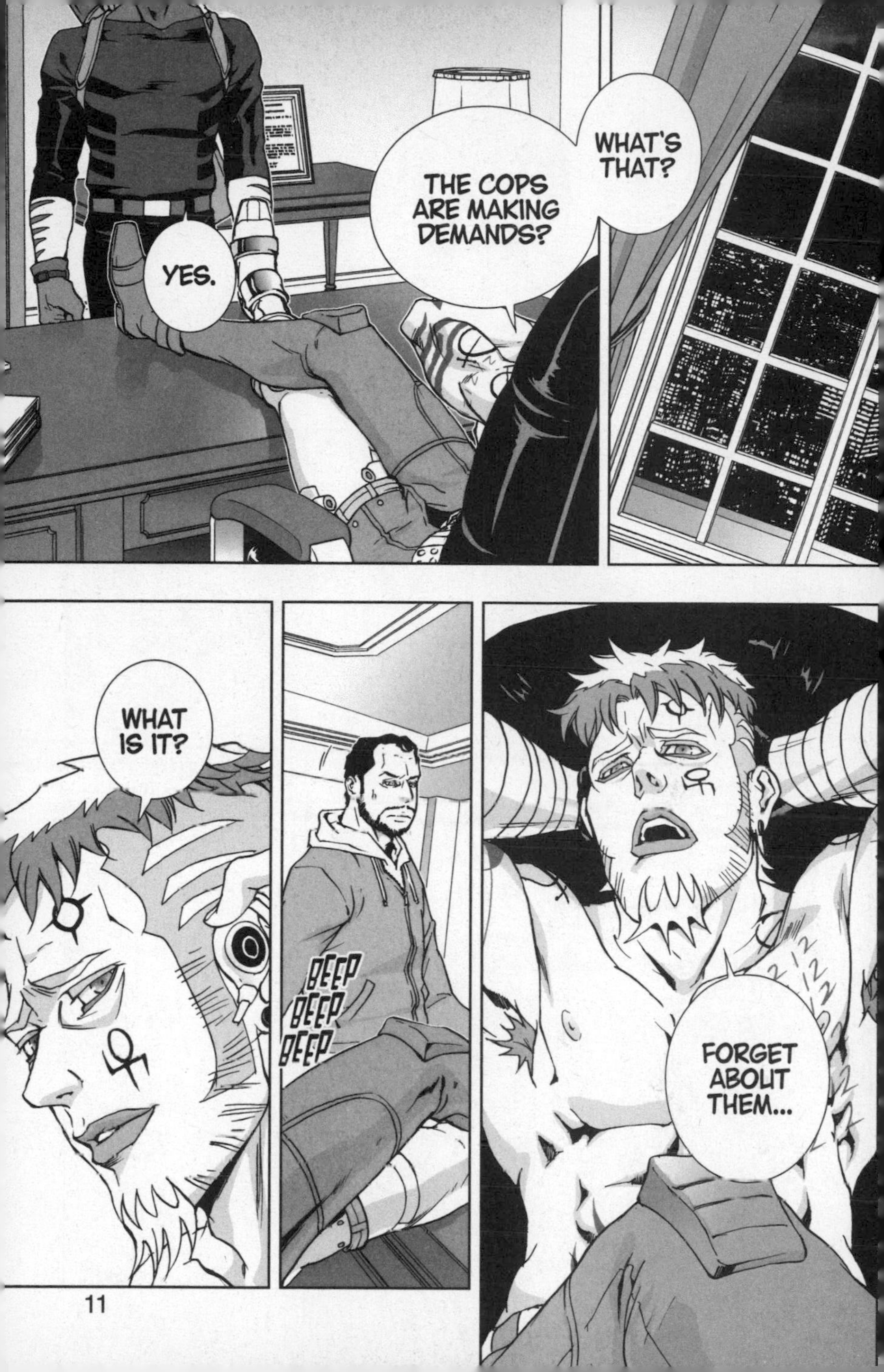
WHAT'S THAT?
THE COPS ARE MAKING DEMANDS?
YES.
FORGET ABOUT THEM...
BEEP BEEP BEEP
WHAT IS IT?

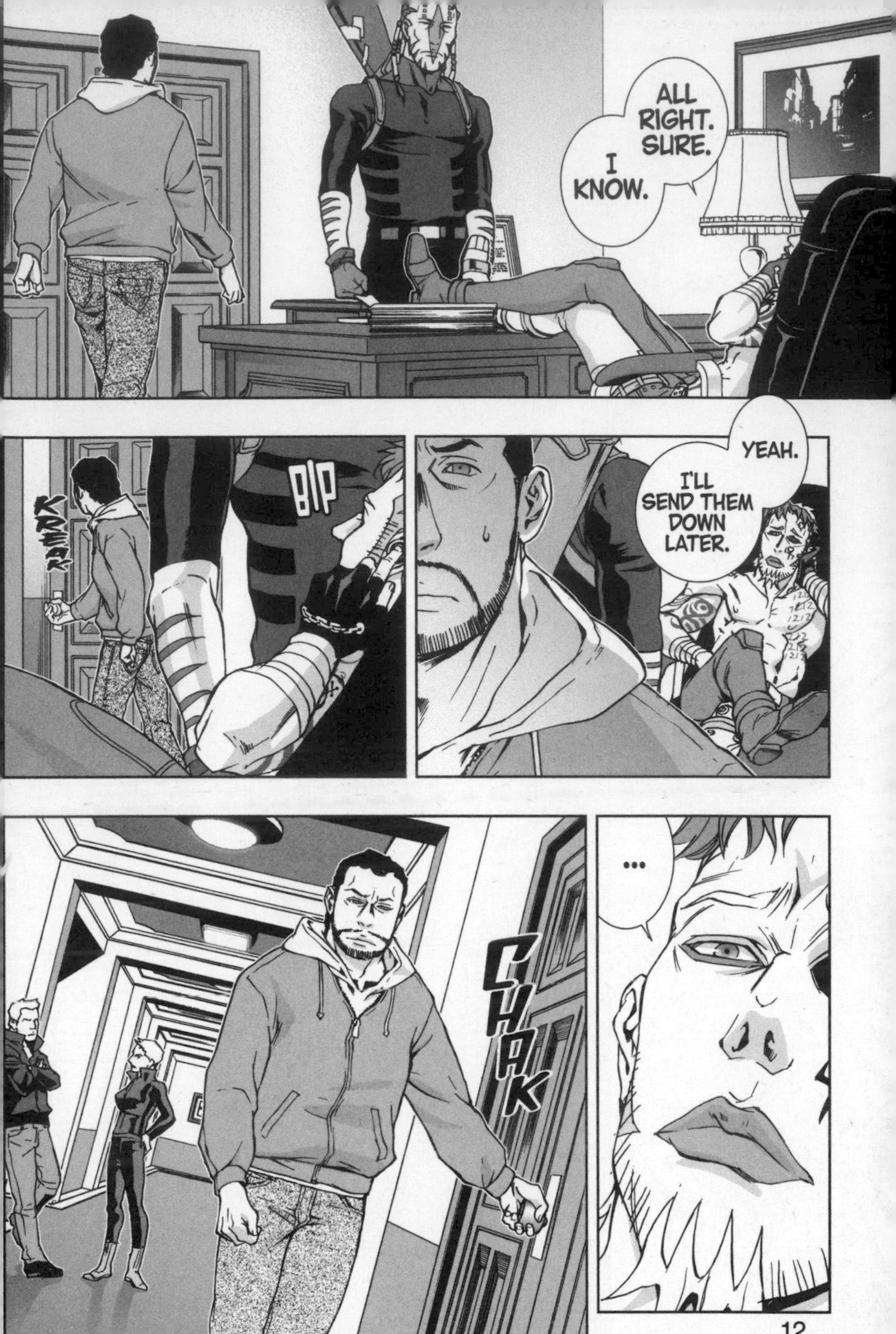
ALL RIGHT. SURE.
I KNOW.
YEAH.
I'LL SEND THEM DOWN LATER.
BIP
KREAK
...
CHAK

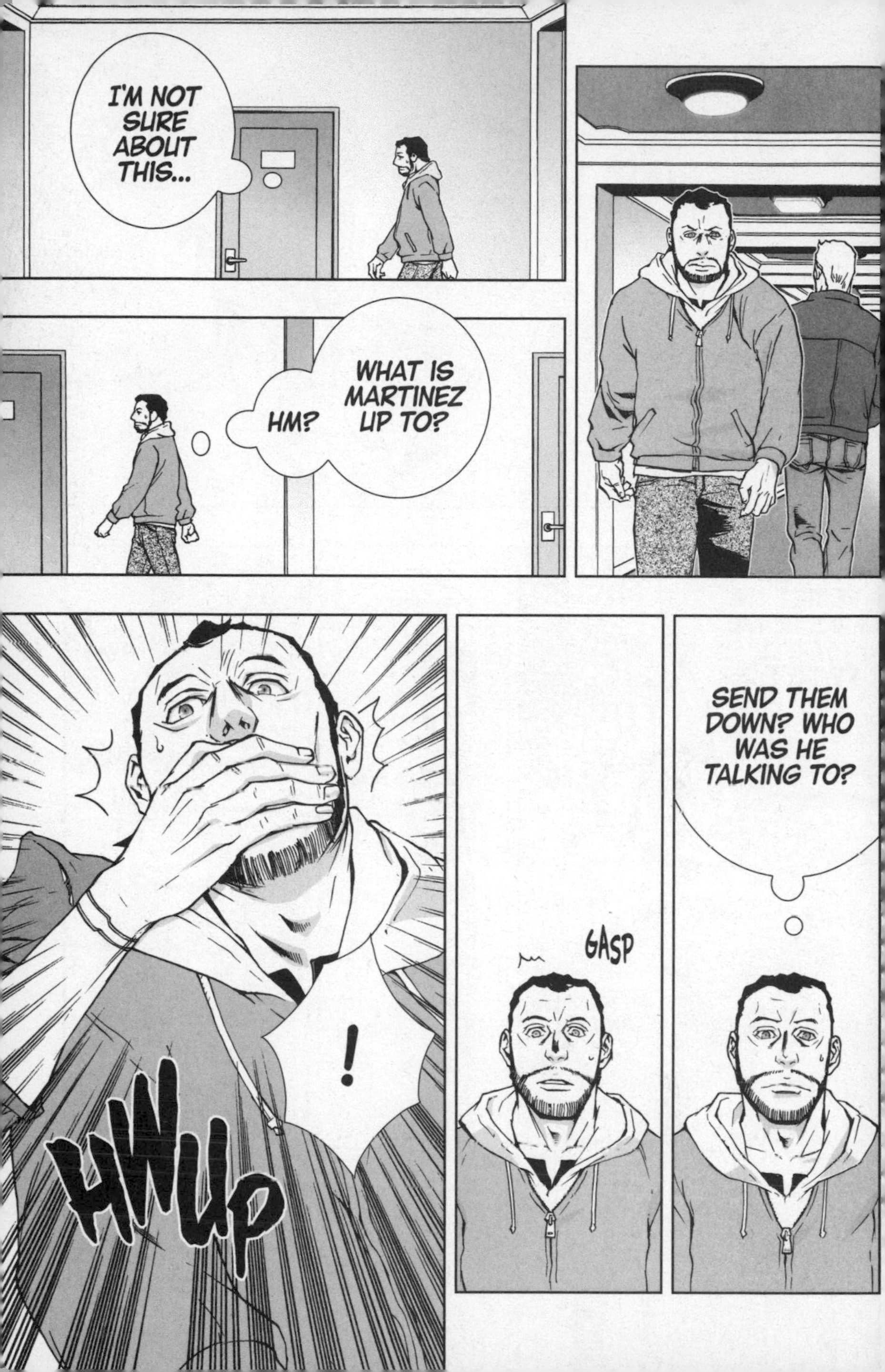
I'M NOT SURE ABOUT THIS...
WHAT IS MARTINEZ UP TO?
HM?
SEND THEM DOWN? WHO WAS HE TALKING TO?
GASP
!
HNUP

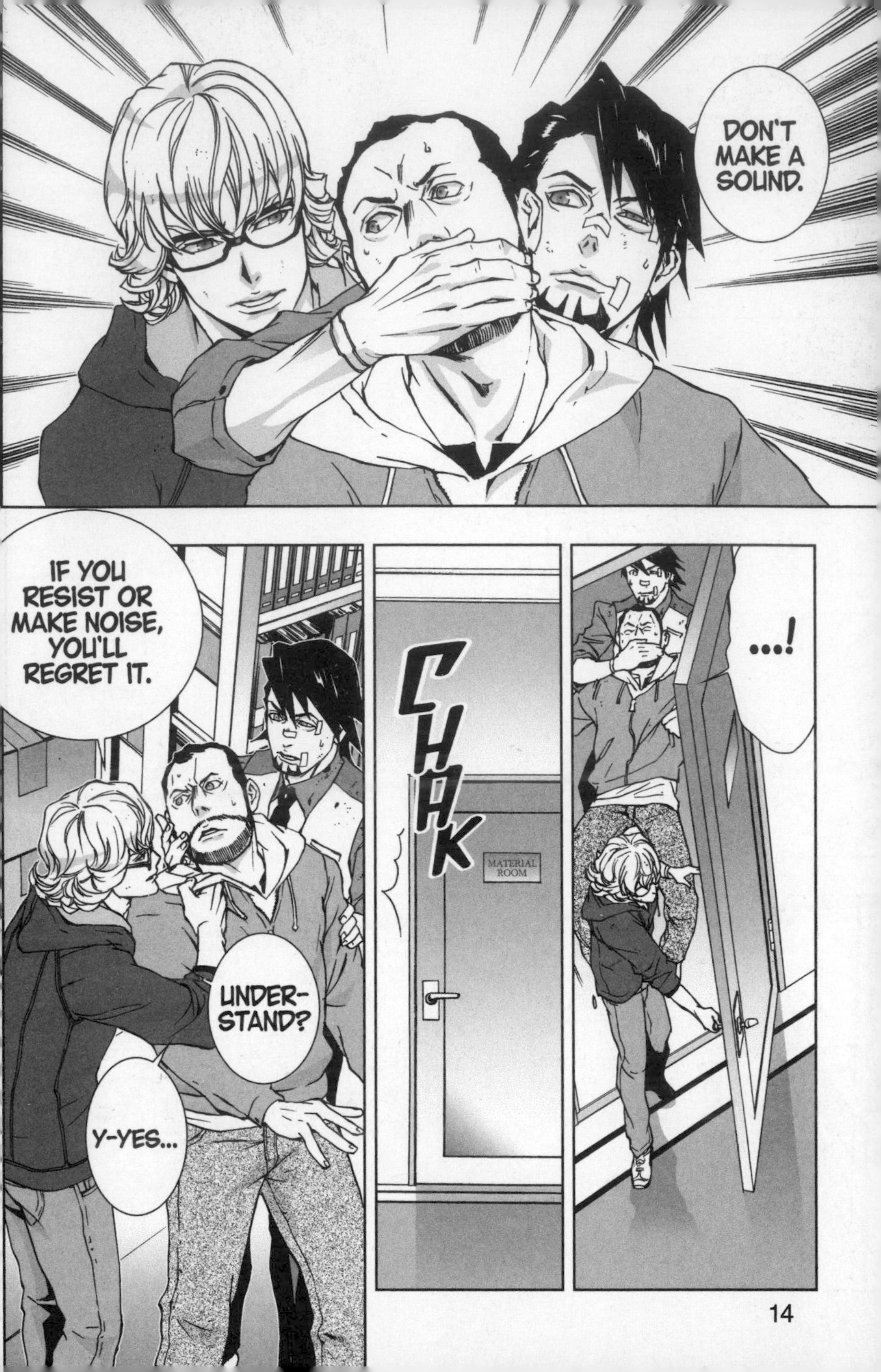

DON'T MAKE A SOUND.
...!
CHAK
MATERIAL ROOM
IF YOU RESIST OR MAKE NOISE, YOU'LL REGRET IT.
UNDER-STAND?
Y-YES...

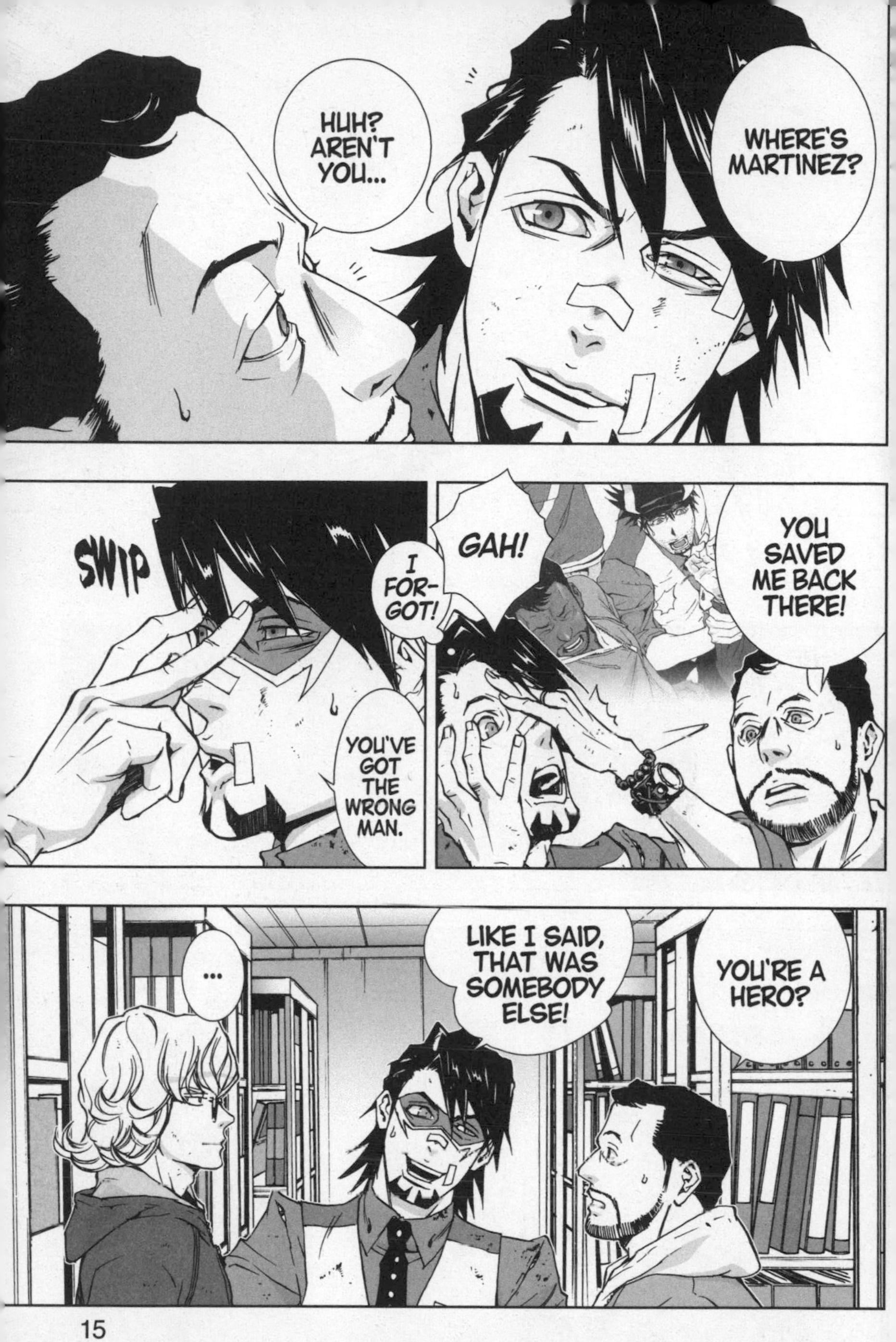
WHERE'S MARTINEZ?
HUH? AREN'T YOU...
YOU SAVED ME BACK THERE!
GAH!
I FOR-GOT!
SWIP
YOU'VE GOT THE WRONG MAN.
YOU'RE A HERO?
LIKE I SAID, THAT WAS SOMEBODY ELSE!
...

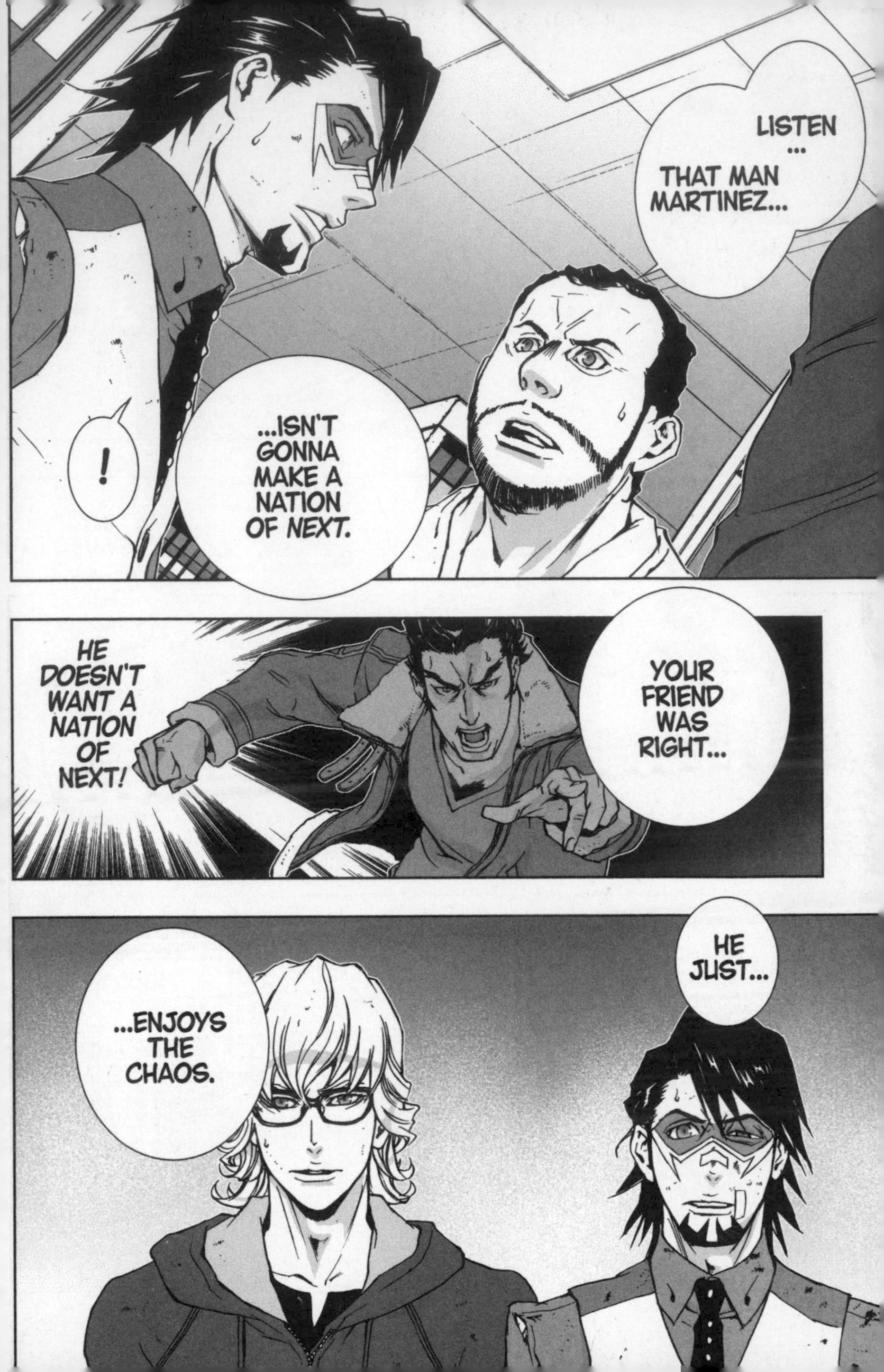
LISTEN ... THAT MAN MARTINEZ...
...ISN'T GONNA MAKE A NATION OF NEXT.
!
YOUR FRIEND WAS RIGHT...
HE DOESN'T WANT A NATION OF NEXT!
HE JUST...
...ENJOYS THE CHAOS.

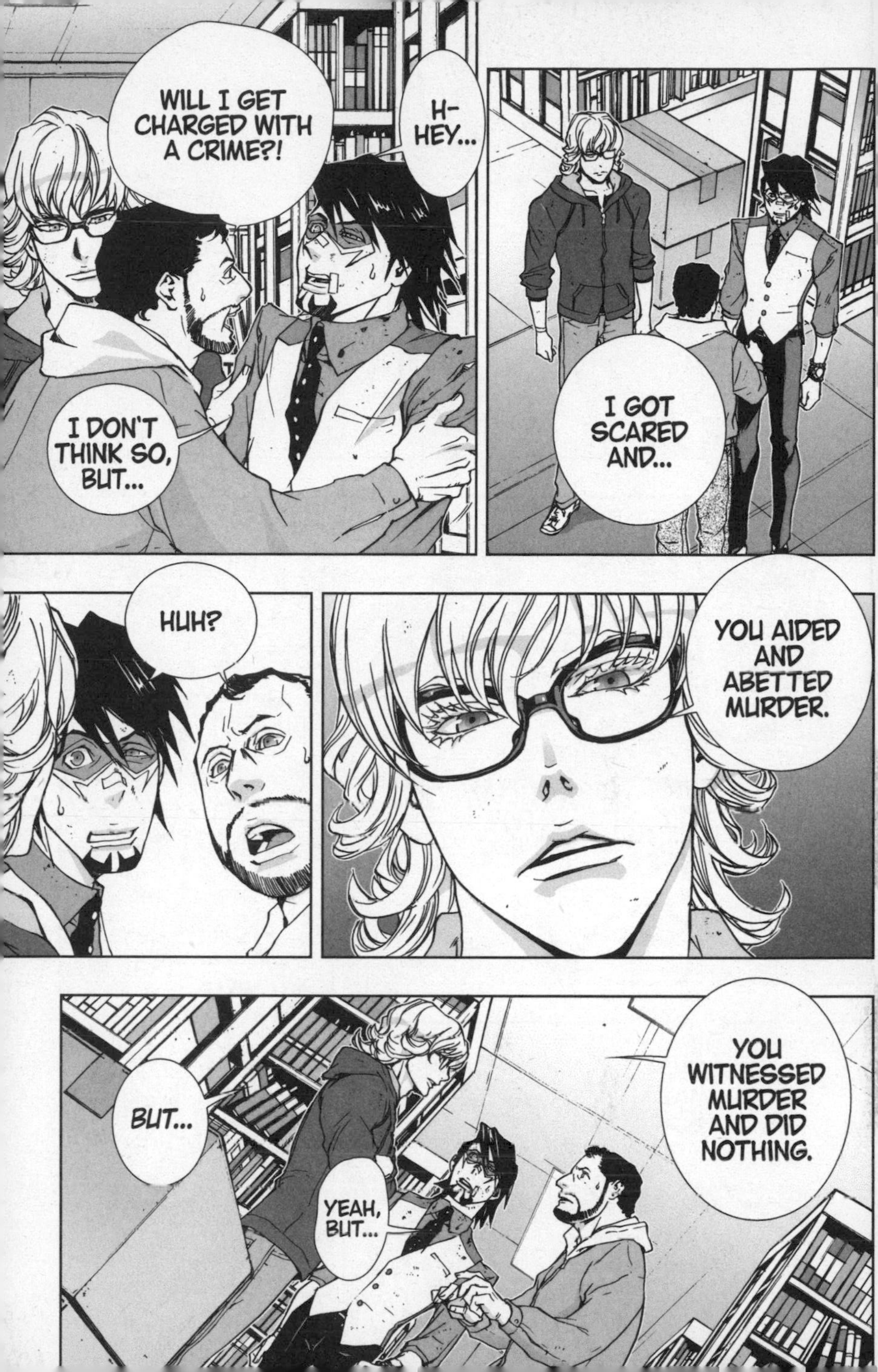
I GOT SCARED AND...
H- HEY...
WILL I GET CHARGED WITH A CRIME?!
I DON'T THINK SO, BUT...
YOU AIDED AND ABETTED MURDER.
HUH?
YOU WITNESSED MURDER AND DID NOTHING.
BUT...
YEAH, BUT...

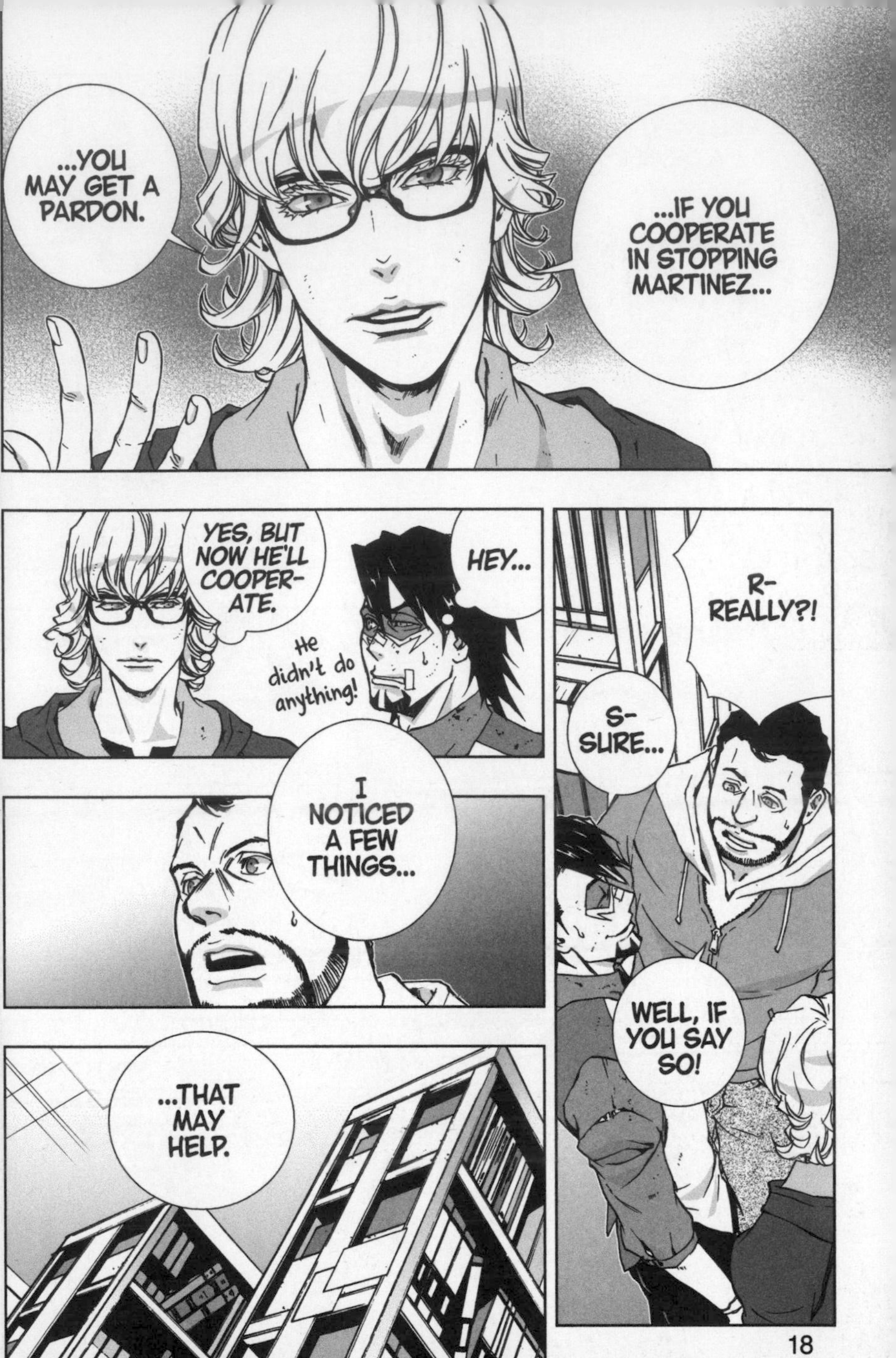
...IF YOU COOPERATE IN STOPPING MARTINEZ...
...YOU MAY GET A PARDON.
R-REALLY?!
S-SURE...
WELL, IF YOU SAY SO!
HEY...
YES, BUT NOW HE'LL COOPER-ATE.
He didn't do anything!
I NOTICED A FEW THINGS...
...THAT MAY HELP.

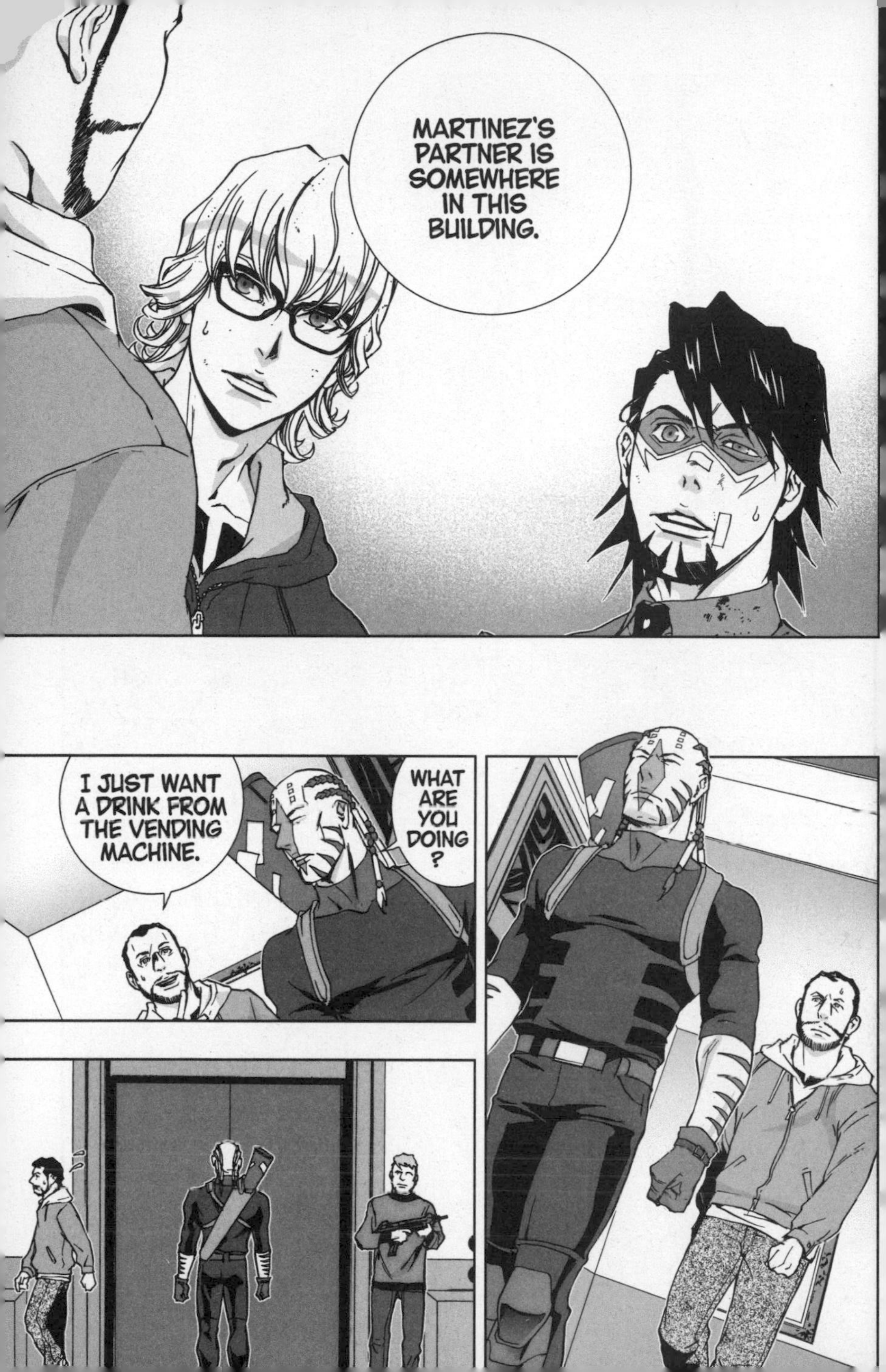
MARTINEZ'S PARTNER IS SOMEWHERE IN THIS BUILDING.
WHAT ARE YOU DOING?
I JUST WANT A DRINK FROM THE VENDING MACHINE.

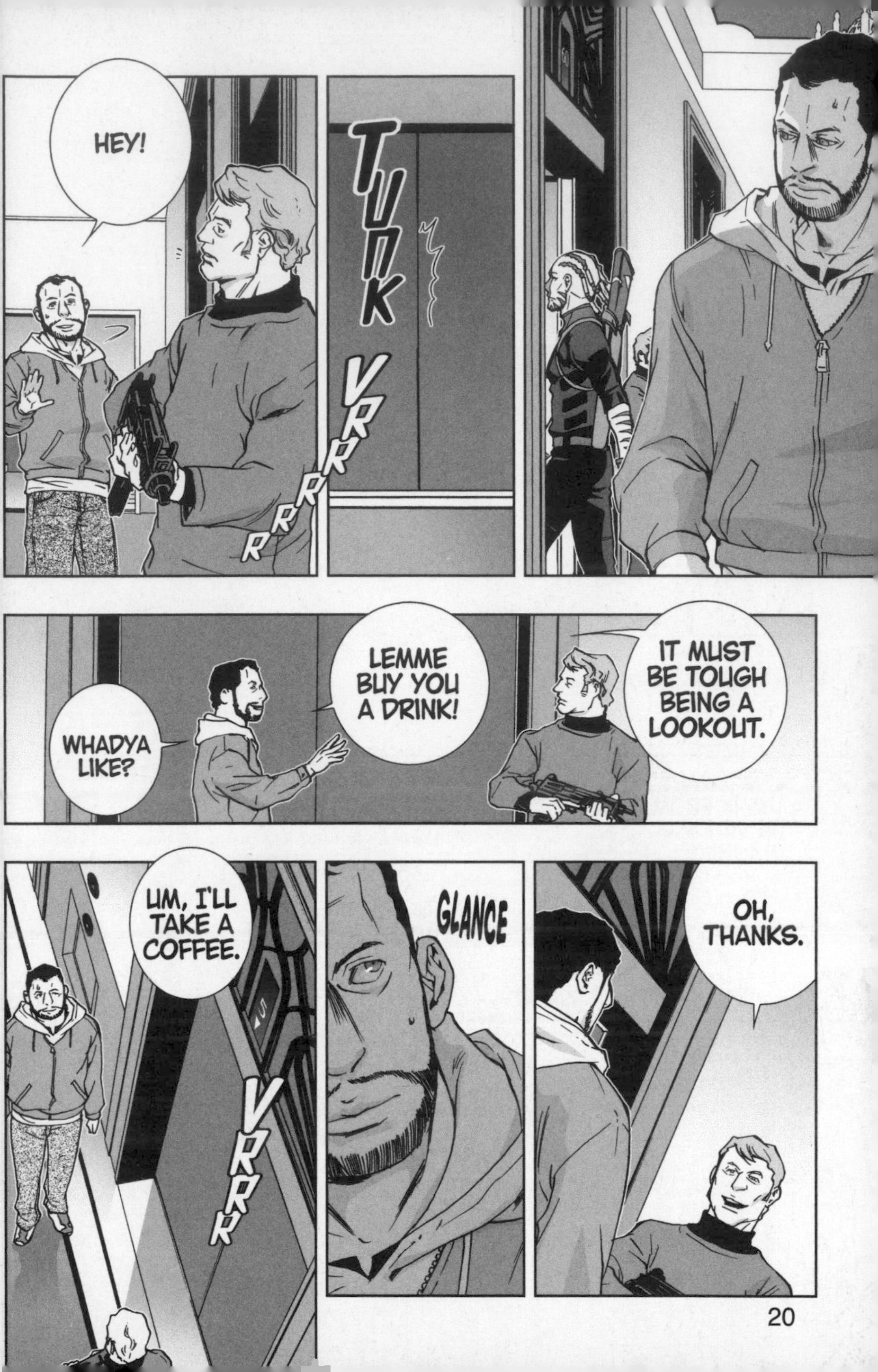
TUNK
VRRRRRR
HEY!
IT MUST BE TOUGH BEING A LOOKOUT.
LEMME BUY YOU A DRINK!
WHADYA LIKE?
OH, THANKS.
GLANCE
UM, I'LL TAKE A COFFEE.
VRRRR

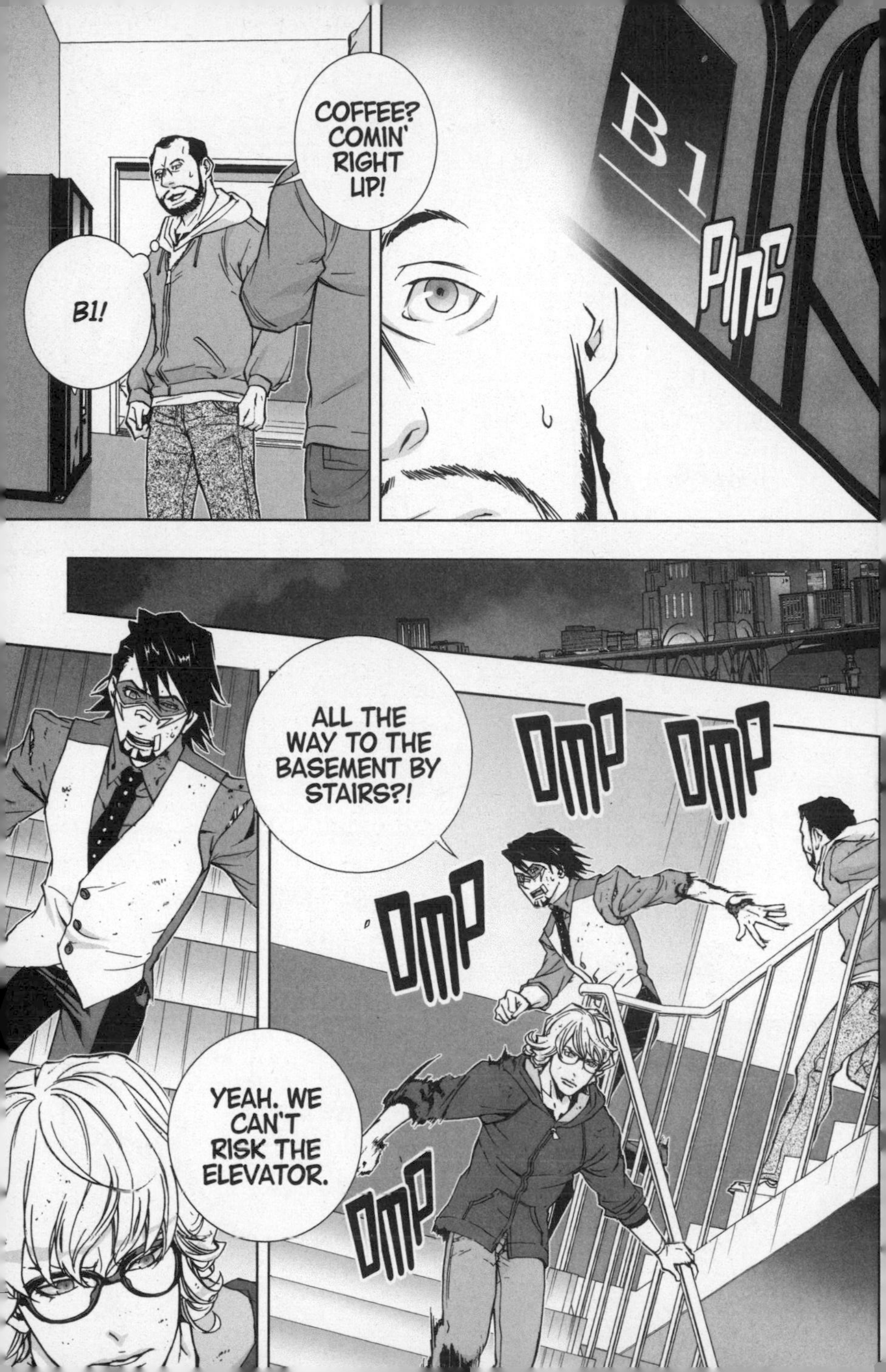

B1
PING
COFFEE? COMIN' RIGHT UP!
B1!
OMP OMP
ALL THE WAY TO THE BASEMENT BY STAIRS?!
OMP
YEAH. WE CAN'T RISK THE ELEVATOR.
OMP

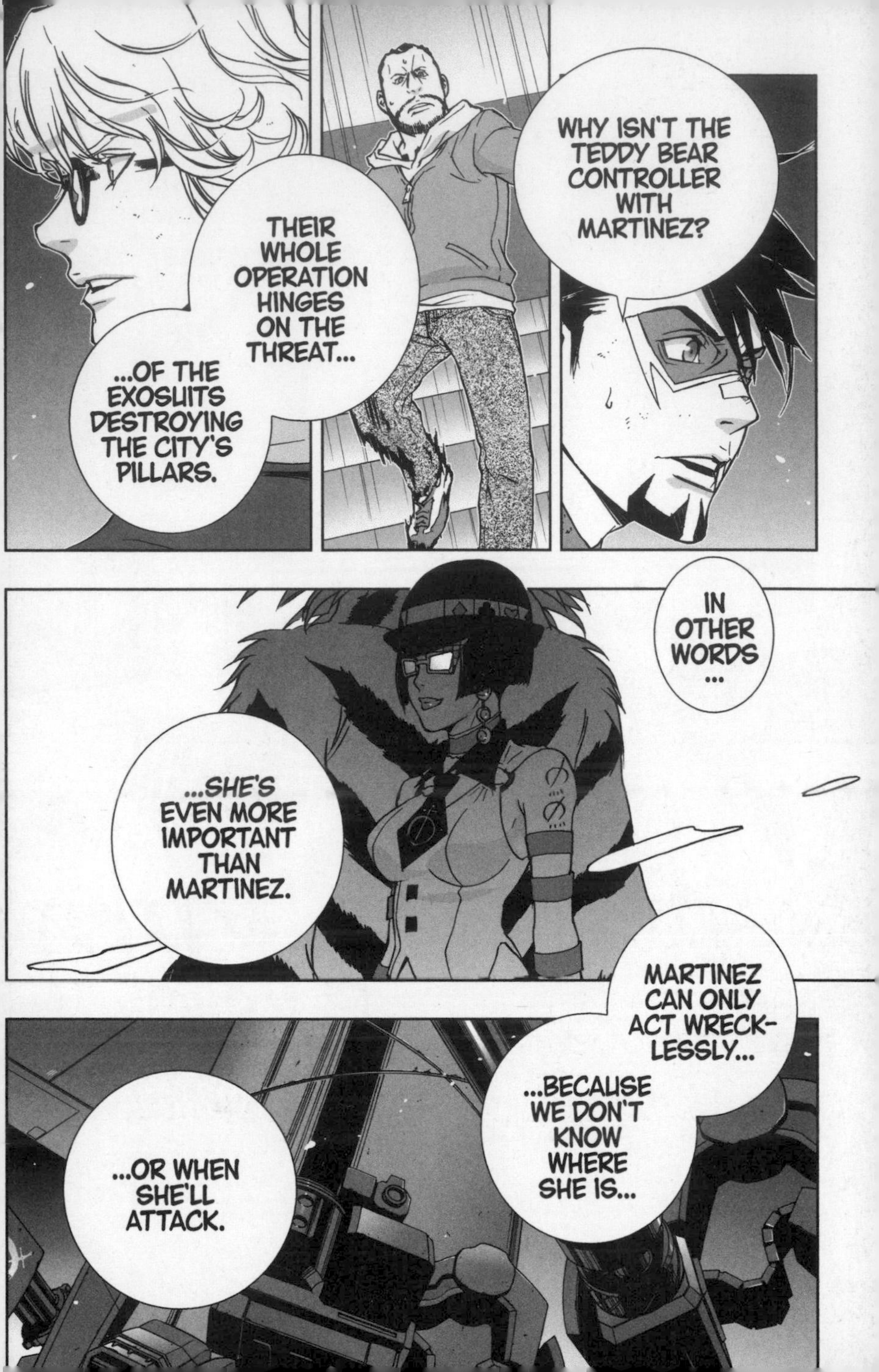
WHY ISN'T THE TEDDY BEAR CONTROLLER WITH MARTINEZ?
THEIR WHOLE OPERATION HINGES ON THE THREAT...
...OF THE EXOSUITS DESTROYING THE CITY'S PILLARS.
IN OTHER WORDS...
...SHE'S EVEN MORE IMPORTANT THAN MARTINEZ.
MARTINEZ CAN ONLY ACT WRECK-LESSLY...
...BECAUSE WE DON'T KNOW WHERE SHE IS...
...OR WHEN SHE'LL ATTACK.

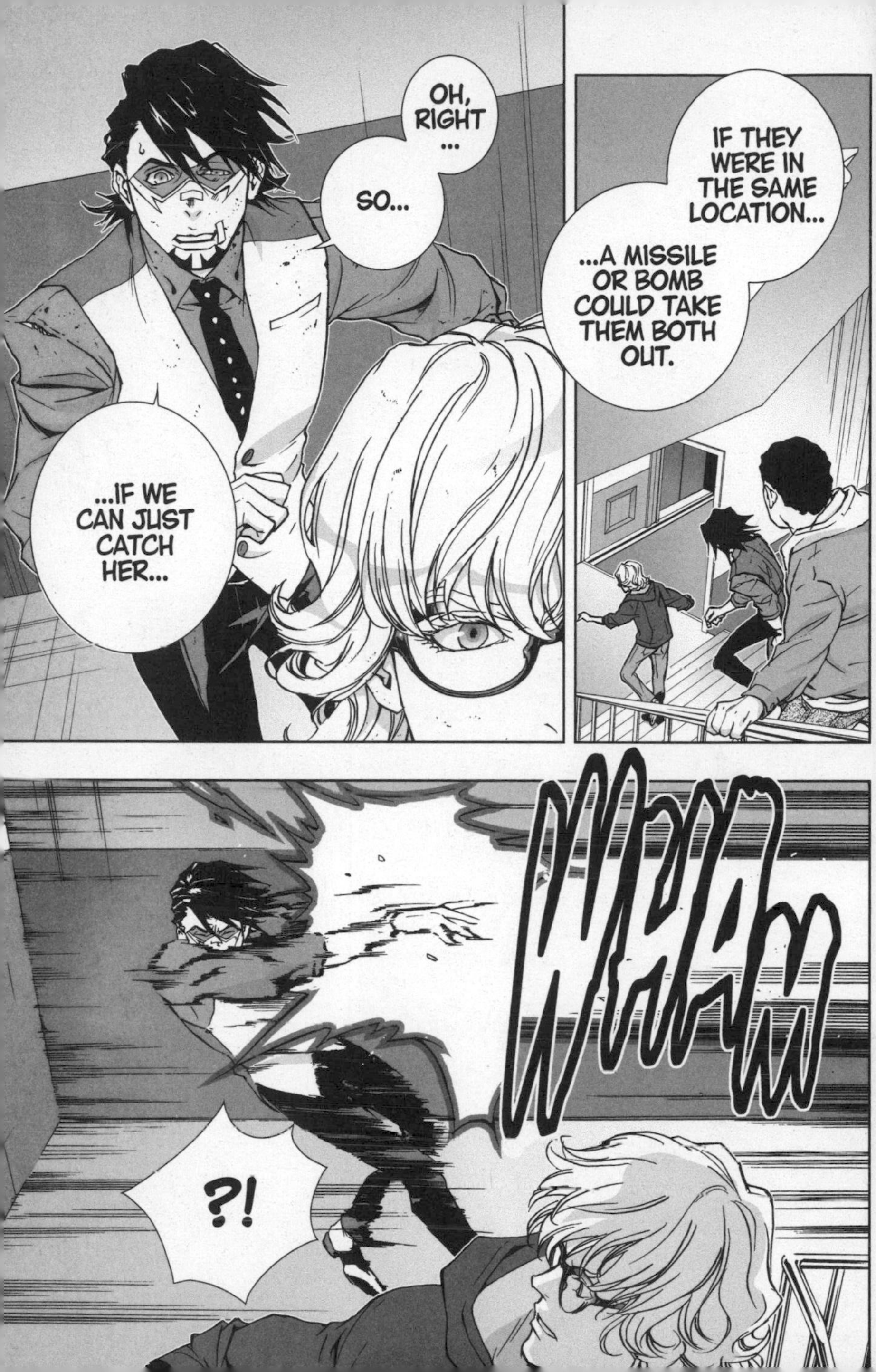
IF THEY WERE IN THE SAME LOCATION...
...A MISSILE OR BOMB COULD TAKE THEM BOTH OUT.
OH, RIGHT ...
SO...
...IF WE CAN JUST CATCH HER...
?!

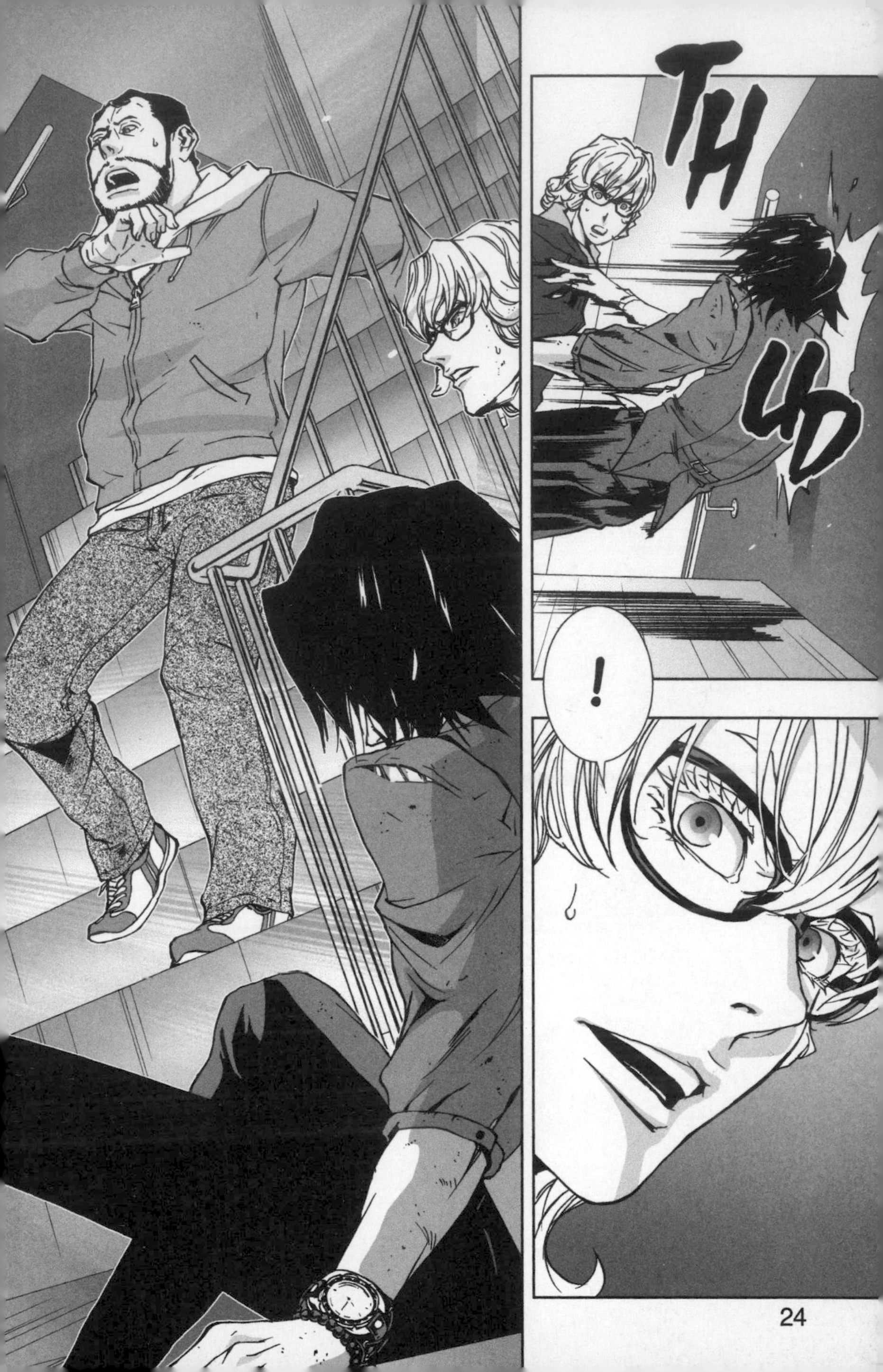
THUD
!

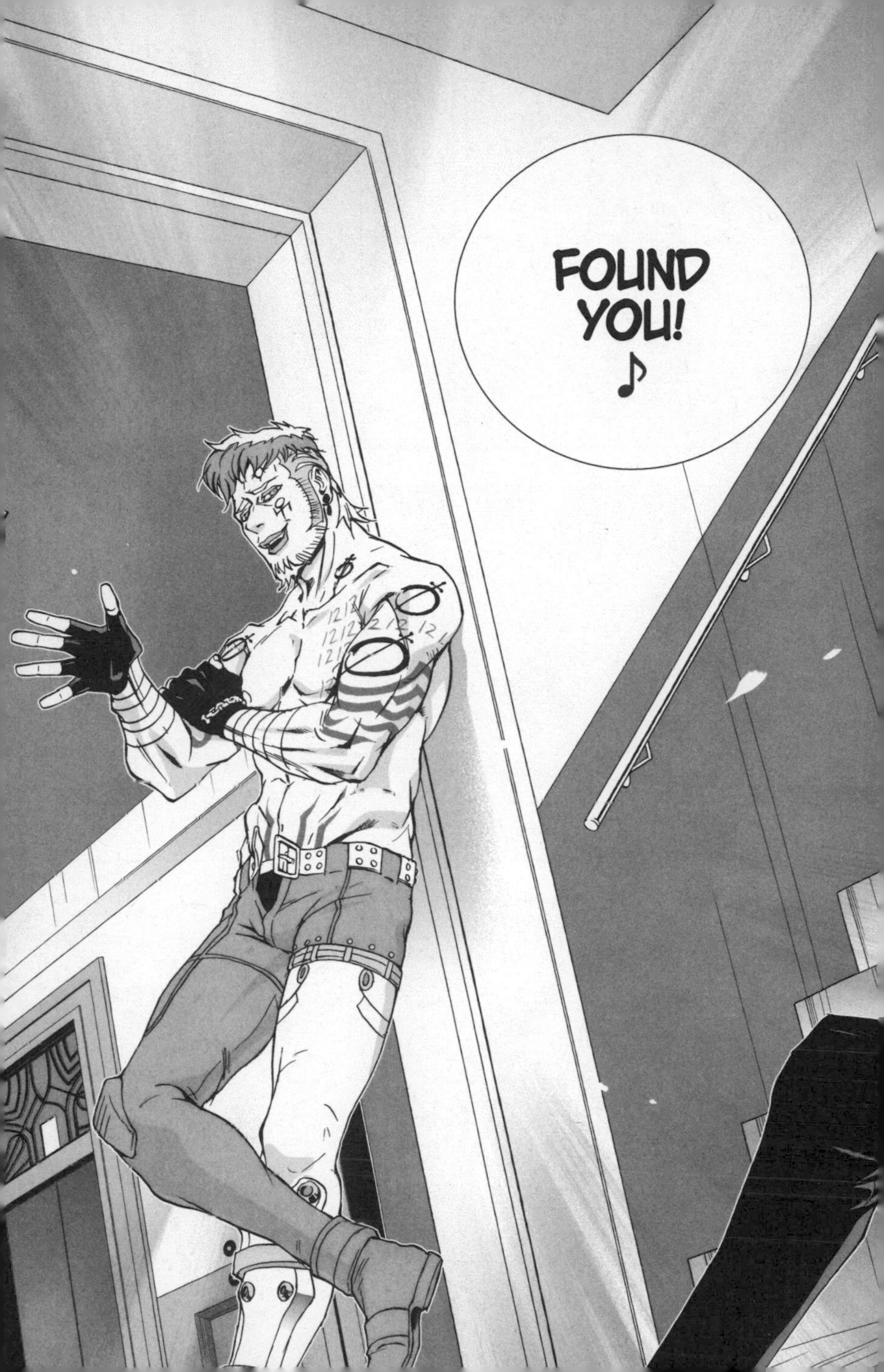
FOUND YOU! ♪

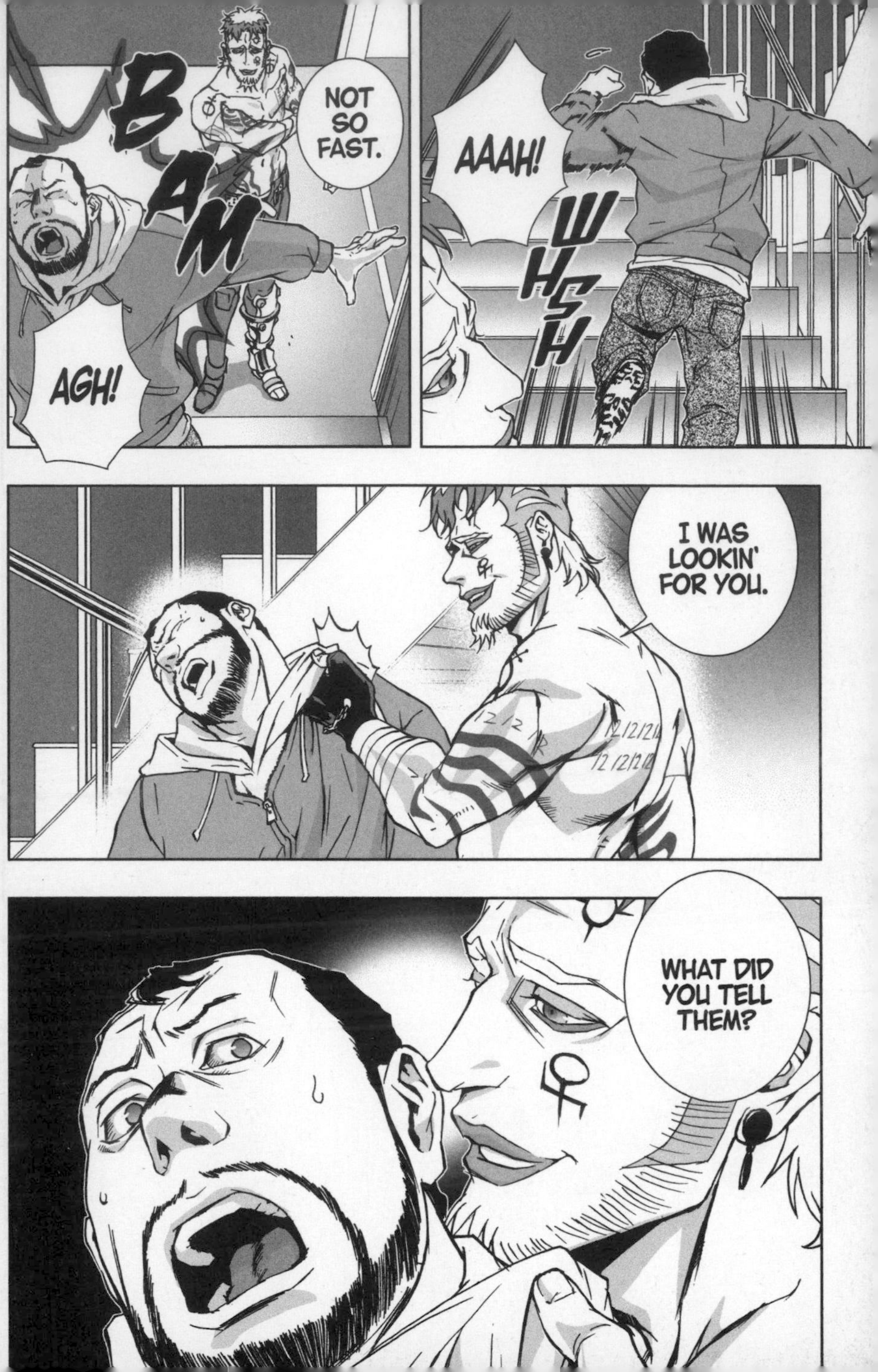
AAAH!
WHSH
NOT SO FAST.
BAM
AGH!
I WAS LOOKIN' FOR YOU.
WHAT DID YOU TELL THEM?

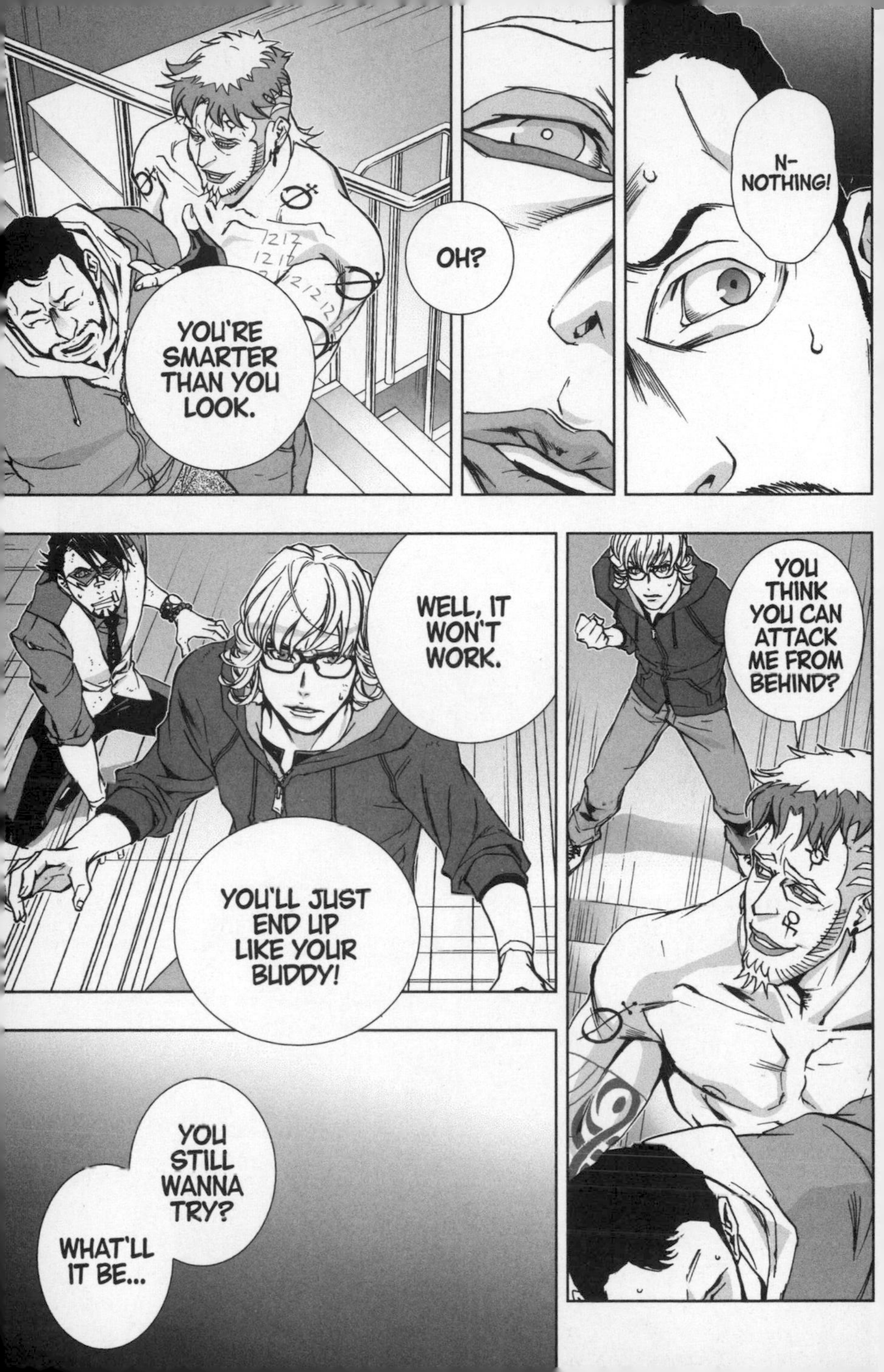
N-NOTHING!
OH?
YOU'RE SMARTER THAN YOU LOOK.
YOU THINK YOU CAN ATTACK ME FROM BEHIND?
WELL, IT WON'T WORK.
YOU'LL JUST END UP LIKE YOUR BUDDY!
YOU STILL WANNA TRY?
WHAT'LL IT BE...

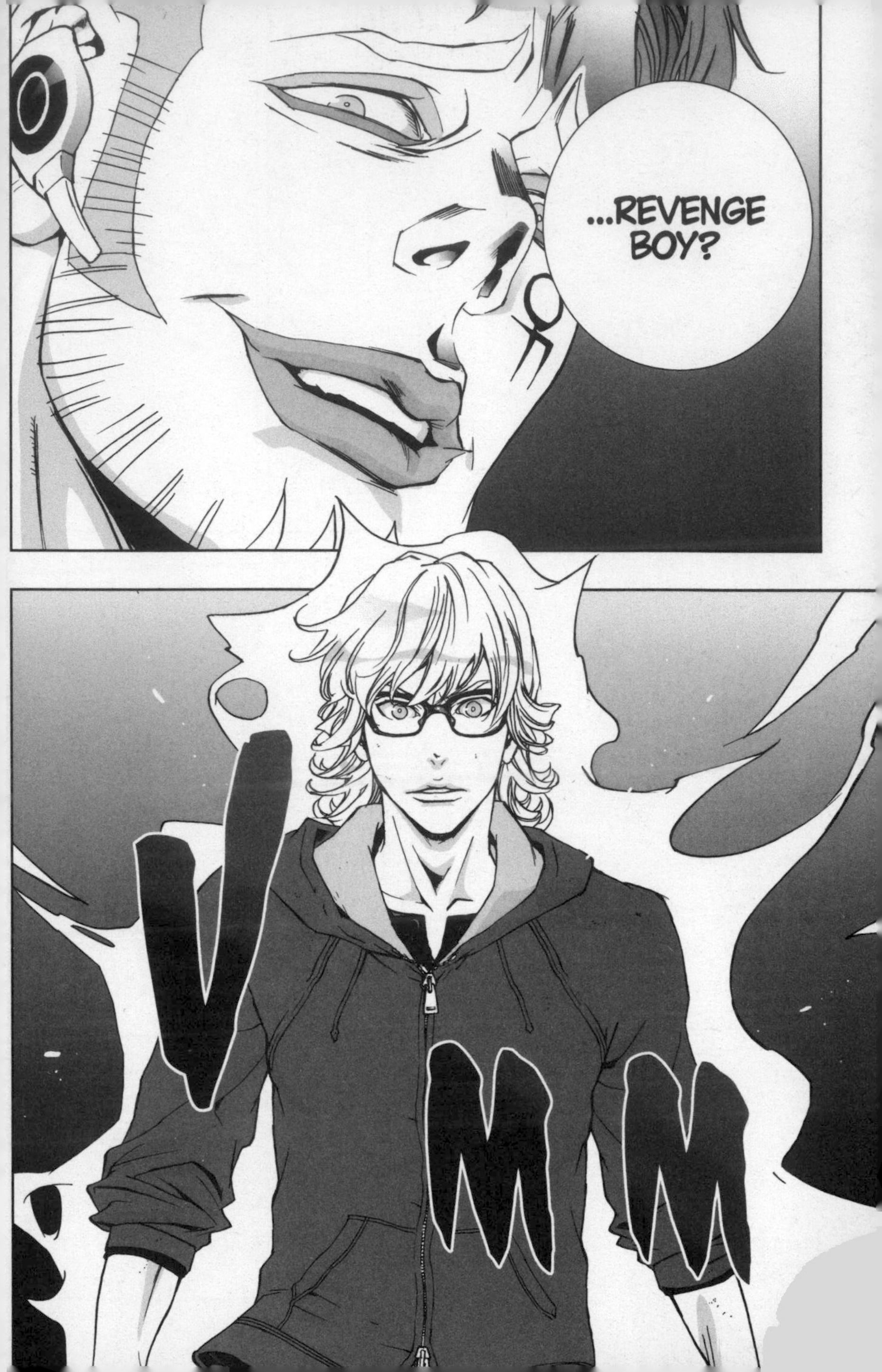
...REVENGE BOY?
VMM

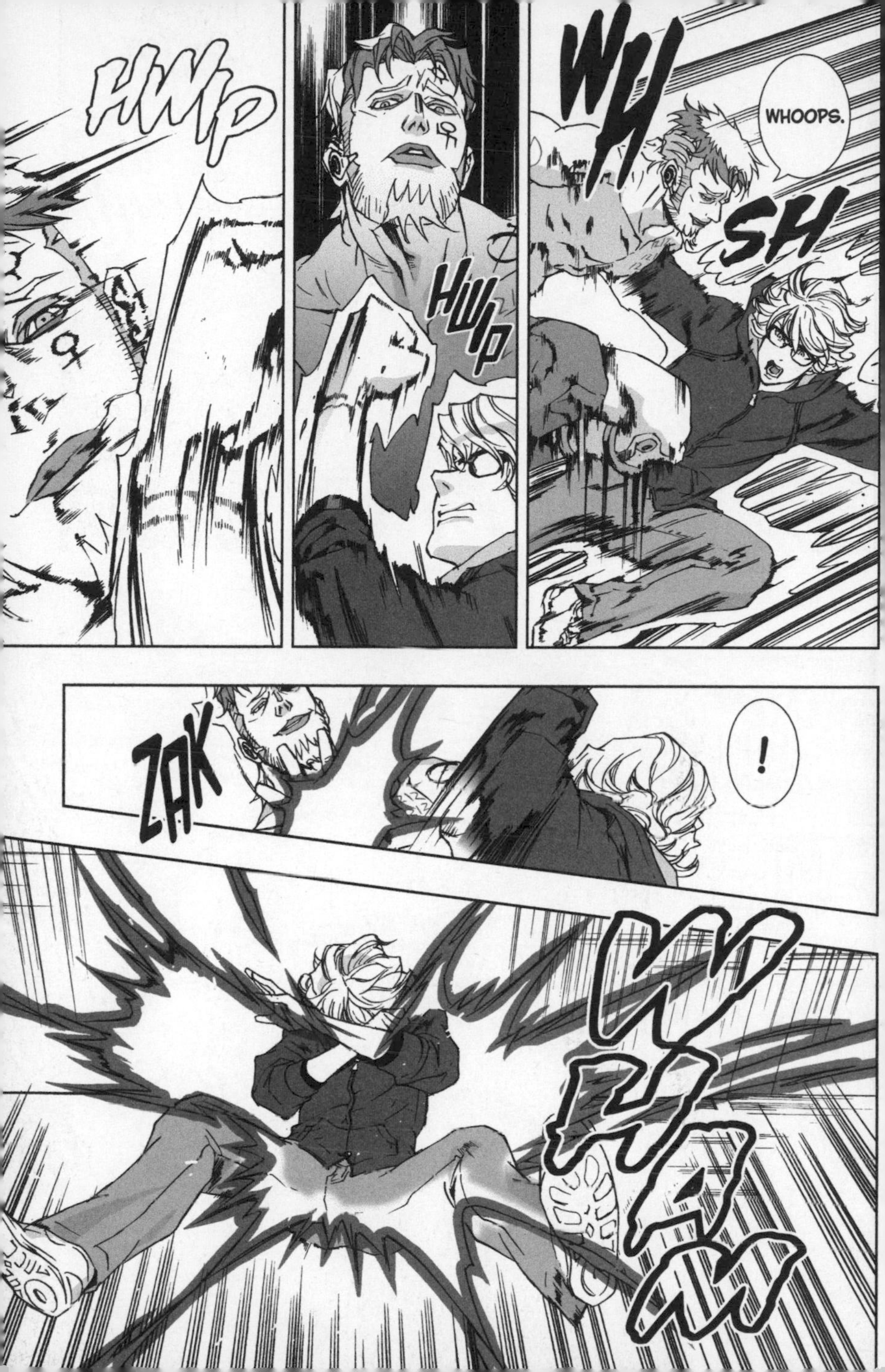
WHOOPS.
WH
SH
HWIP
HWIP
!
ZAK
WHAM

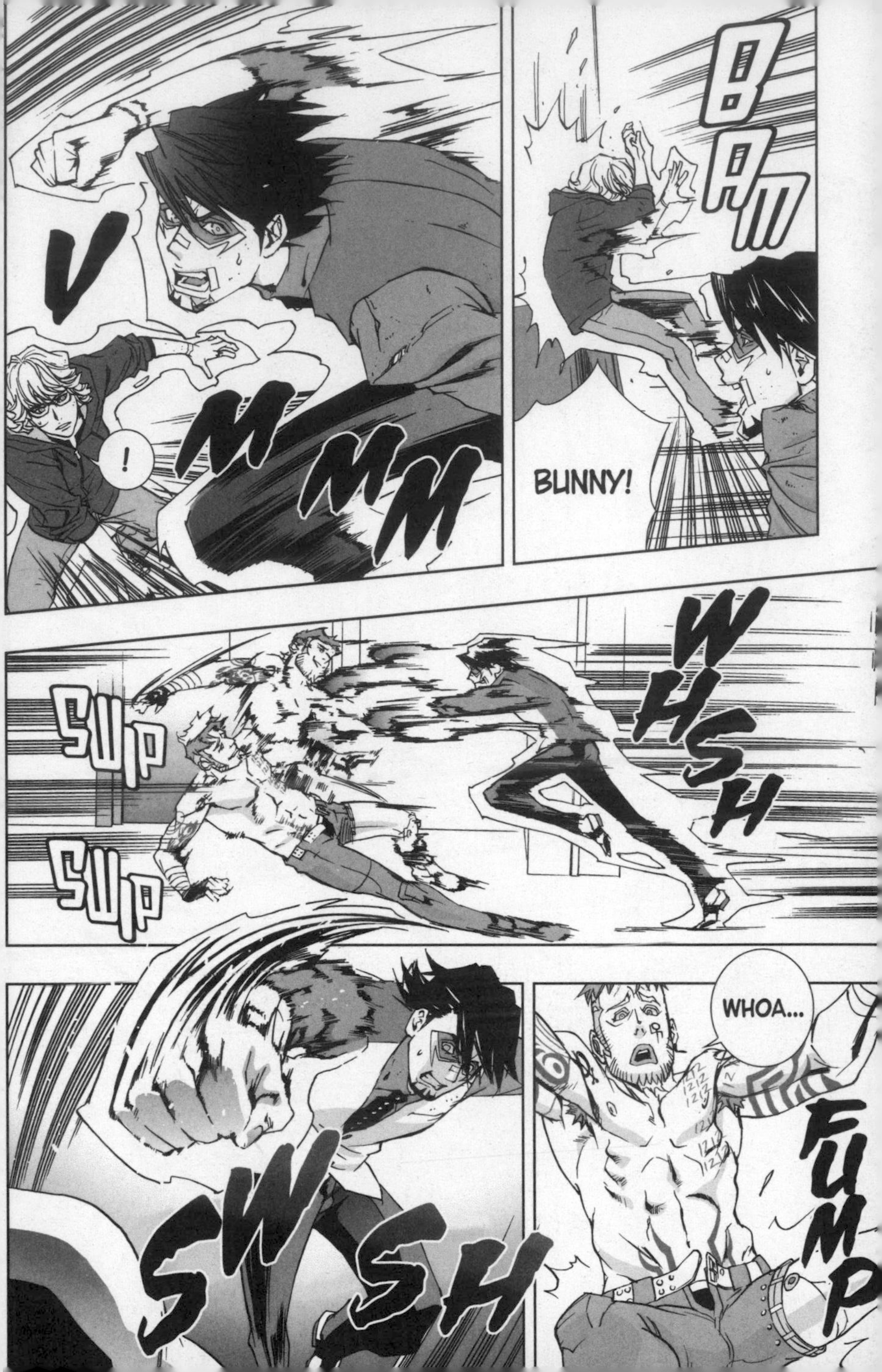
BAM
BUNNY!
VMMM
!
WHSH
SWIP
SWIP
WHOA...
FUMP
SWSH

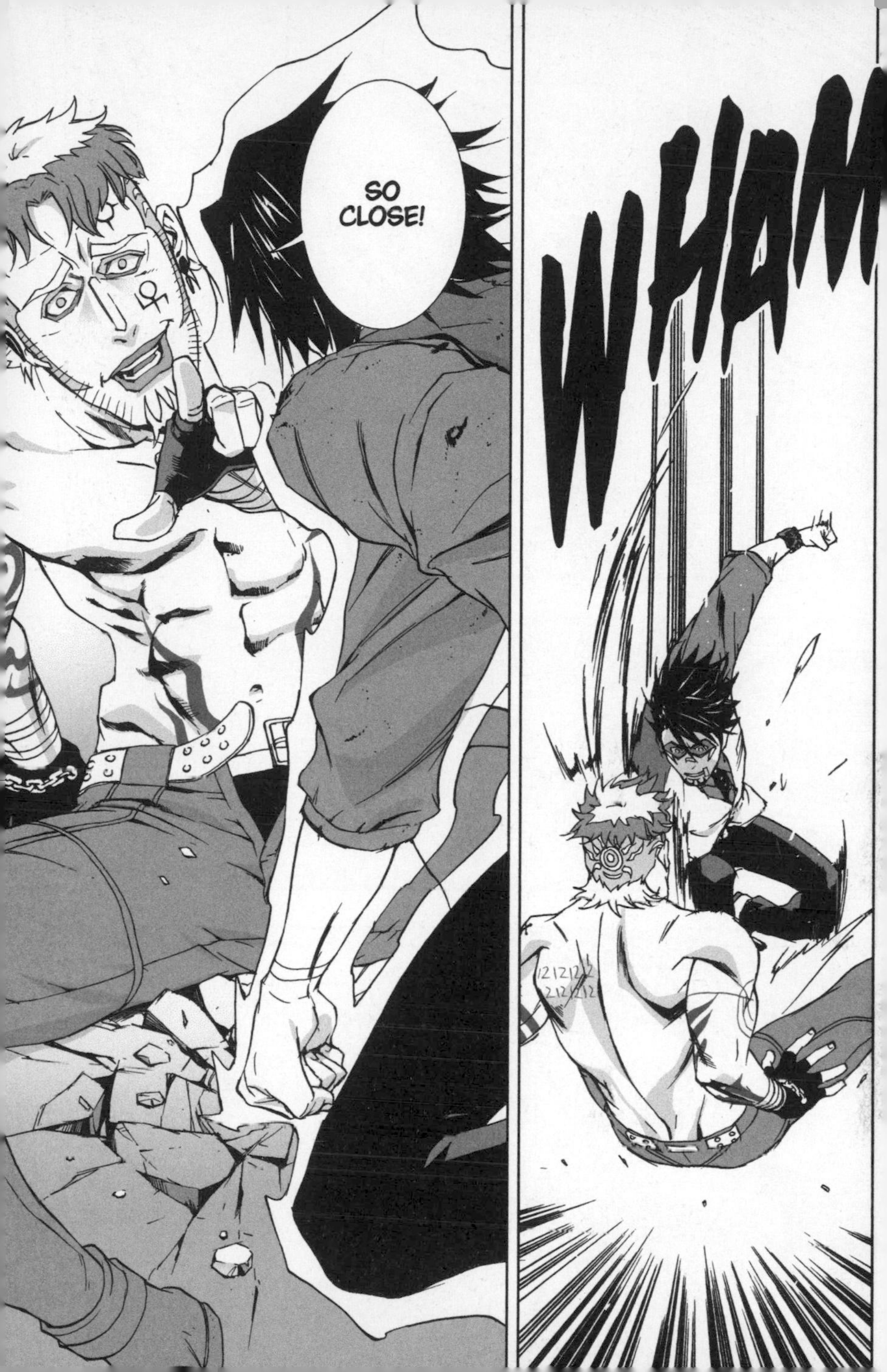
WHAM
SO CLOSE!

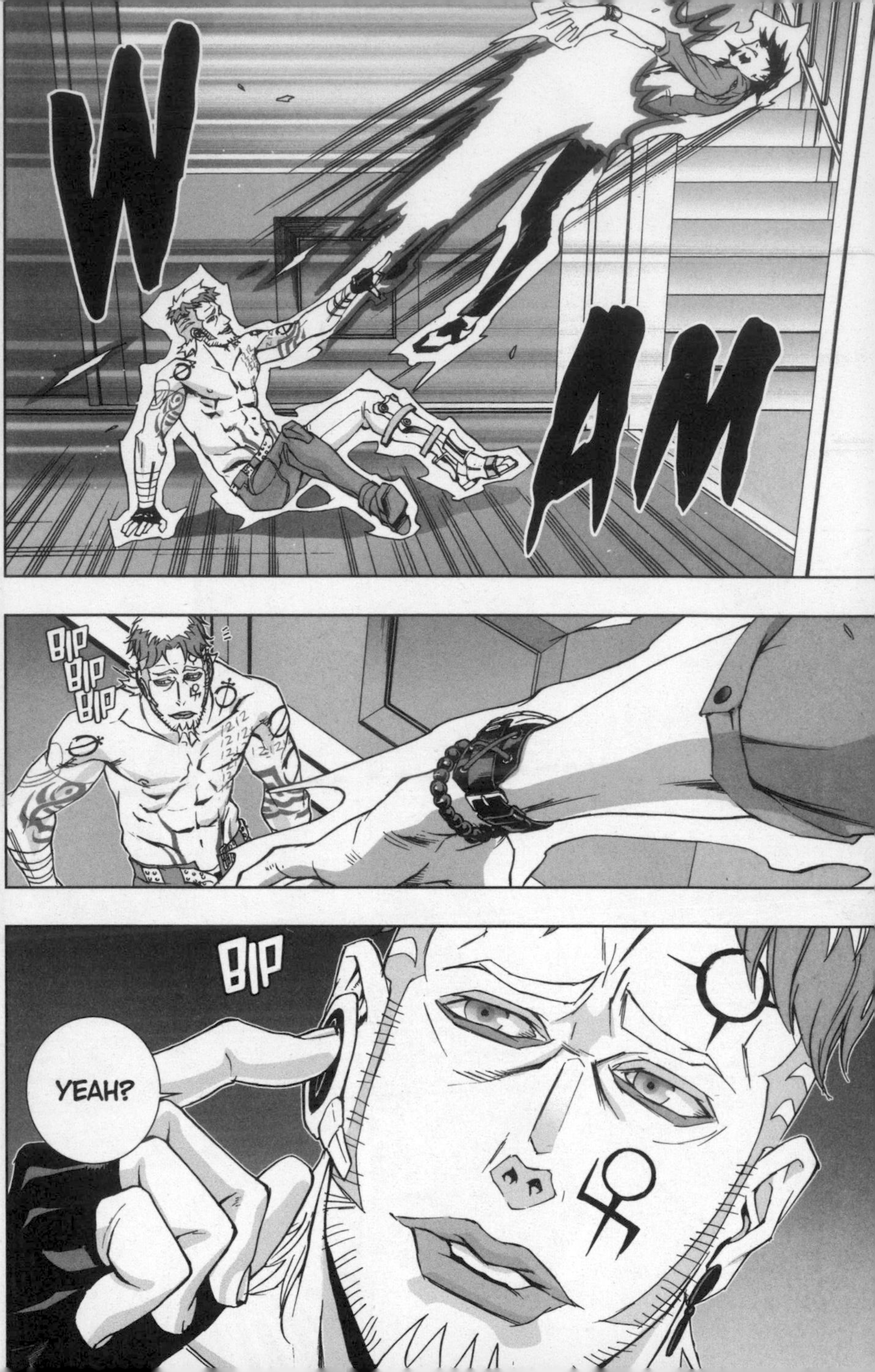
WAM
BIP BIP BIP
BIP
YEAH?

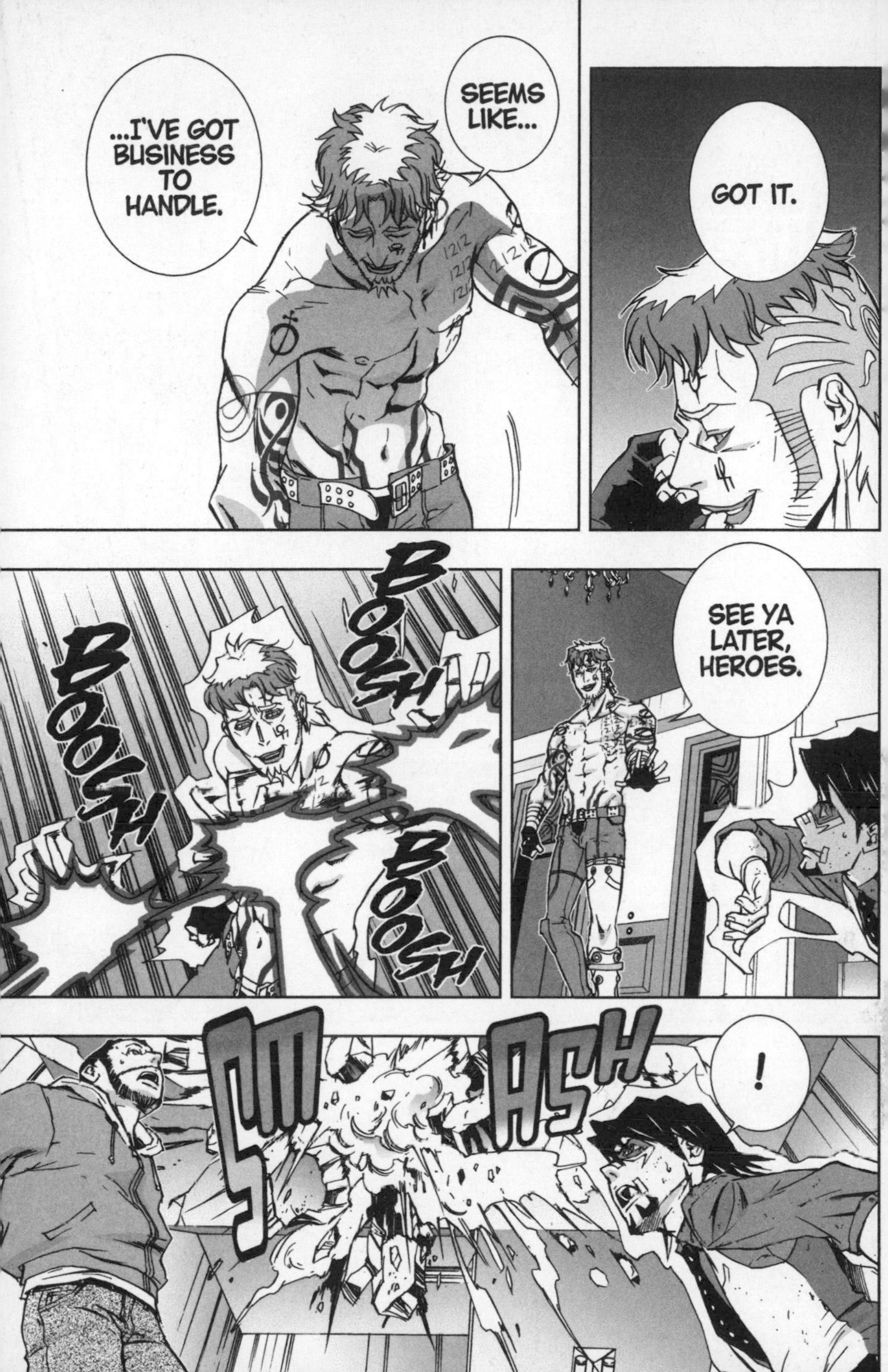
GOT IT.
SEEMS LIKE...
...I'VE GOT BUSINESS TO HANDLE.
SEE YA LATER, HEROES.
BOOSH
BOOSH
BOOSH
!
SMASH

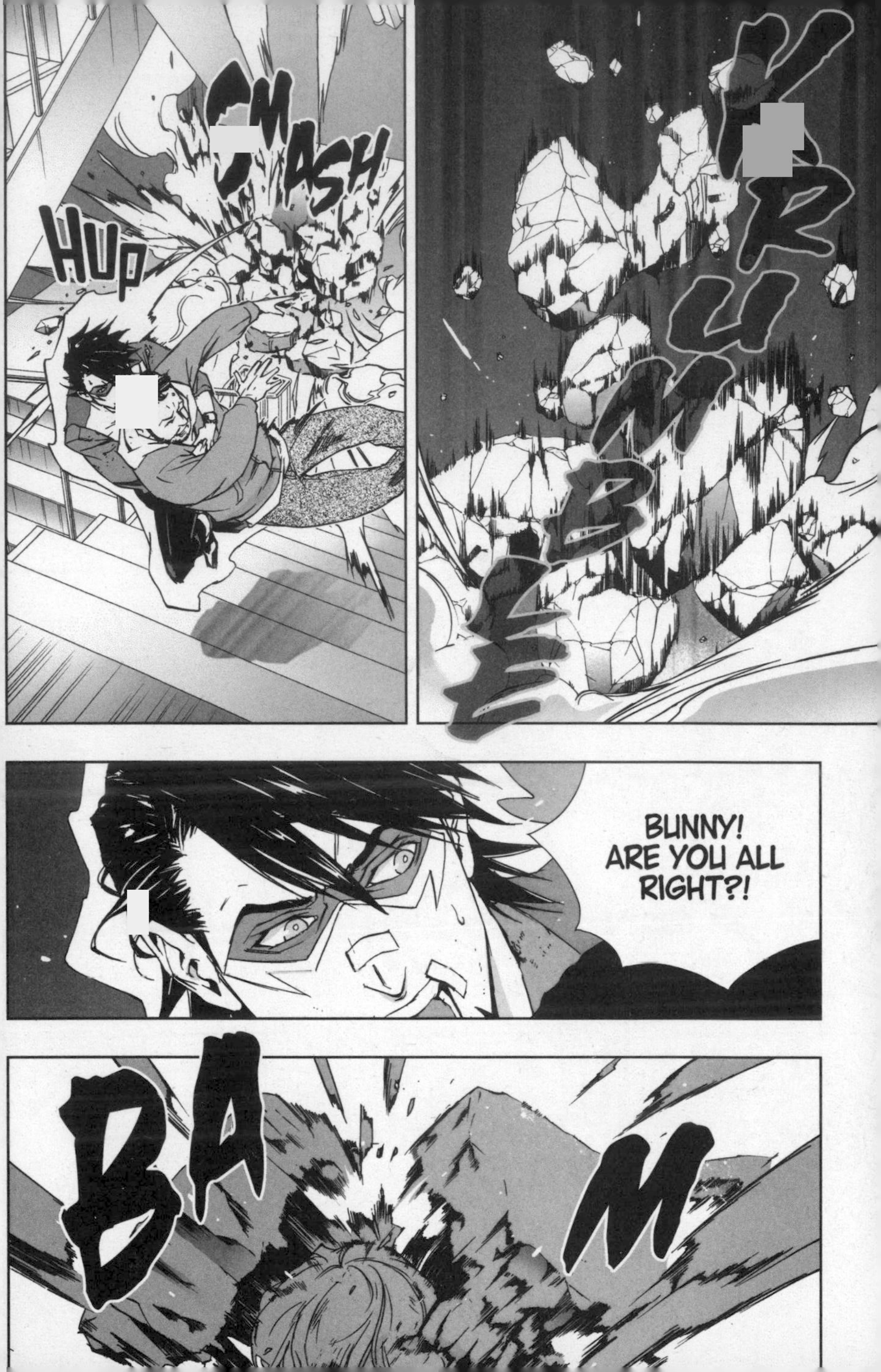
HUP
BUNNY! ARE YOU ALL RIGHT?!
BAM

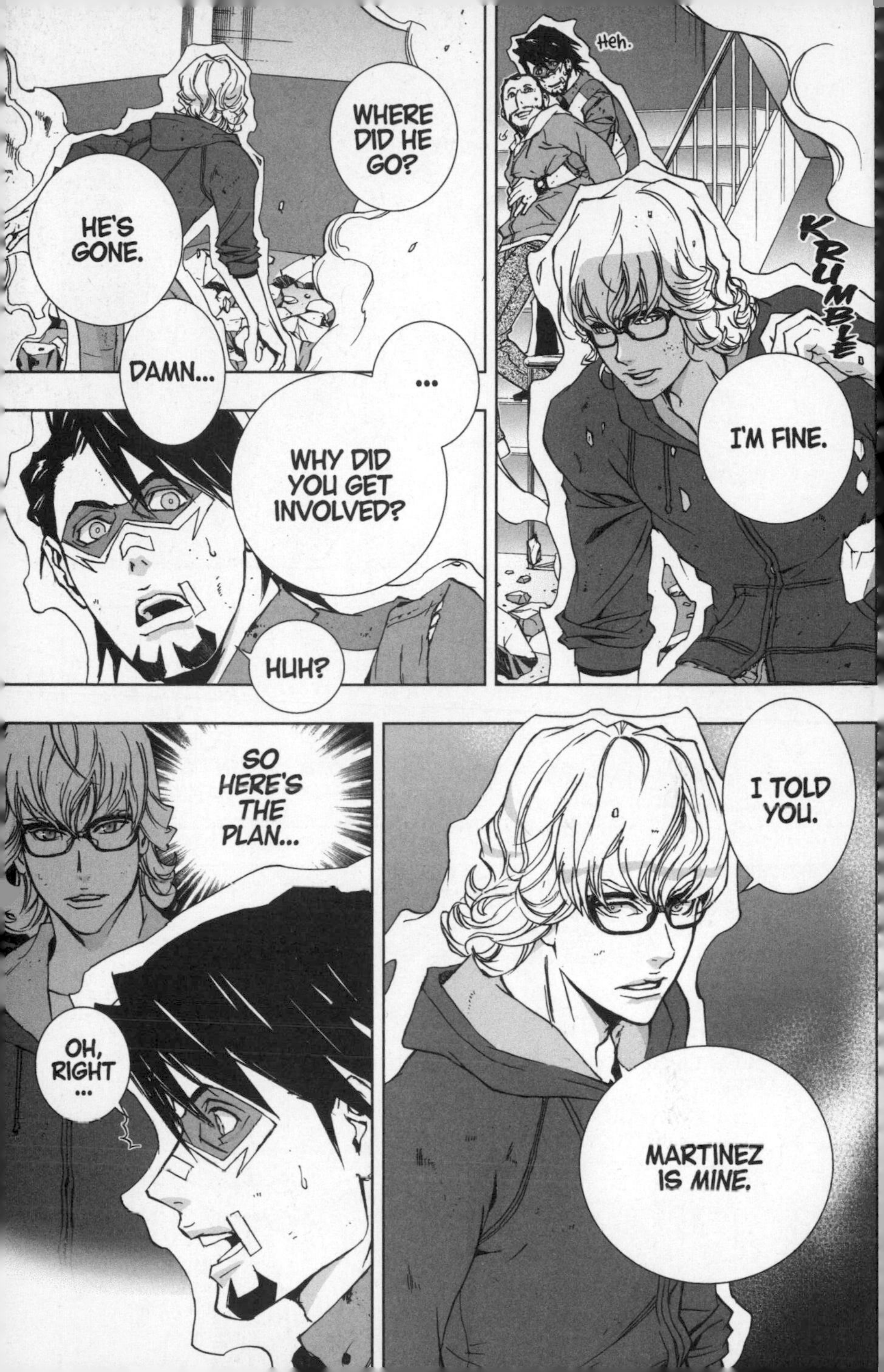
Heh.
KRUMBLE
I'M FINE.
WHERE DID HE GO?
HE'S GONE.
DAMN...
...
WHY DID YOU GET INVOLVED?
HUH?
I TOLD YOU.
MARTINEZ IS MINE.
SO HERE'S THE PLAN...
OH, RIGHT ...

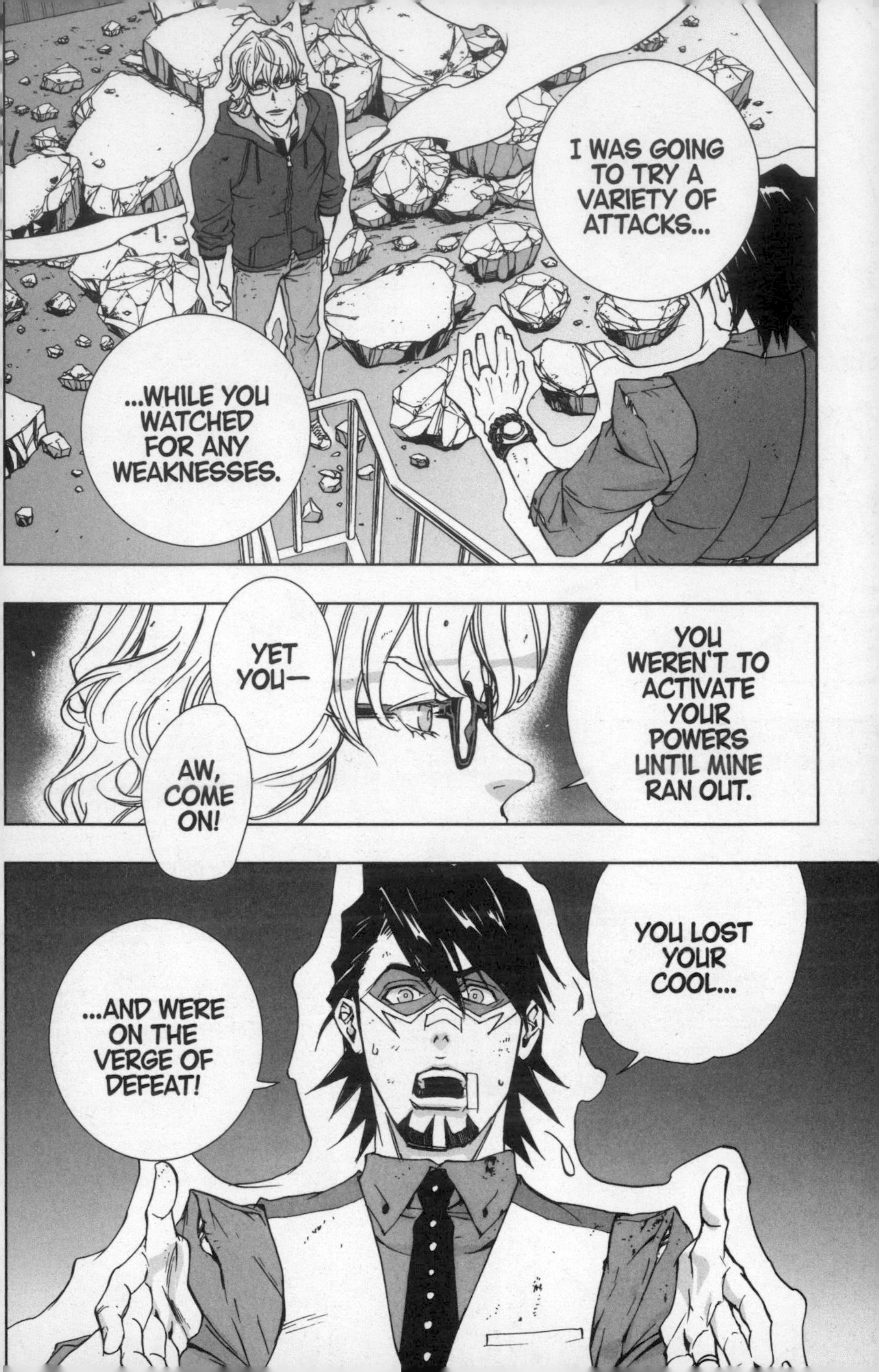
I WAS GOING TO TRY A VARIETY OF ATTACKS...
...WHILE YOU WATCHED FOR ANY WEAKNESSES.
YOU WEREN'T TO ACTIVATE YOUR POWERS UNTIL MINE RAN OUT.
YET YOU—
AW, COME ON!
YOU LOST YOUR COOL...
...AND WERE ON THE VERGE OF DEFEAT!

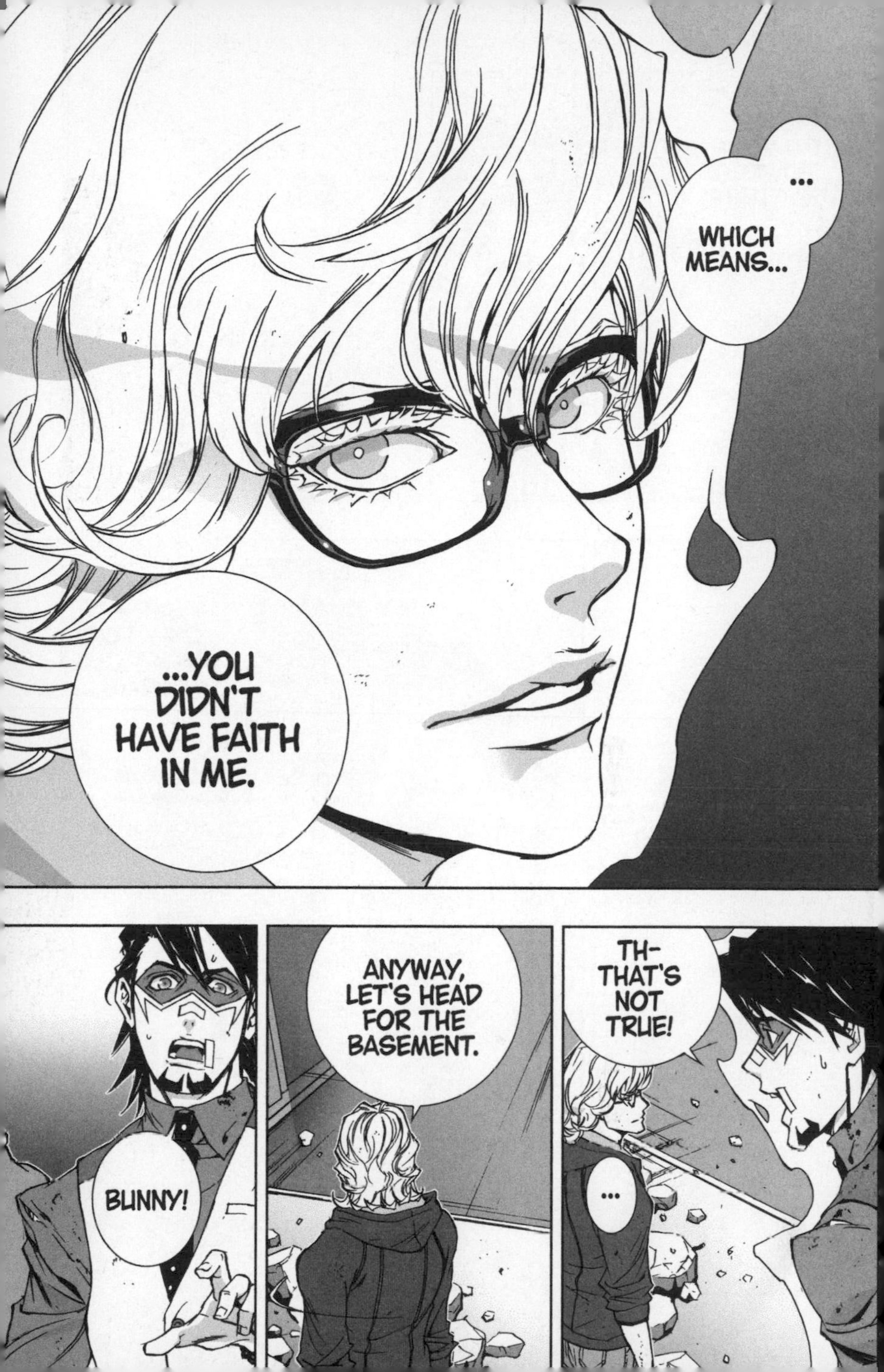
...
WHICH MEANS...
...YOU DIDN'T HAVE FAITH IN ME.
TH-THAT'S NOT TRUE!
...
ANYWAY, LET'S HEAD FOR THE BASEMENT.
BUNNY!

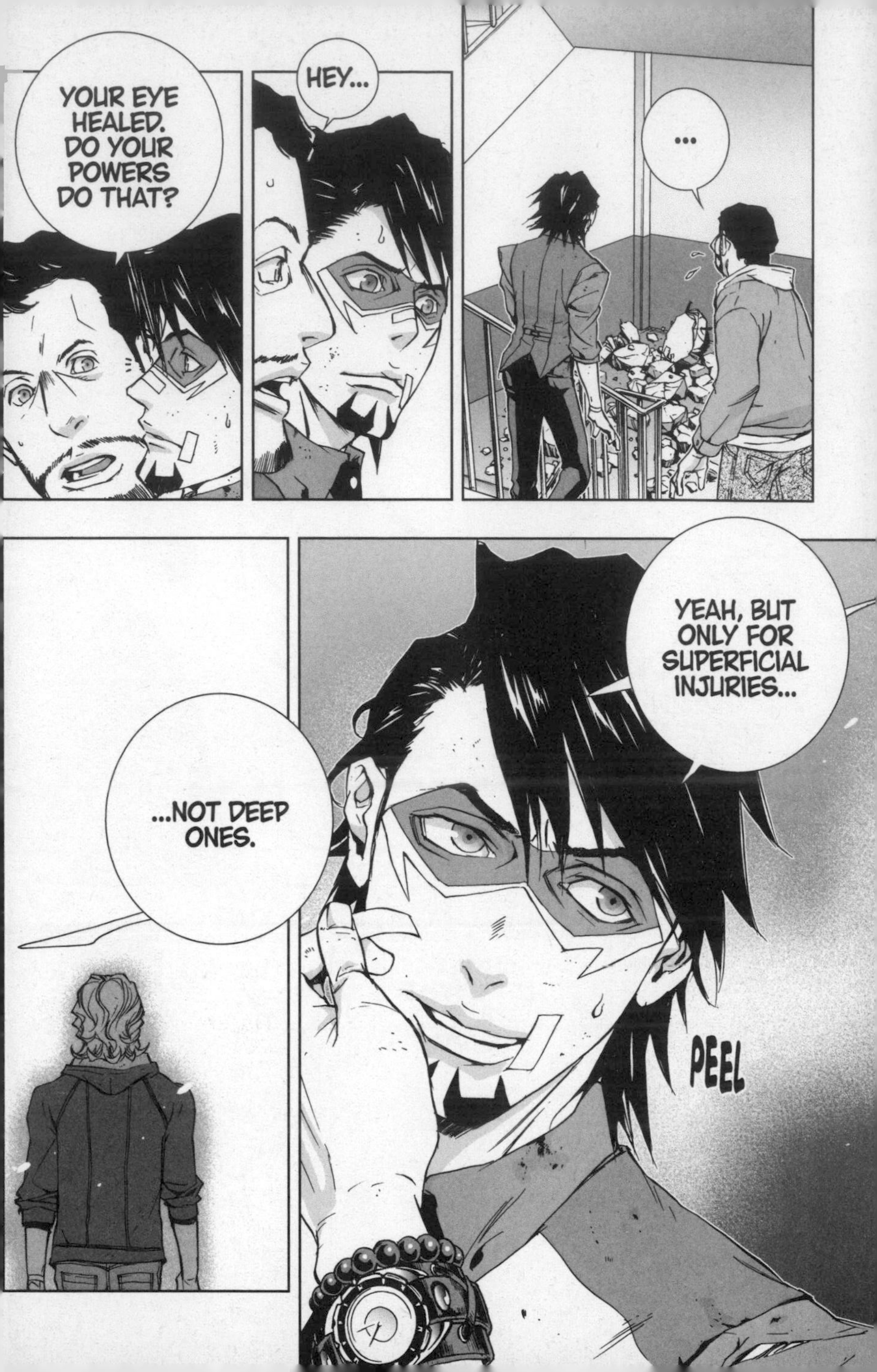
...
HEY...
YOUR EYE HEALED. DO YOUR POWERS DO THAT?
YEAH, BUT ONLY FOR SUPERFICIAL INJURIES...
...NOT DEEP ONES.
PEEL

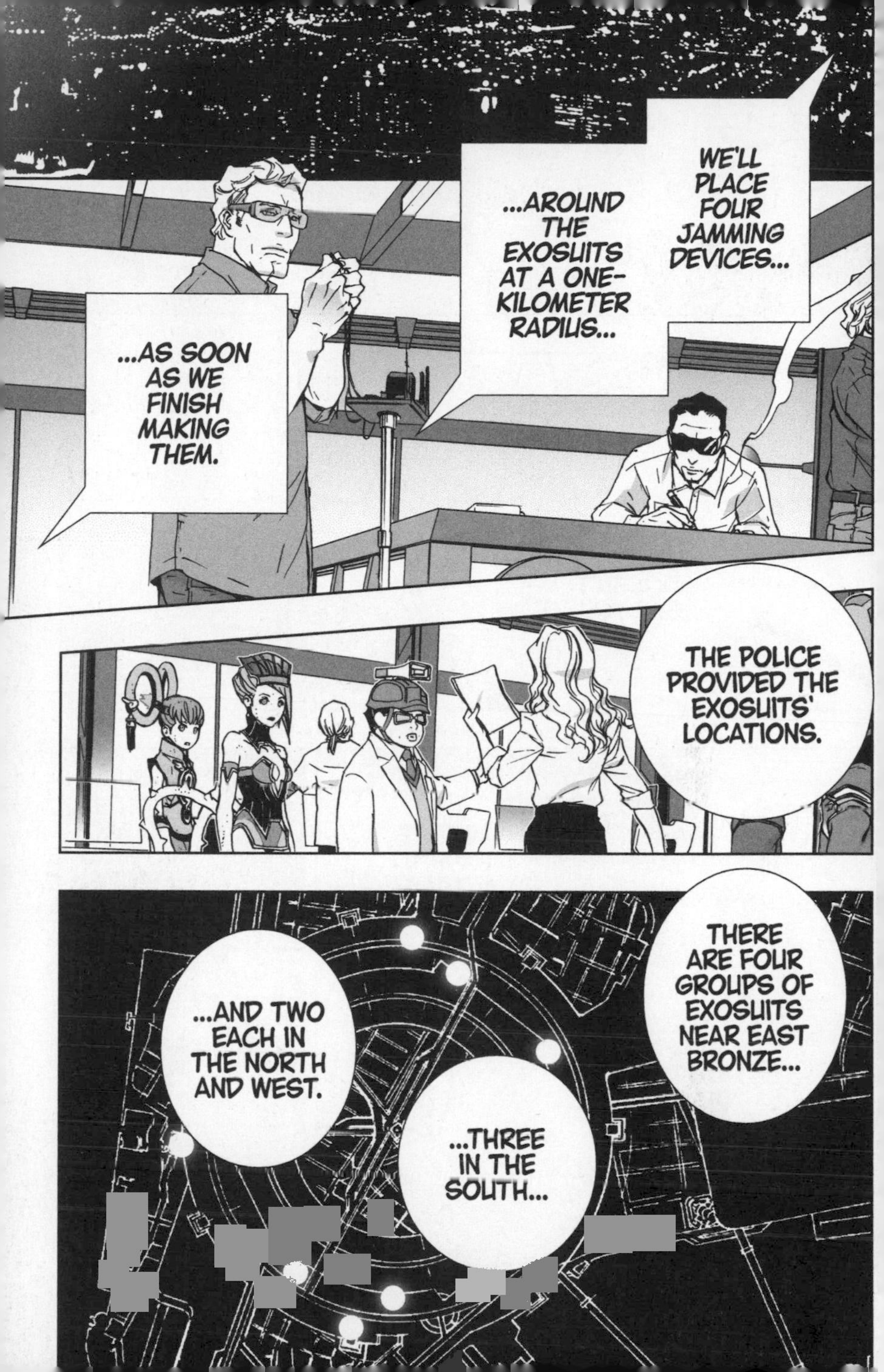
WE'LL PLACE FOUR JAMMING DEVICES...
...AROUND THE EXOSUITS AT A ONE-KILOMETER RADIUS...
...AS SOON AS WE FINISH MAKING THEM.
THE POLICE PROVIDED THE EXOSUITS' LOCATIONS.
THERE ARE FOUR GROUPS OF EXOSUITS NEAR EAST BRONZE...
...THREE IN THE SOUTH...
...AND TWO EACH IN THE NORTH AND WEST.

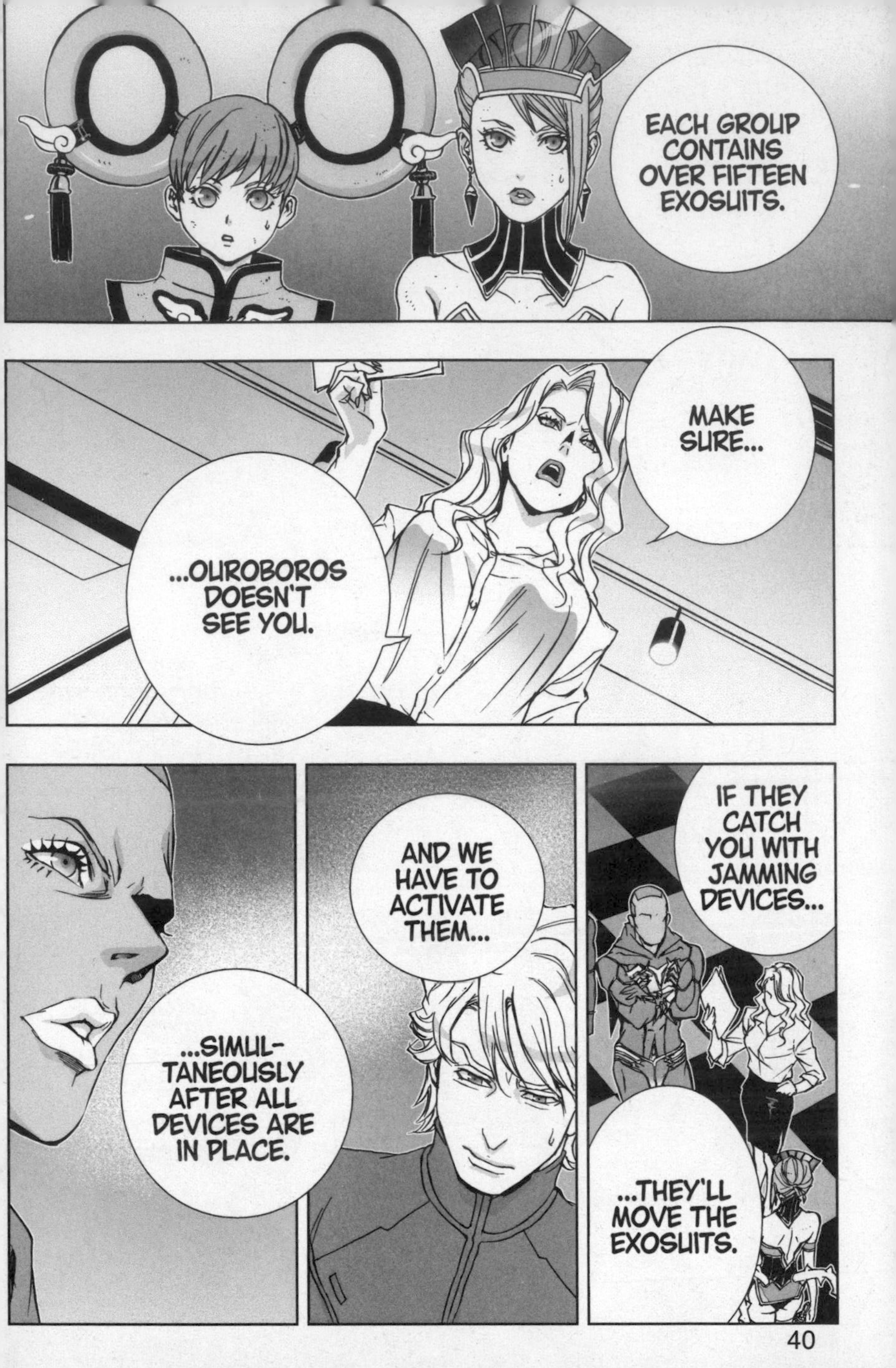
EACH GROUP CONTAINS OVER FIFTEEN EXOSUITS.
MAKE SURE...
...OUROBOROS DOESN'T SEE YOU.
IF THEY CATCH YOU WITH JAMMING DEVICES...
...THEY'LL MOVE THE EXOSUITS.
AND WE HAVE TO ACTIVATE THEM...
...SIMUL-TANEOUSLY AFTER ALL DEVICES ARE IN PLACE.

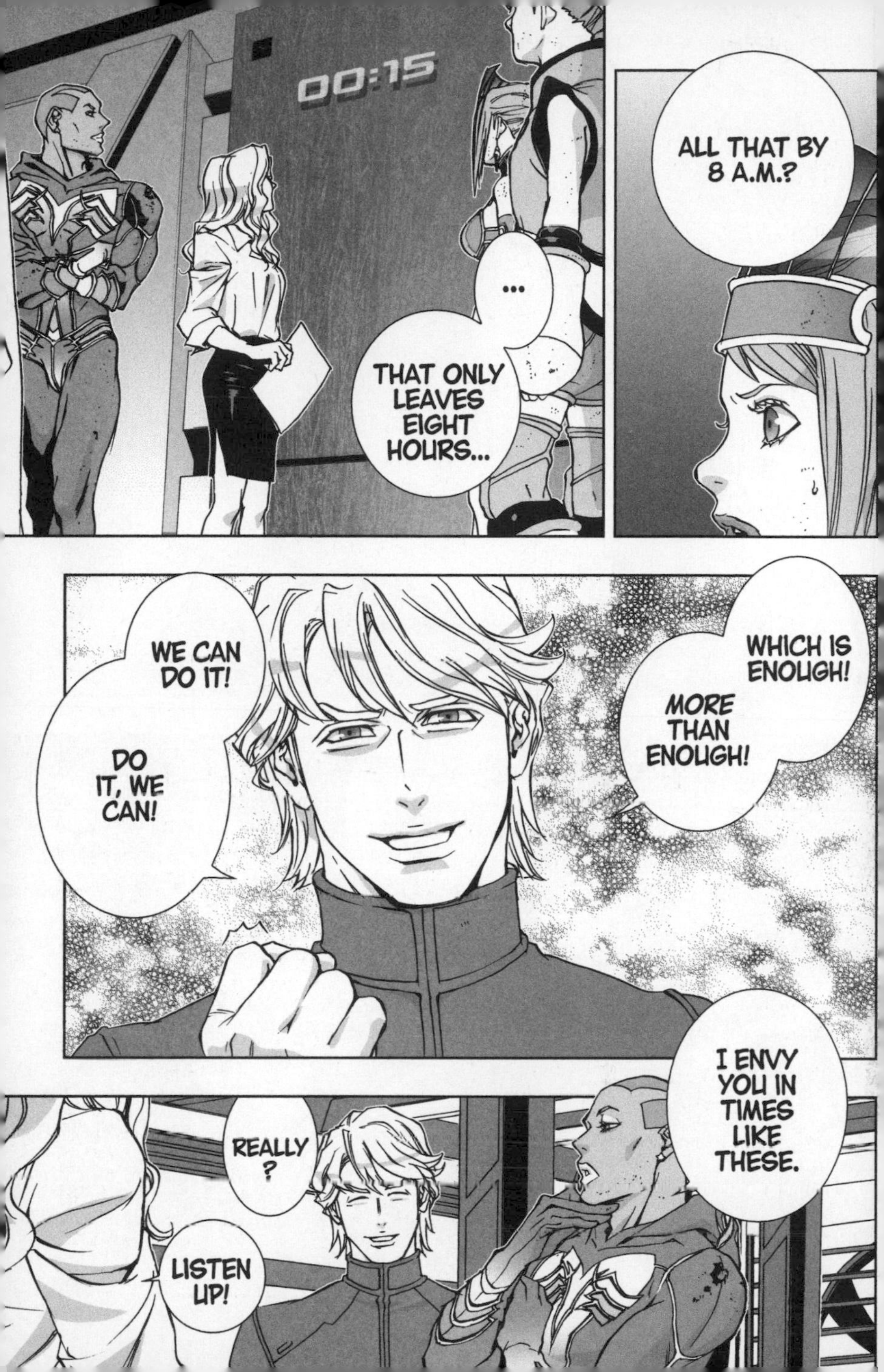
00:15
ALL THAT BY 8 A.M.?
...
THAT ONLY LEAVES EIGHT HOURS...
WHICH IS ENOUGH!
MORE THAN ENOUGH!
WE CAN DO IT!
DO IT, WE CAN!
I ENVY YOU IN TIMES LIKE THESE.
REALLY?
LISTEN UP!

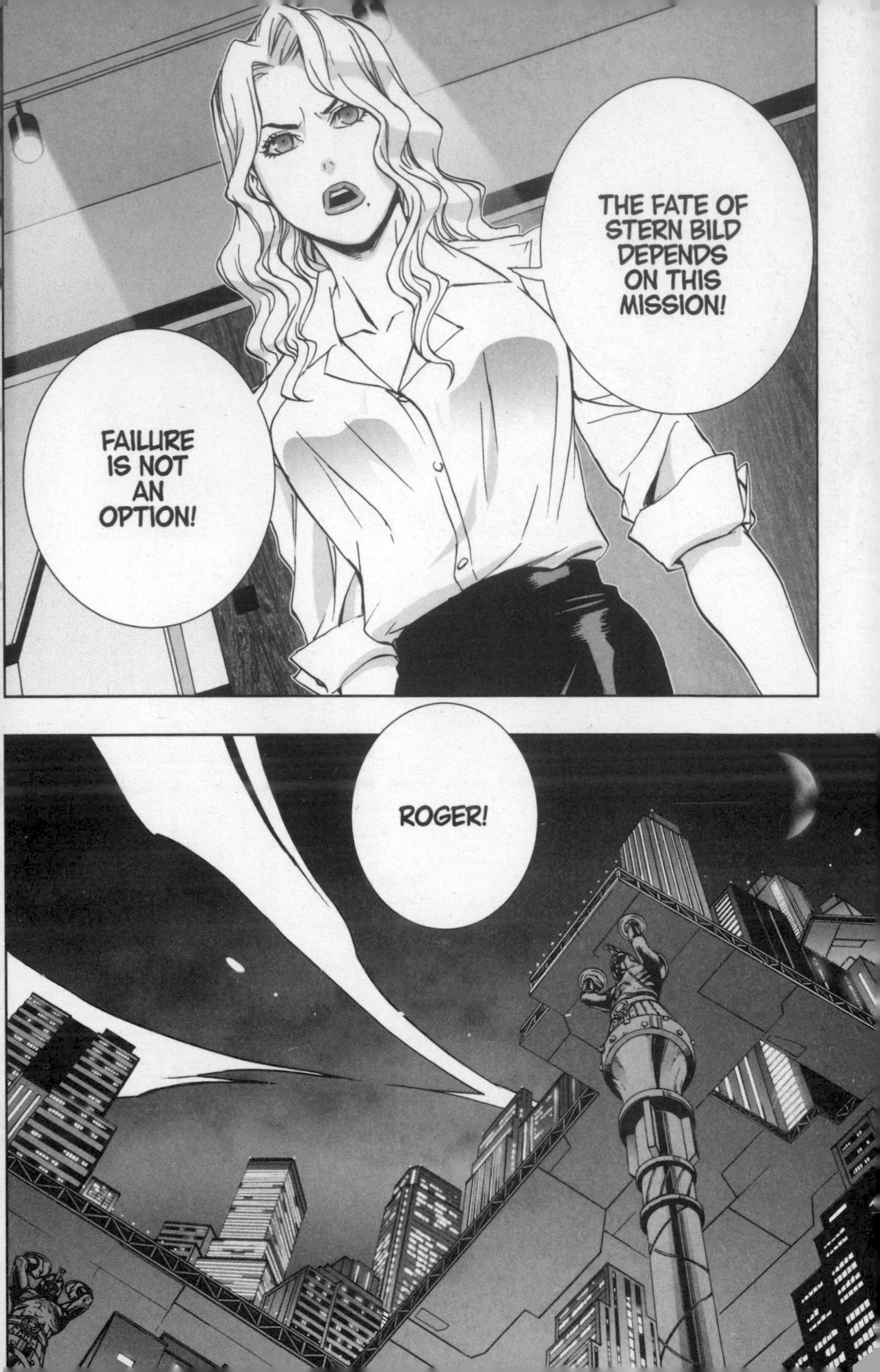
THE FATE OF STERN BILD DEPENDS ON THIS MISSION!
FAILURE IS NOT AN OPTION!
ROGER!

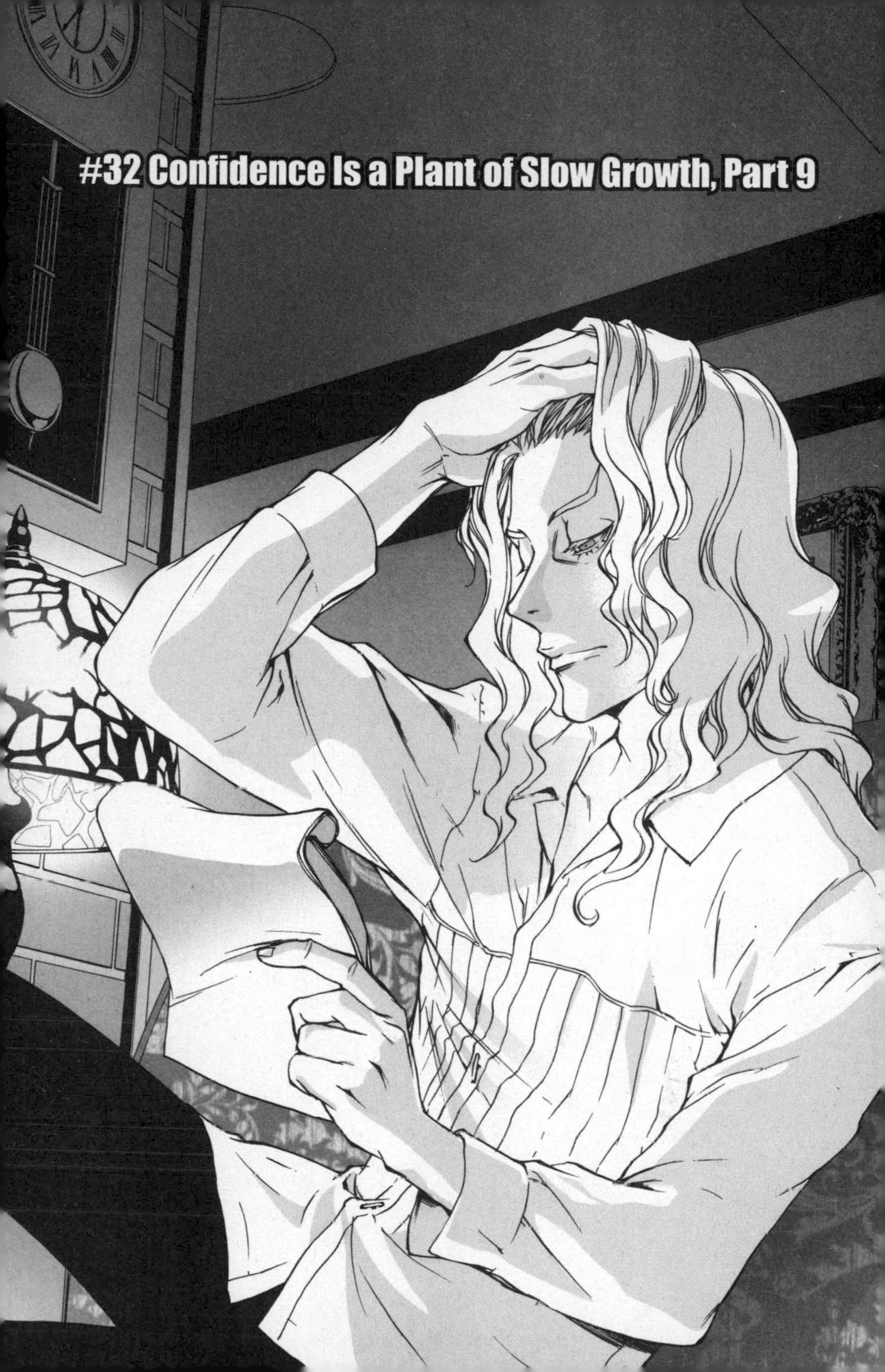
#32 Confidence Is a Plant of Slow Growth, Part 9

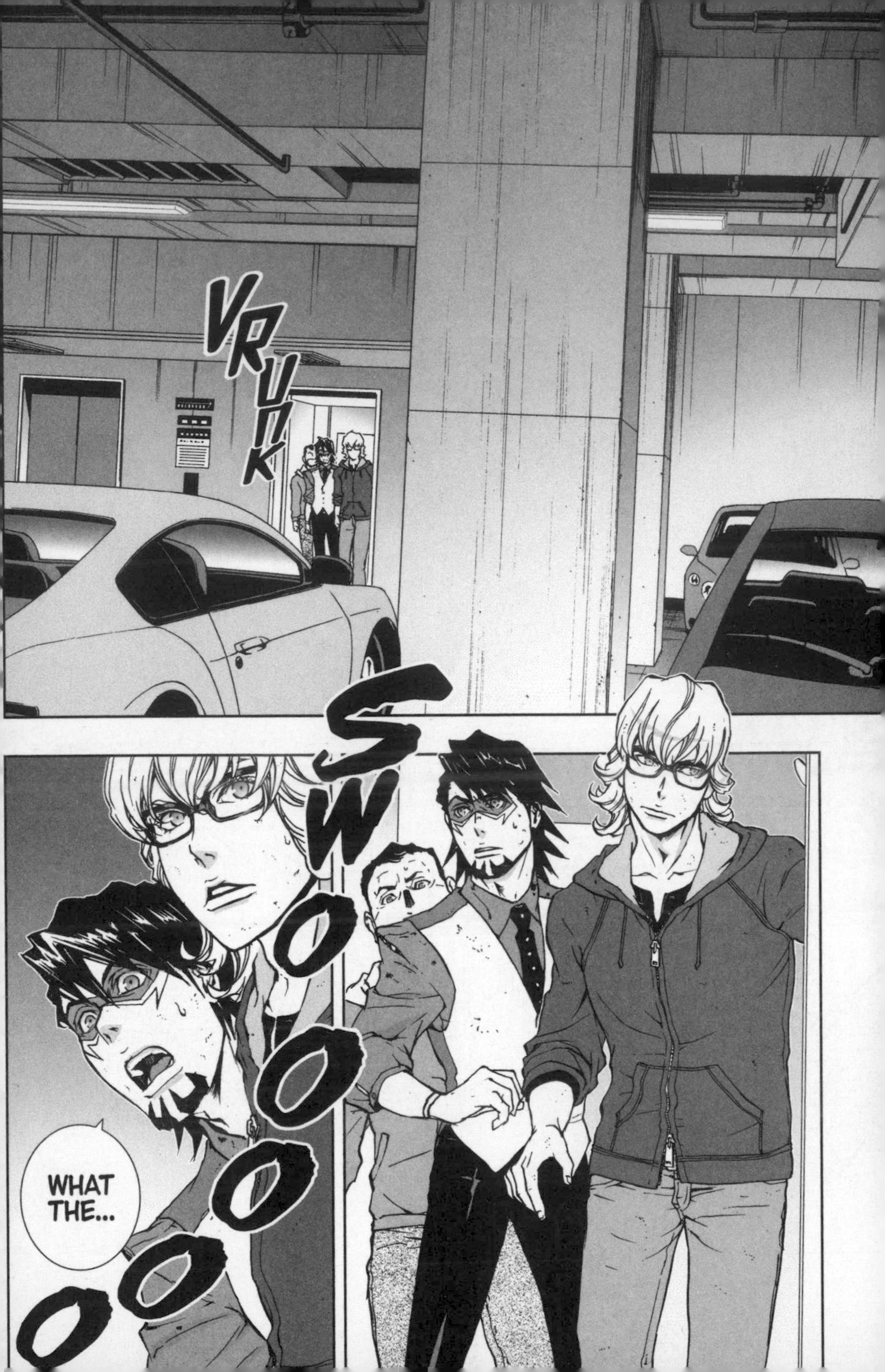
VRUNK
SWOOOOOOOO
WHAT THE...

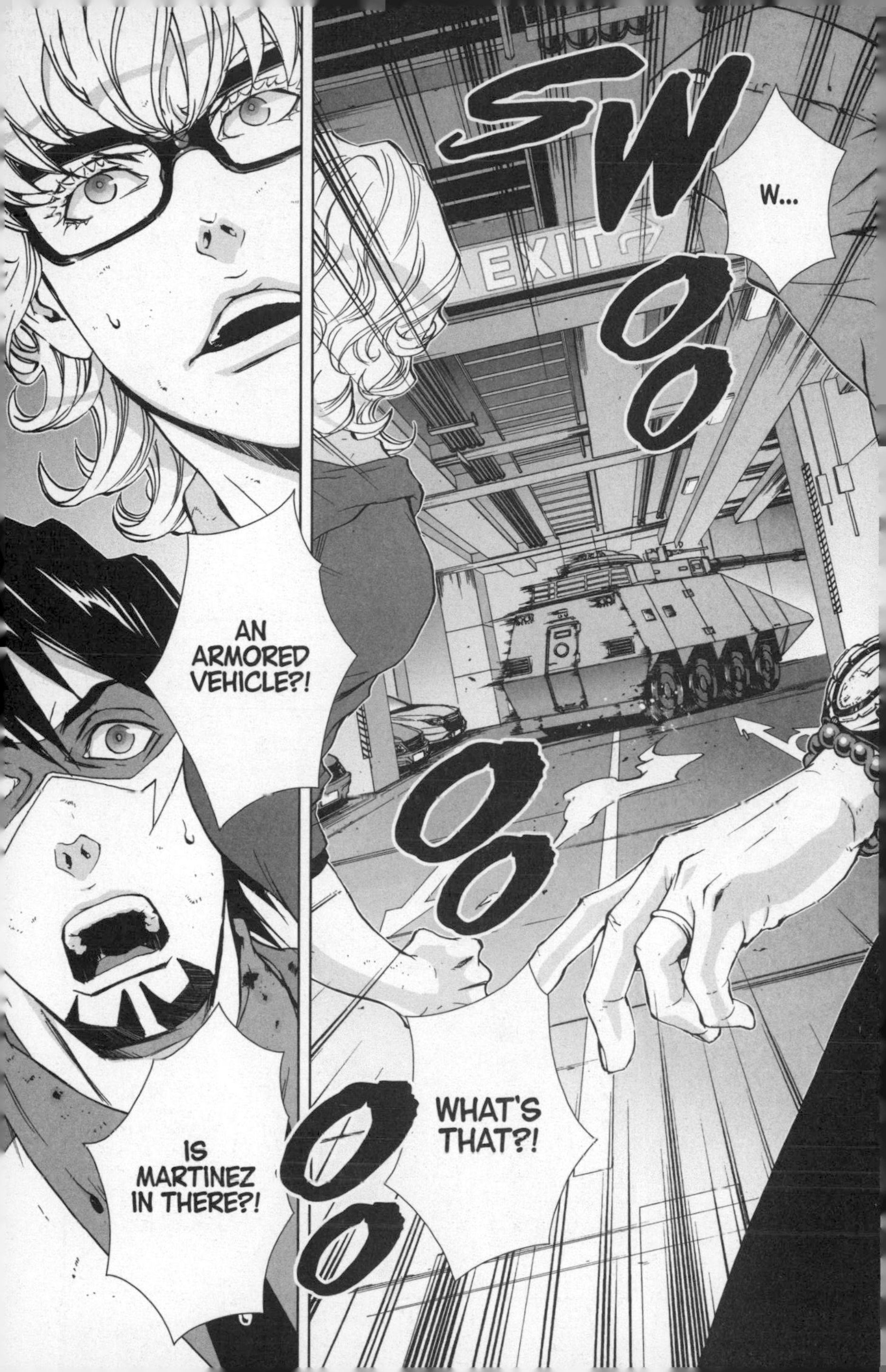
W...
SWOOOOOO
EXIT
WHAT'S THAT?!
AN ARMORED VEHICLE?!
IS MARTINEZ IN THERE?!

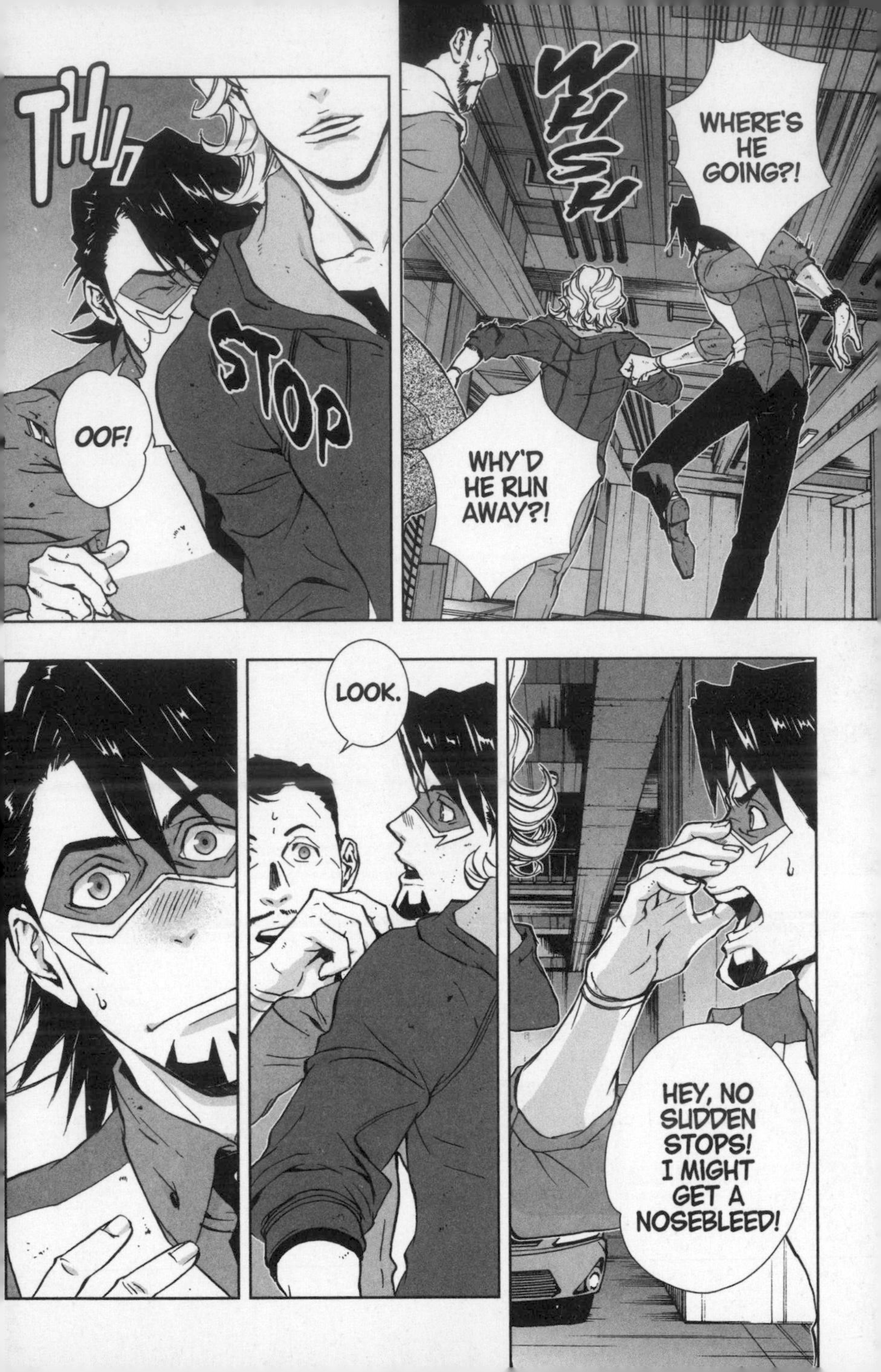
WHSH
WHERE'S HE GOING?!
WHY'D HE RUN AWAY?!
THU
STOP
OOF!
HEY, NO SUDDEN STOPS! I MIGHT GET A NOSEBLEED!
LOOK.

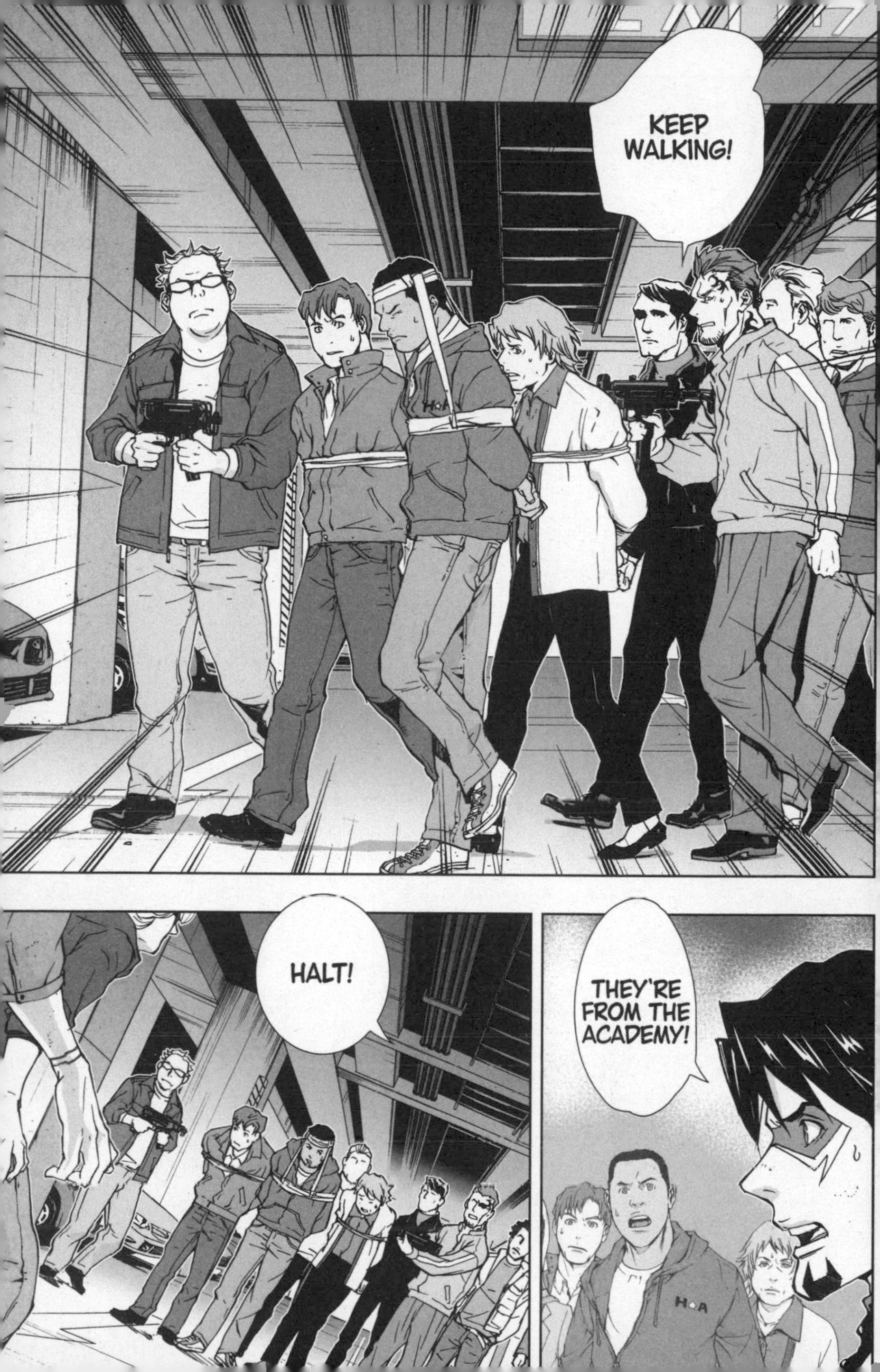
KEEP WALKING!
THEY'RE FROM THE ACADEMY!
HALT!

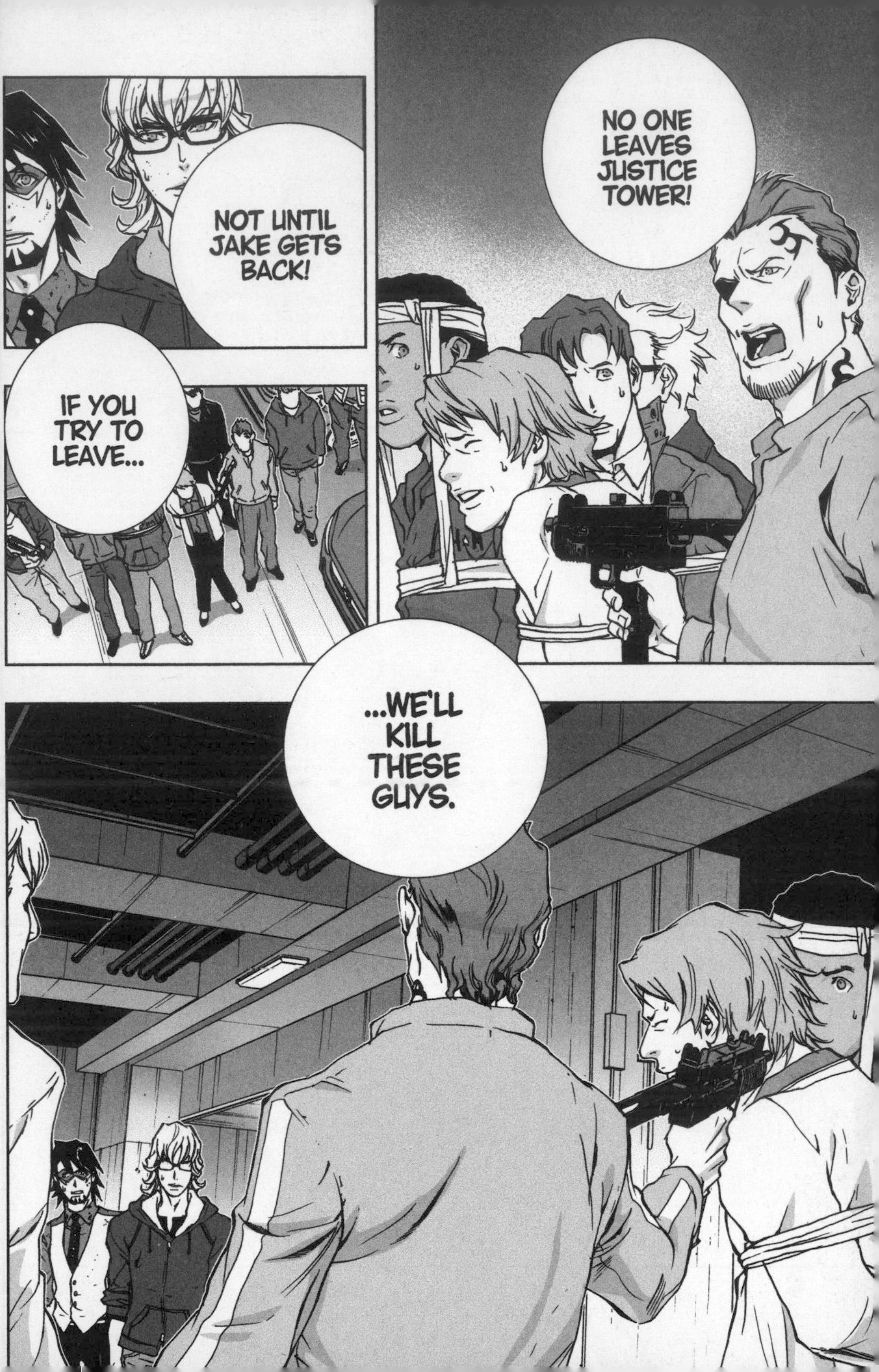
NO ONE LEAVES JUSTICE TOWER!
NOT UNTIL JAKE GETS BACK!
IF YOU TRY TO LEAVE...
...WE'LL KILL THESE GUYS.

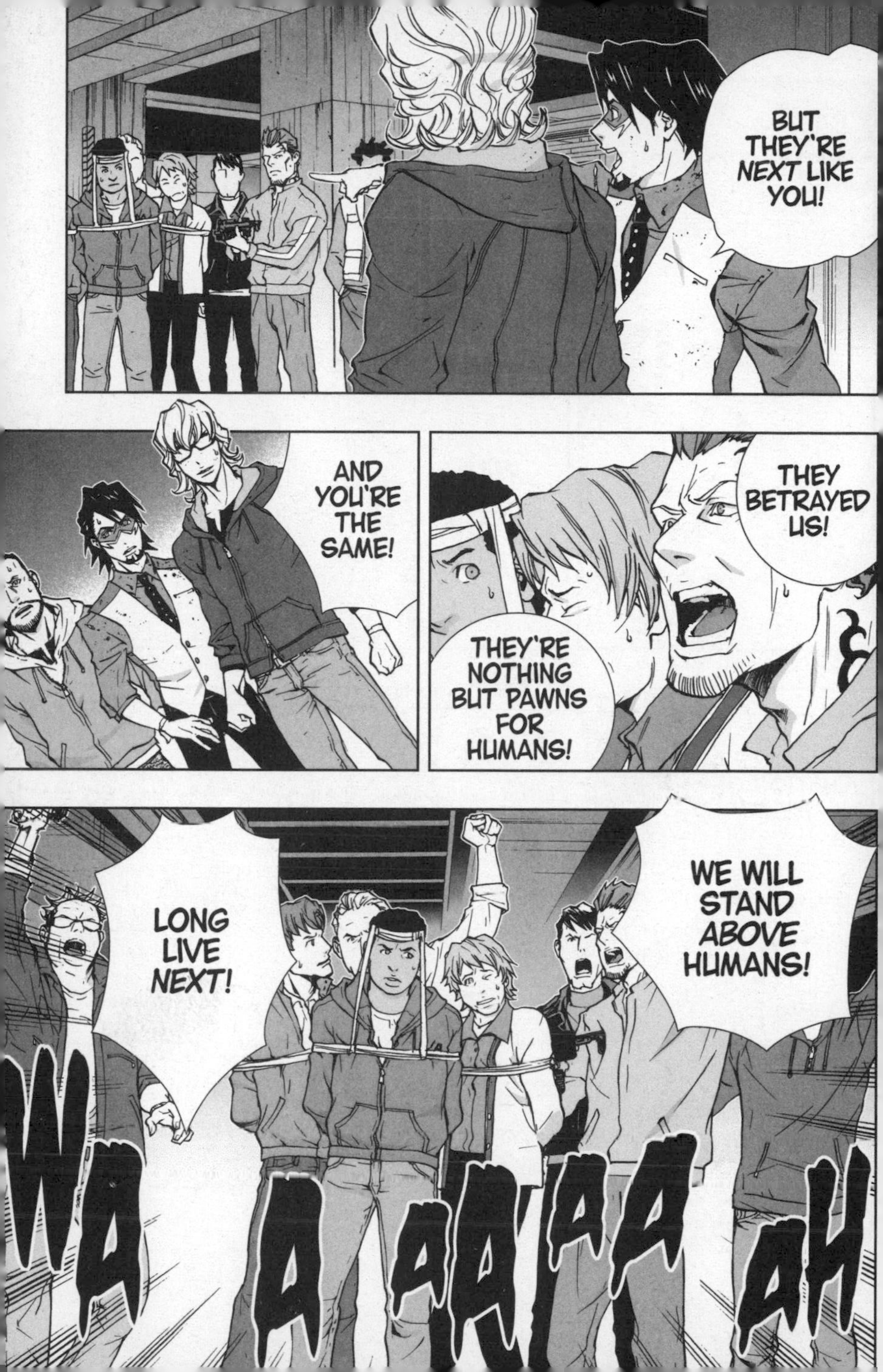
BUT THEY'RE NEXT LIKE YOU!
THEY BETRAYED US!
THEY'RE NOTHING BUT PAWNS FOR HUMANS!
AND YOU'RE THE SAME!
WE WILL STAND ABOVE HUMANS!
LONG LIVE NEXT!
WAAAAAAAH

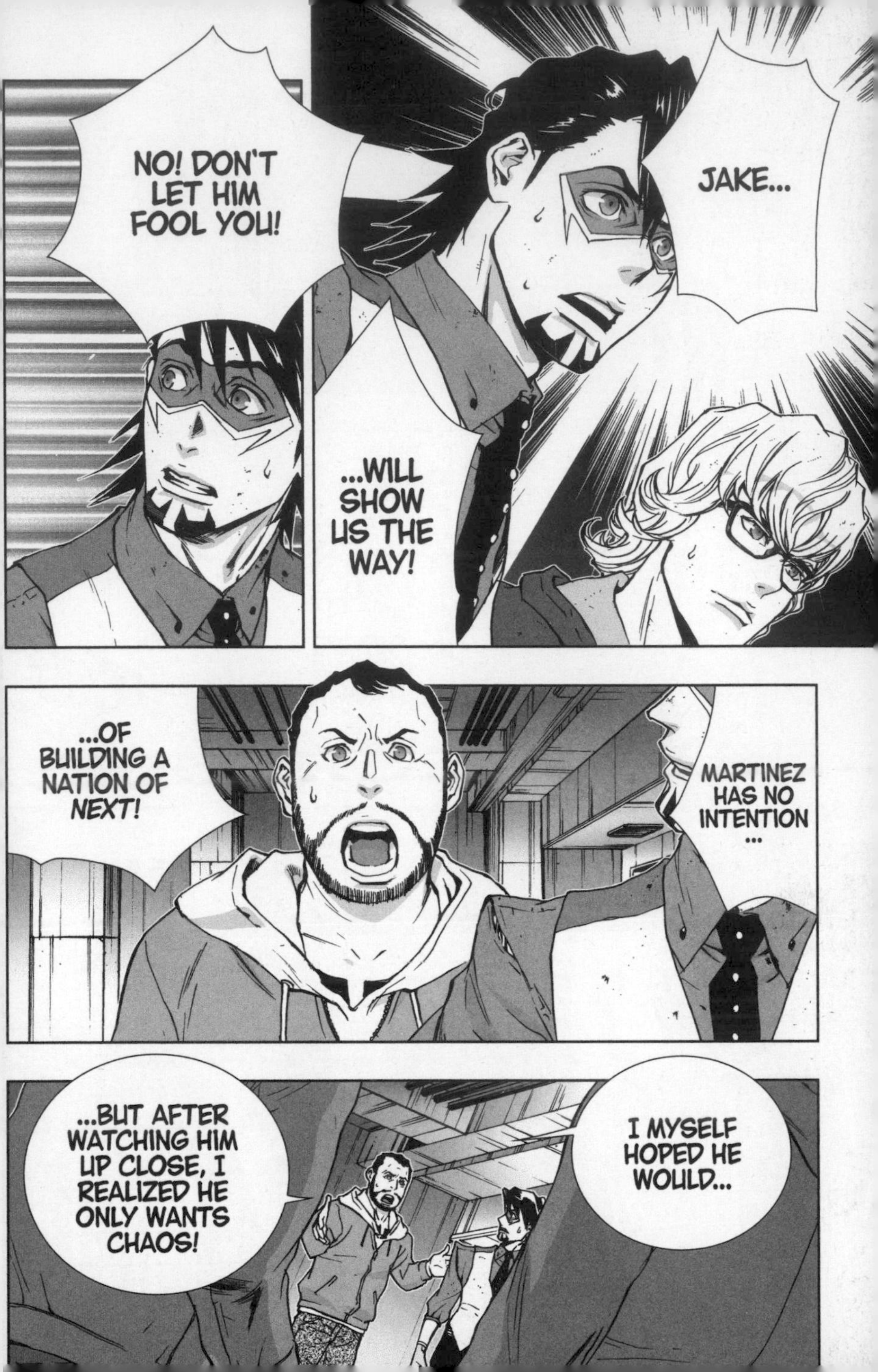
JAKE...
...WILL SHOW US THE WAY!
NO! DON'T LET HIM FOOL YOU!
MARTINEZ HAS NO INTENTION ...
...OF BUILDING A NATION OF NEXT!
I MYSELF HOPED HE WOULD...
...BUT AFTER WATCHING HIM UP CLOSE, I REALIZED HE ONLY WANTS CHAOS!

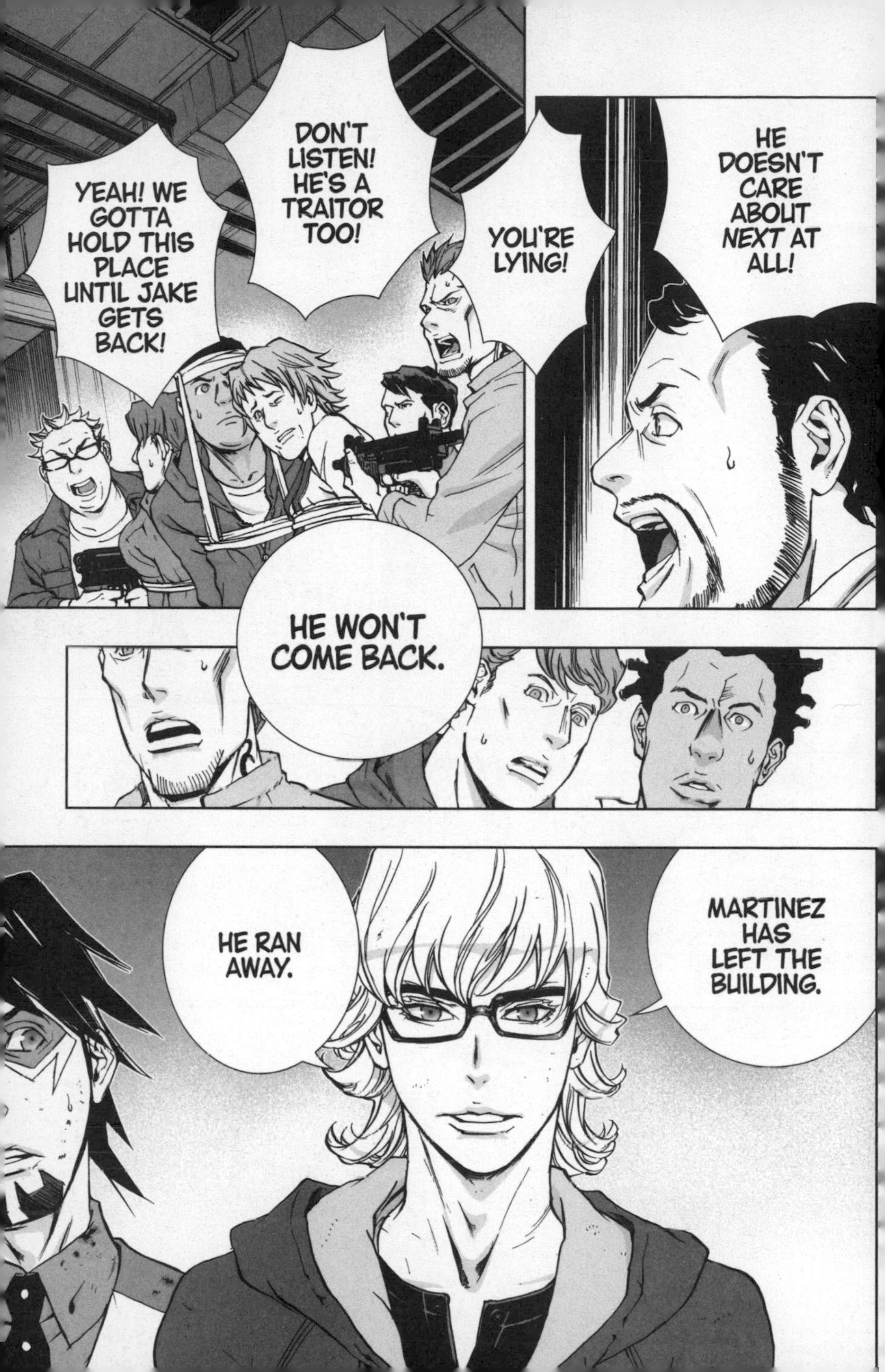
HE DOESN'T CARE ABOUT NEXT AT ALL!
YOU'RE LYING!
DON'T LISTEN! HE'S A TRAITOR TOO!
YEAH! WE GOTTA HOLD THIS PLACE UNTIL JAKE GETS BACK!
HE WON'T COME BACK.
MARTINEZ HAS LEFT THE BUILDING.
HE RAN AWAY.

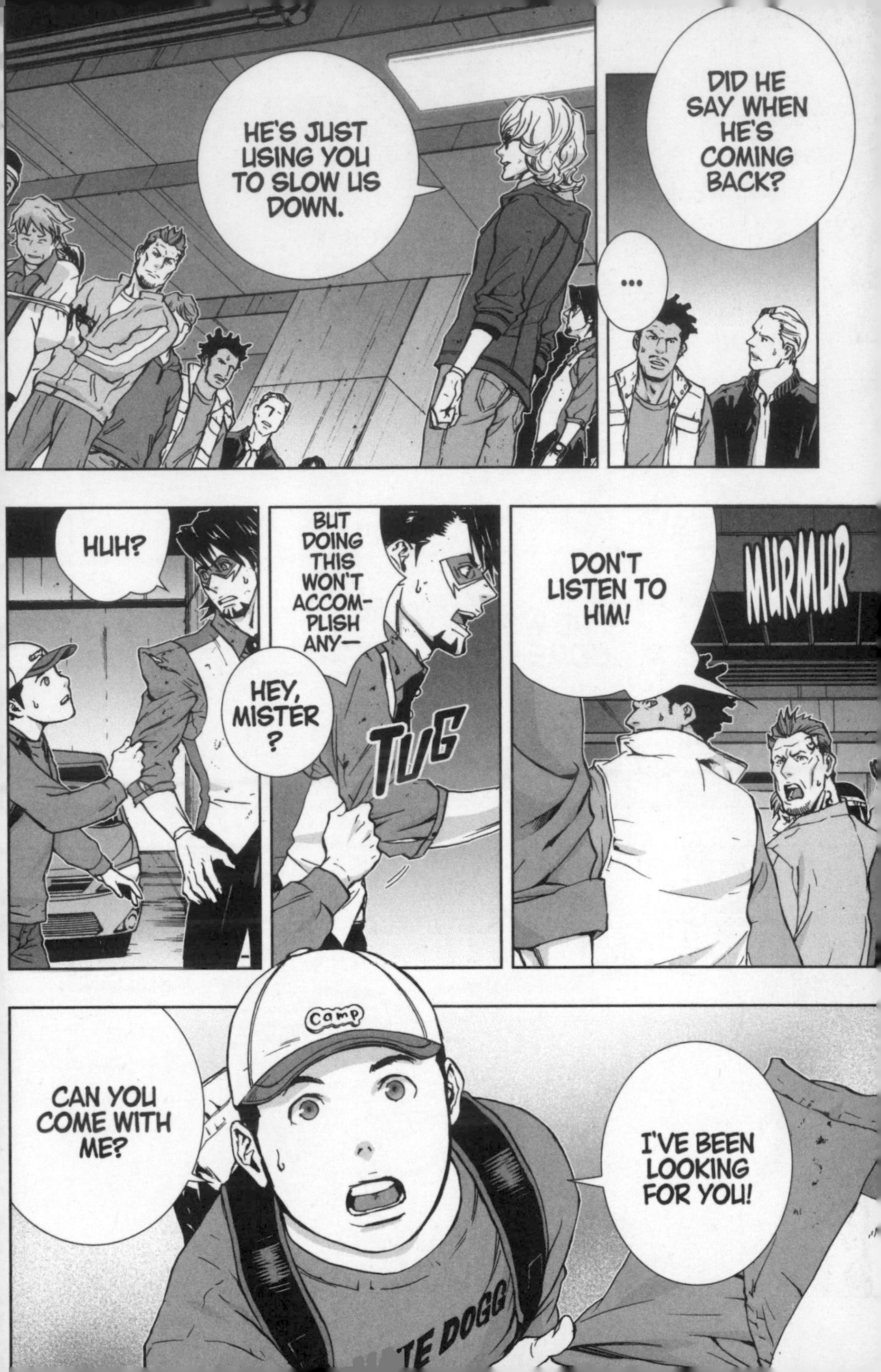
DID HE SAY WHEN HE'S COMING BACK?
...
HE'S JUST USING YOU TO SLOW US DOWN.
MURMUR
DON'T LISTEN TO HIM!
BUT DOING THIS WON'T ACCOM-PLISH ANY—
TUG
HEY, MISTER?
HUH?
I'VE BEEN LOOKING FOR YOU!
camp
CAN YOU COME WITH ME?

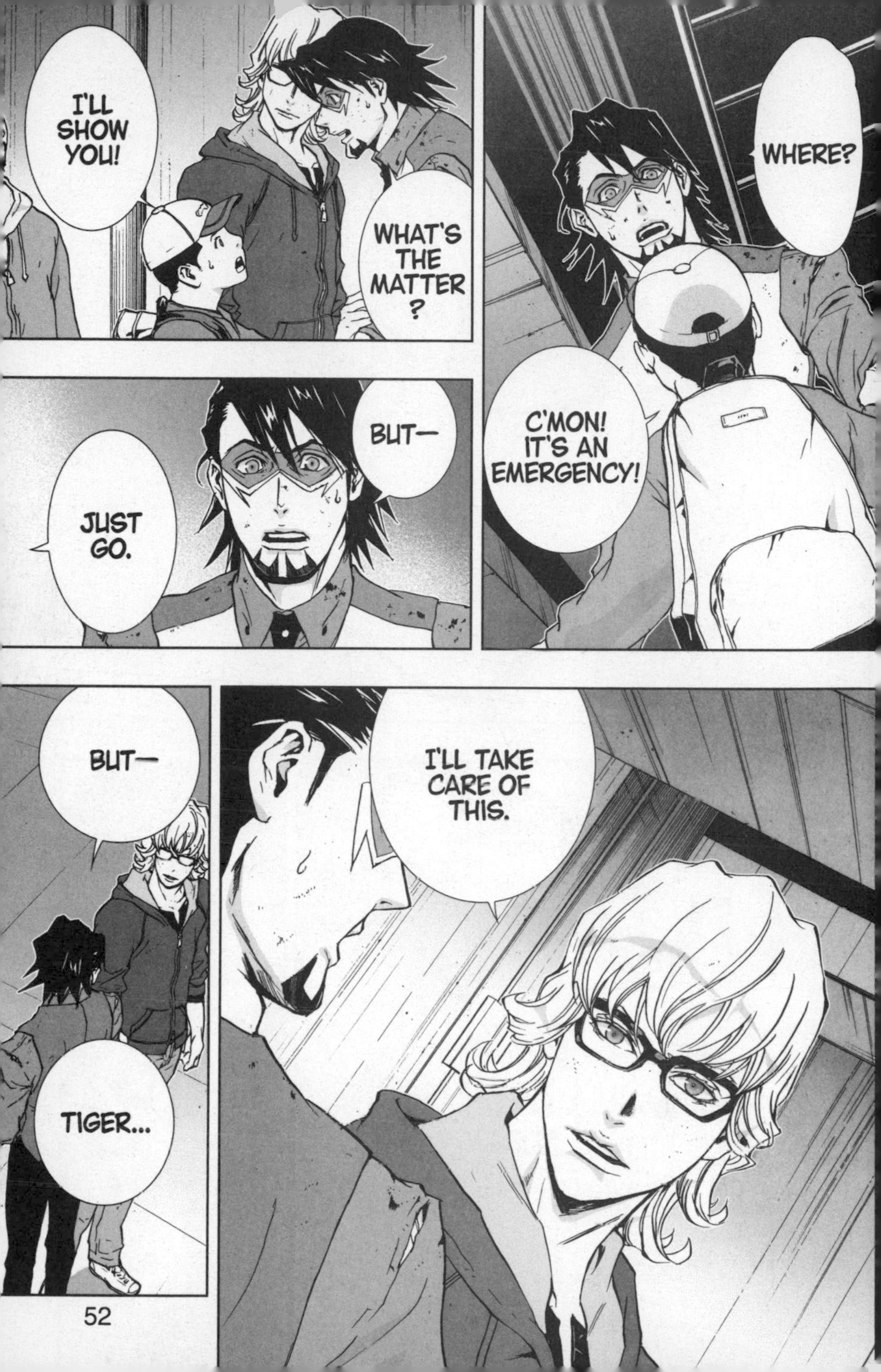
WHERE?
C'MON! IT'S AN EMERGENCY!
WHAT'S THE MATTER?
I'LL SHOW YOU!
BUT—
JUST GO.
I'LL TAKE CARE OF THIS.
BUT—
TIGER...

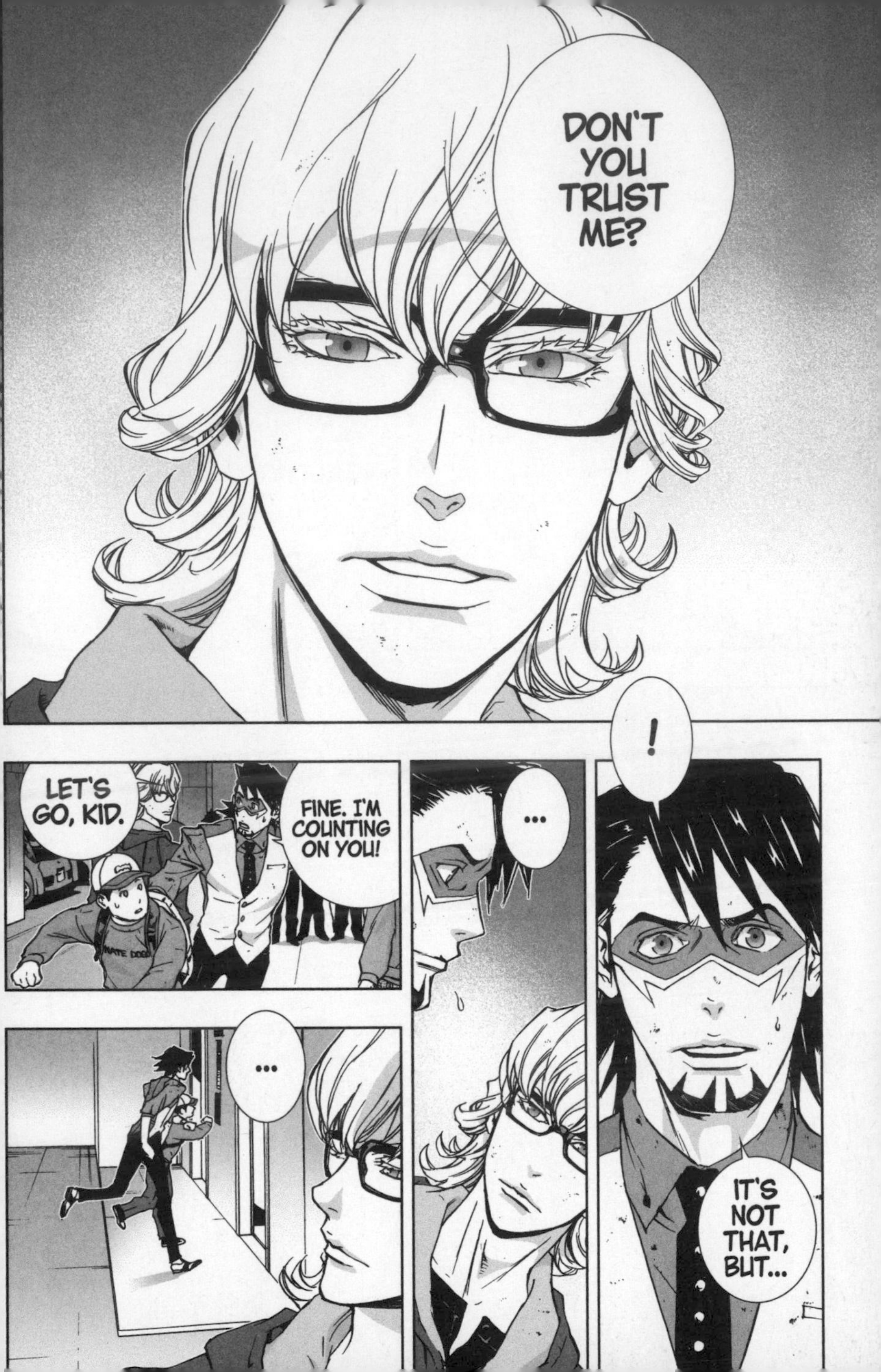
DON'T YOU TRUST ME?
!
IT'S NOT THAT, BUT...
...
FINE. I'M COUNTING ON YOU!
LET'S GO, KID.
...

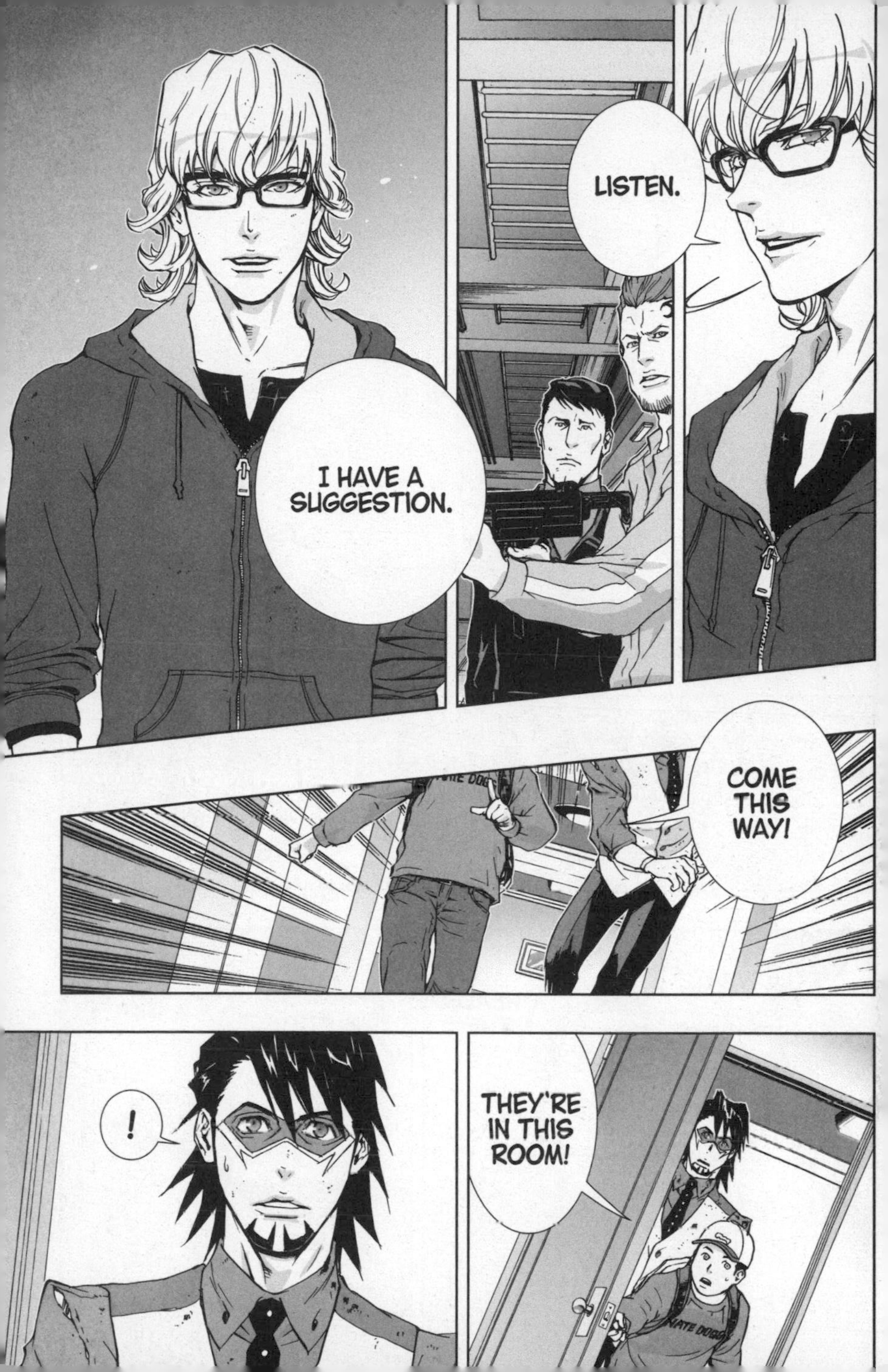
LISTEN.
I HAVE A SUGGESTION.
COME THIS WAY!
THEY'RE IN THIS ROOM!
!

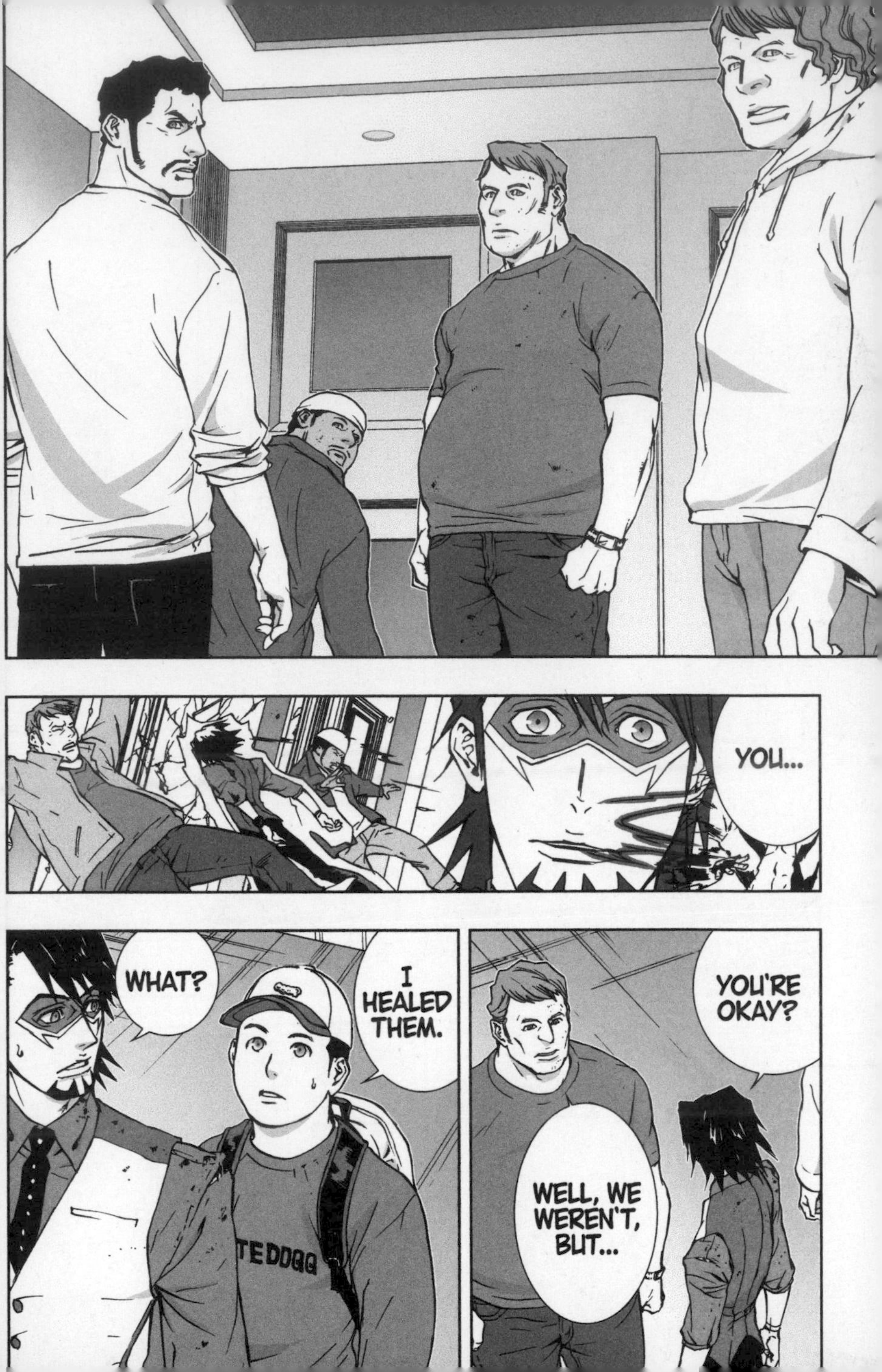
YOU...
YOU'RE OKAY?
WELL, WE WEREN'T, BUT...
I HEALED THEM.
WHAT?

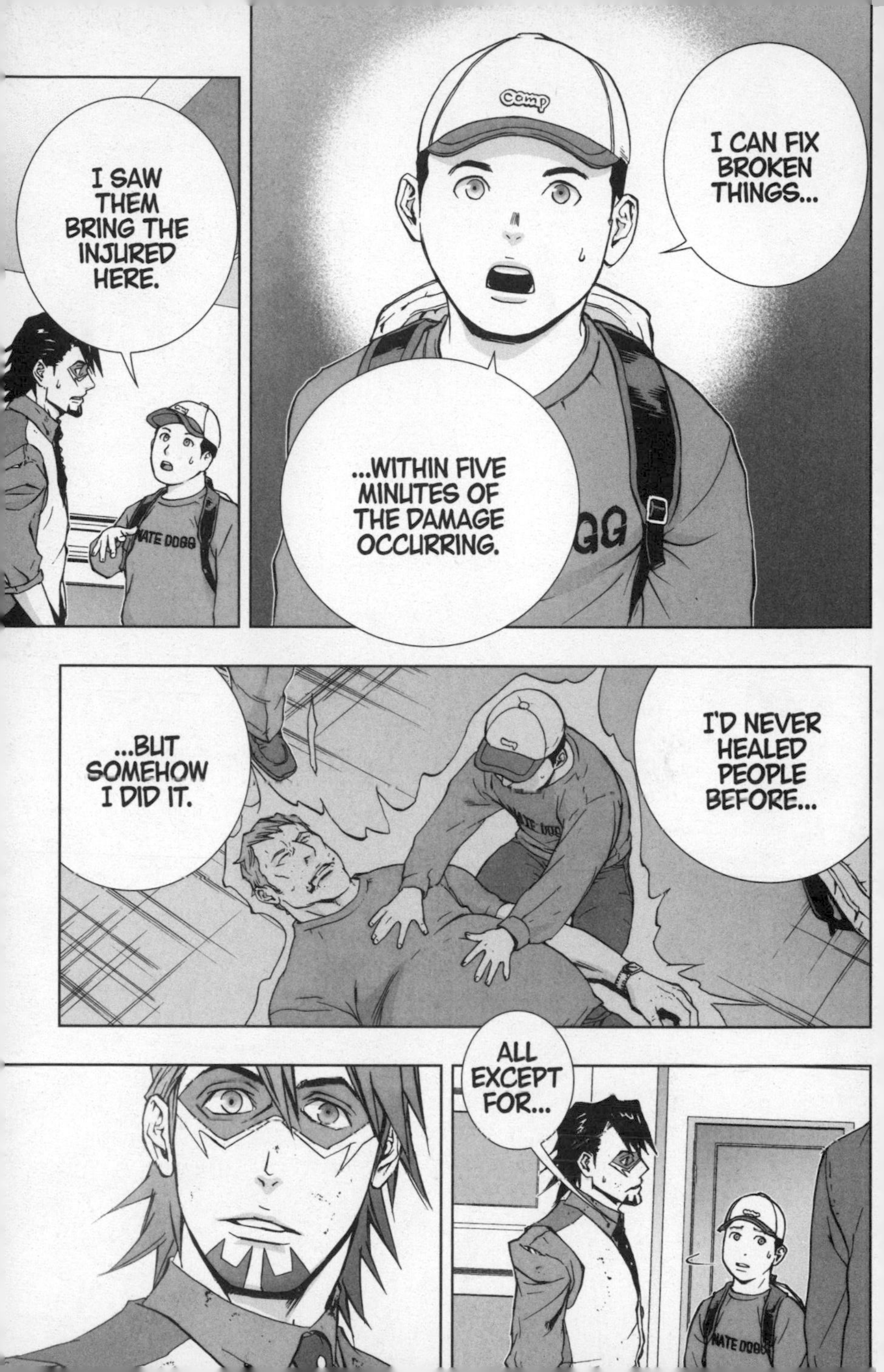
I CAN FIX BROKEN THINGS...
...WITHIN FIVE MINUTES OF THE DAMAGE OCCURRING.
I SAW THEM BRING THE INJURED HERE.
I'D NEVER HEALED PEOPLE BEFORE...
...BUT SOMEHOW I DID IT.
ALL EXCEPT FOR...

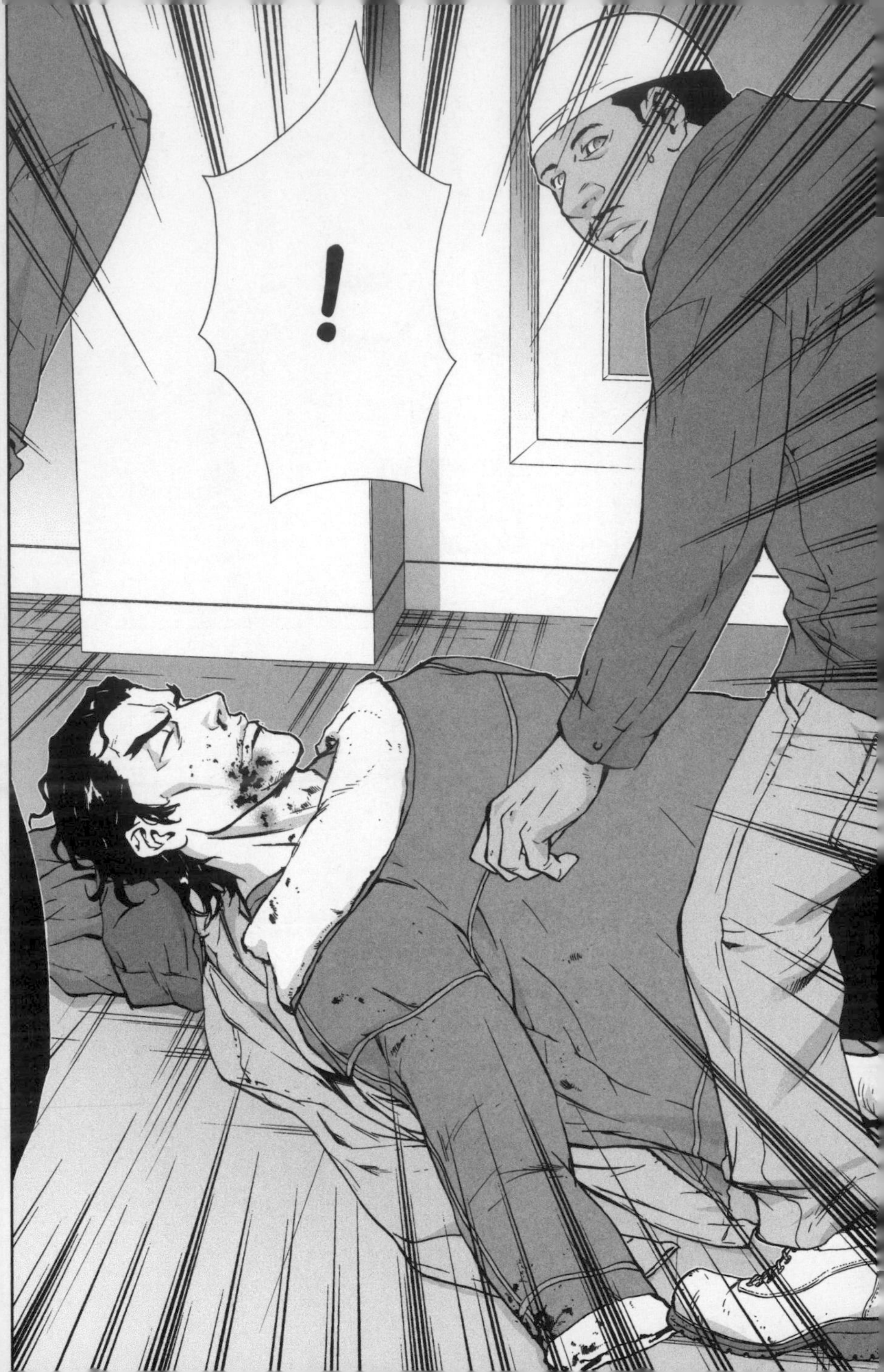
!

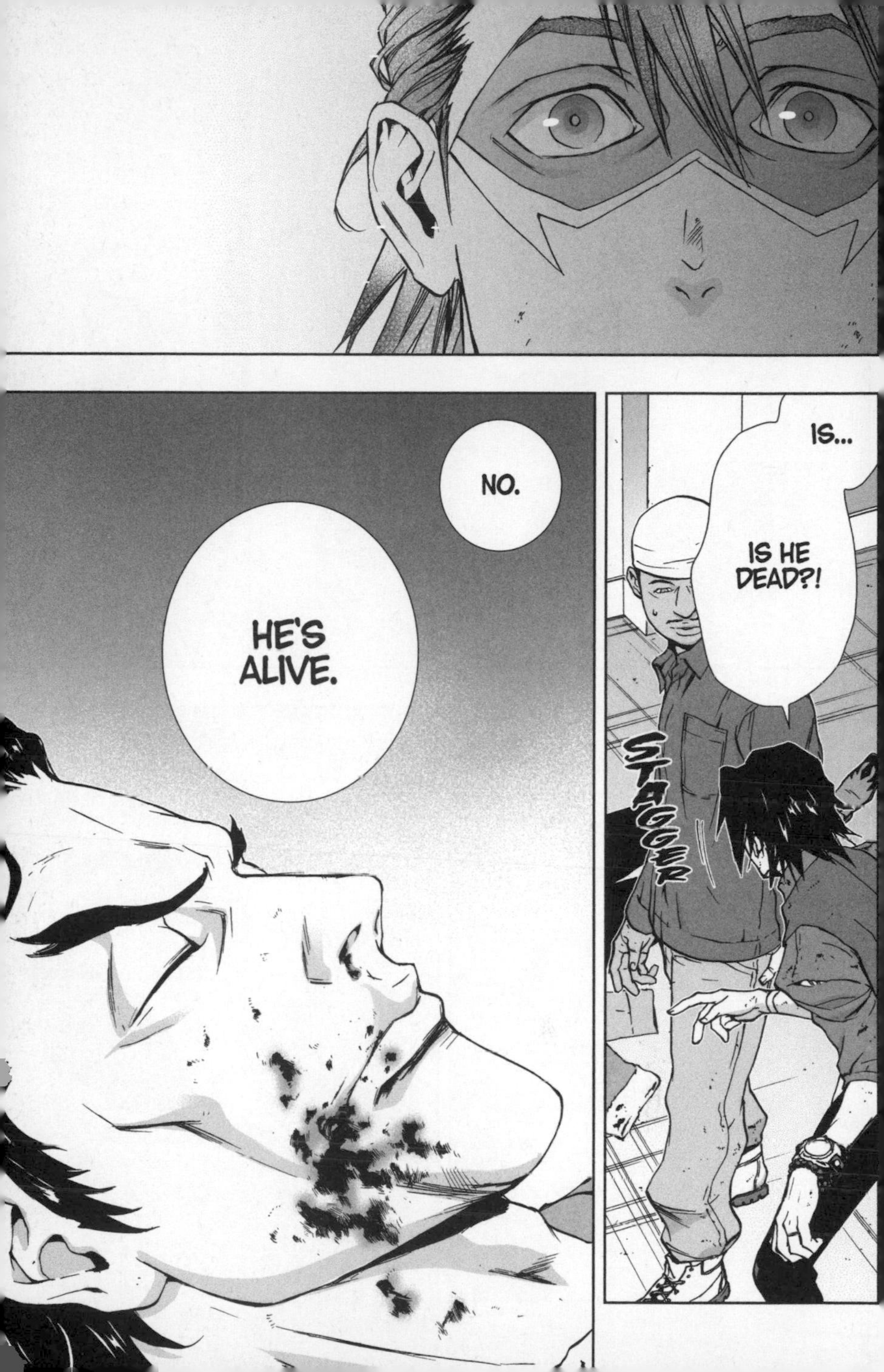
IS...
IS HE DEAD?!
STAGGER
NO.
HE'S ALIVE.

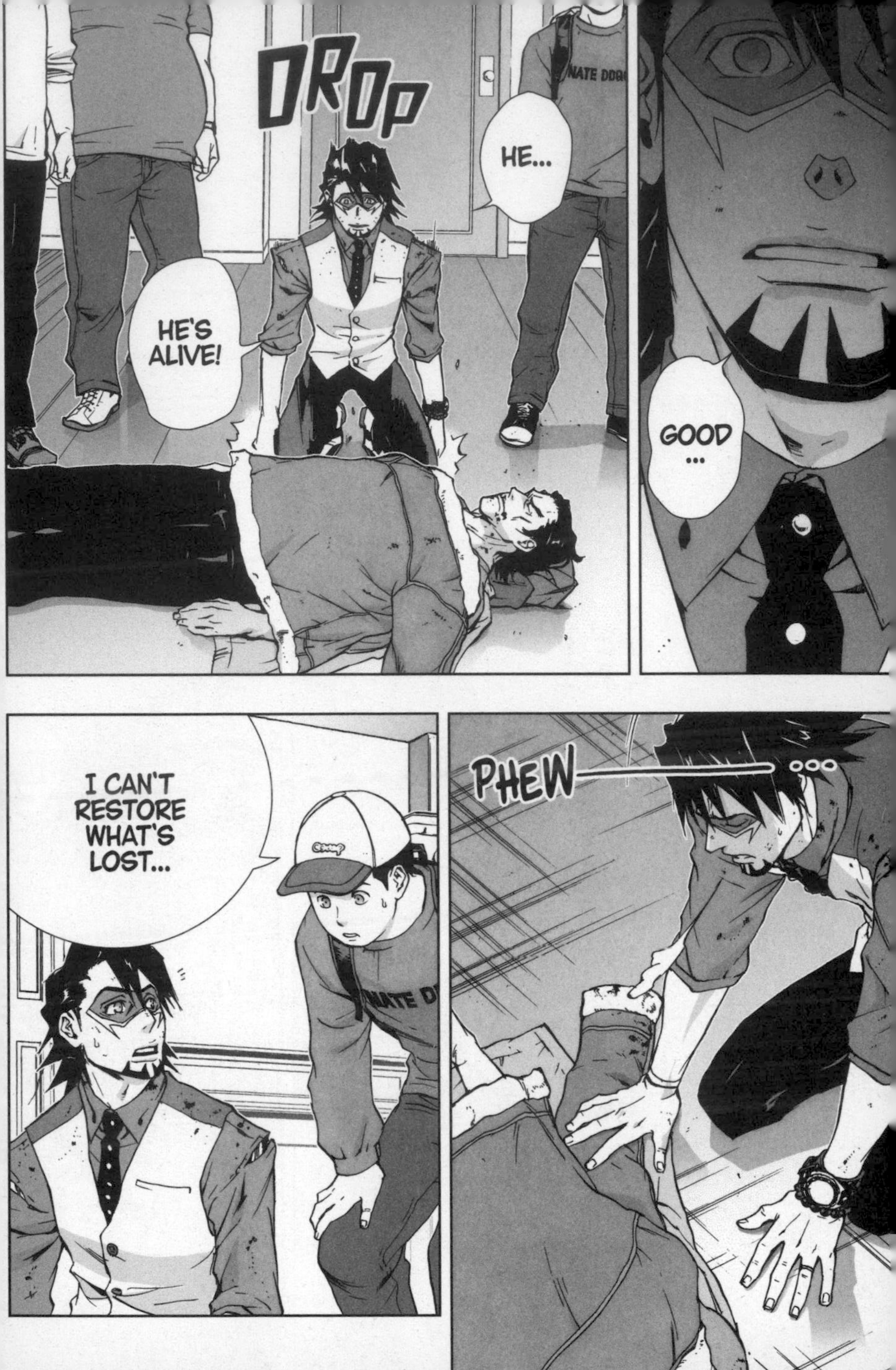
GOOD...
DROP
HE...
HE'S ALIVE!
PHEW
I CAN'T RESTORE WHAT'S LOST...

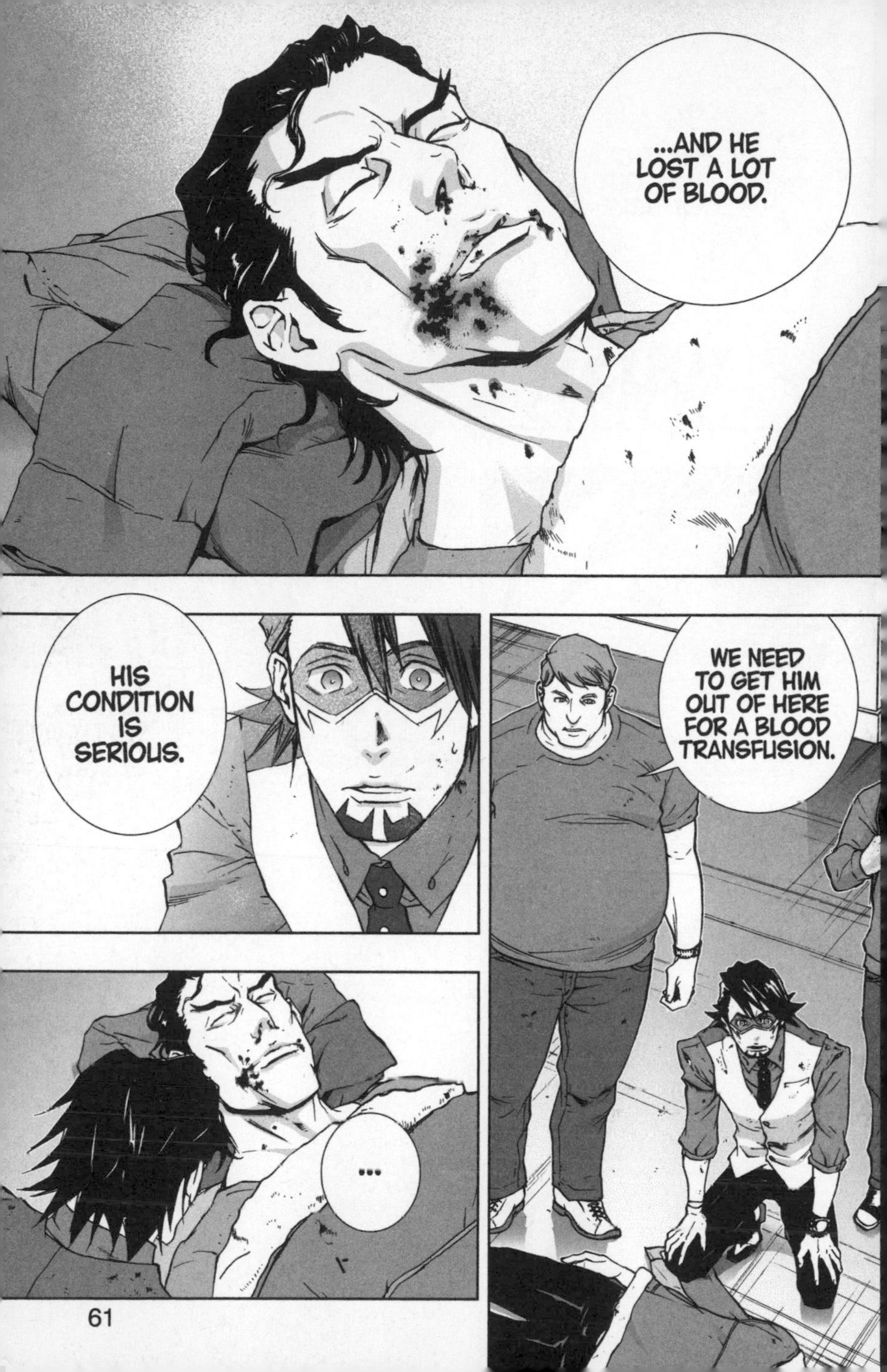
...AND HE LOST A LOT OF BLOOD.
WE NEED TO GET HIM OUT OF HERE FOR A BLOOD TRANSFUSION.
HIS CONDITION IS SERIOUS.
...

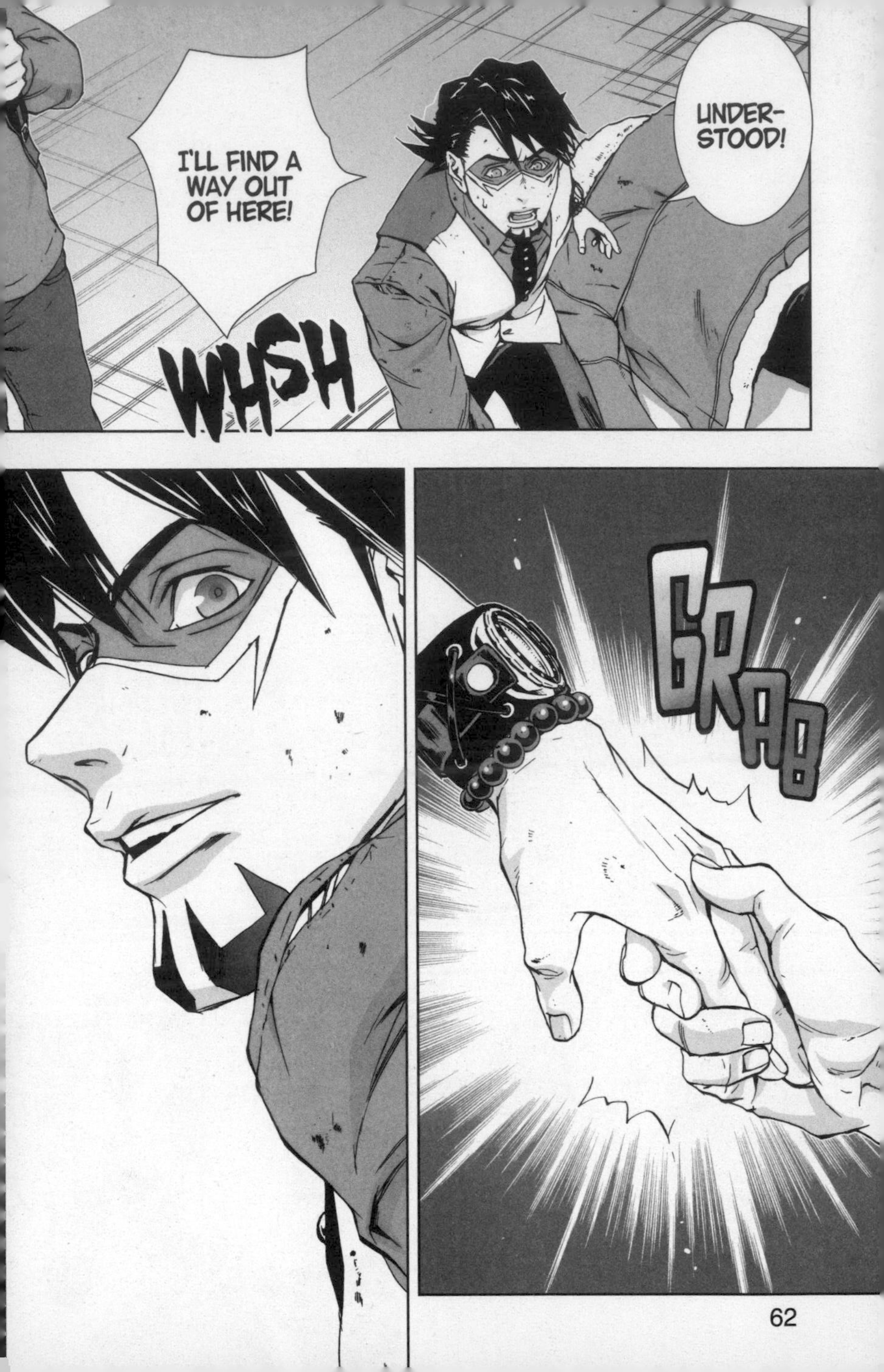
UNDER-
STOOD!
I'LL FIND A WAY OUT OF HERE!
WHSH
GRAB!

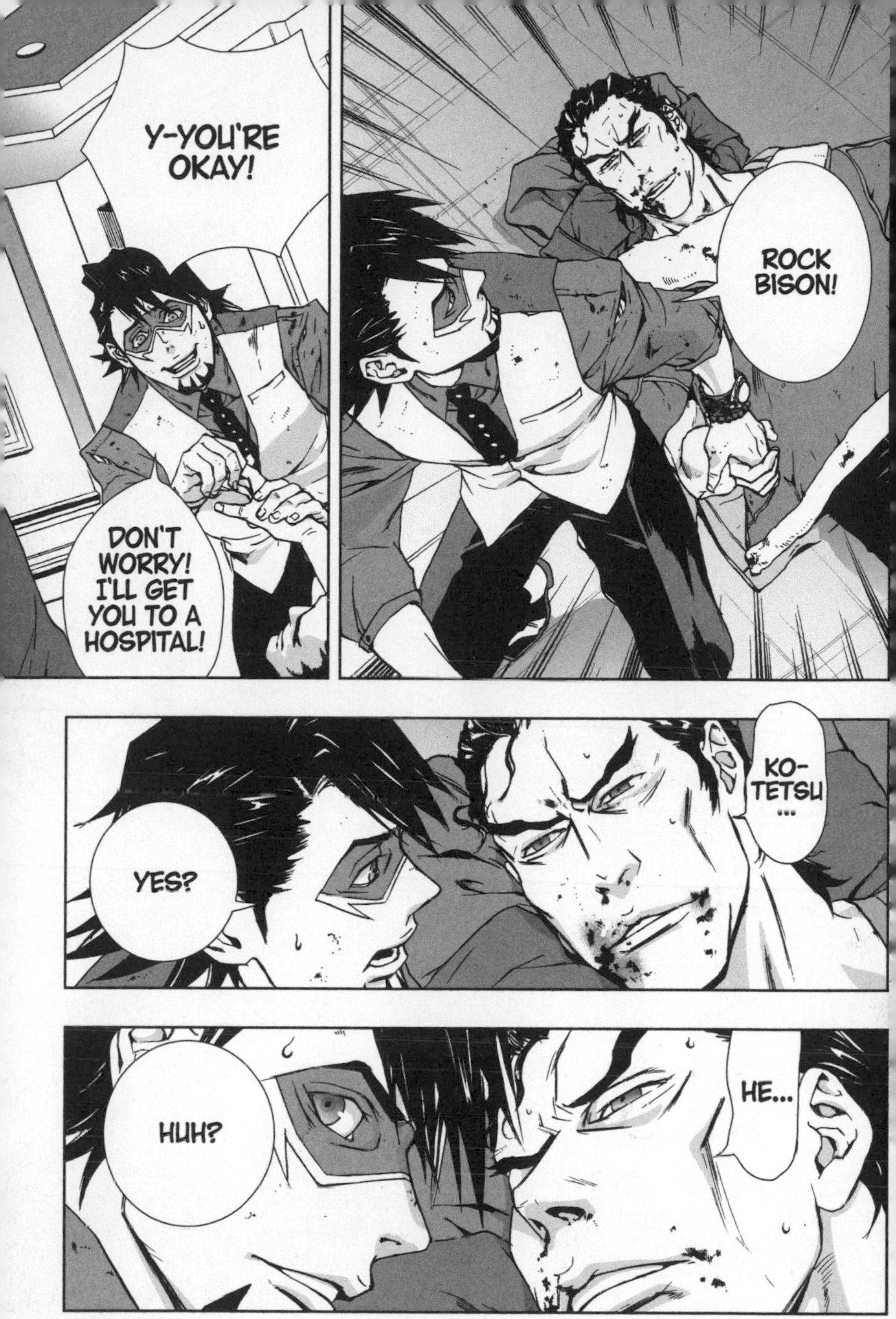
ROCK BISON!
Y-YOU'RE OKAY!
DON'T WORRY! I'LL GET YOU TO A HOSPITAL!
KO-TETSU...
YES?
HE...
HUH?

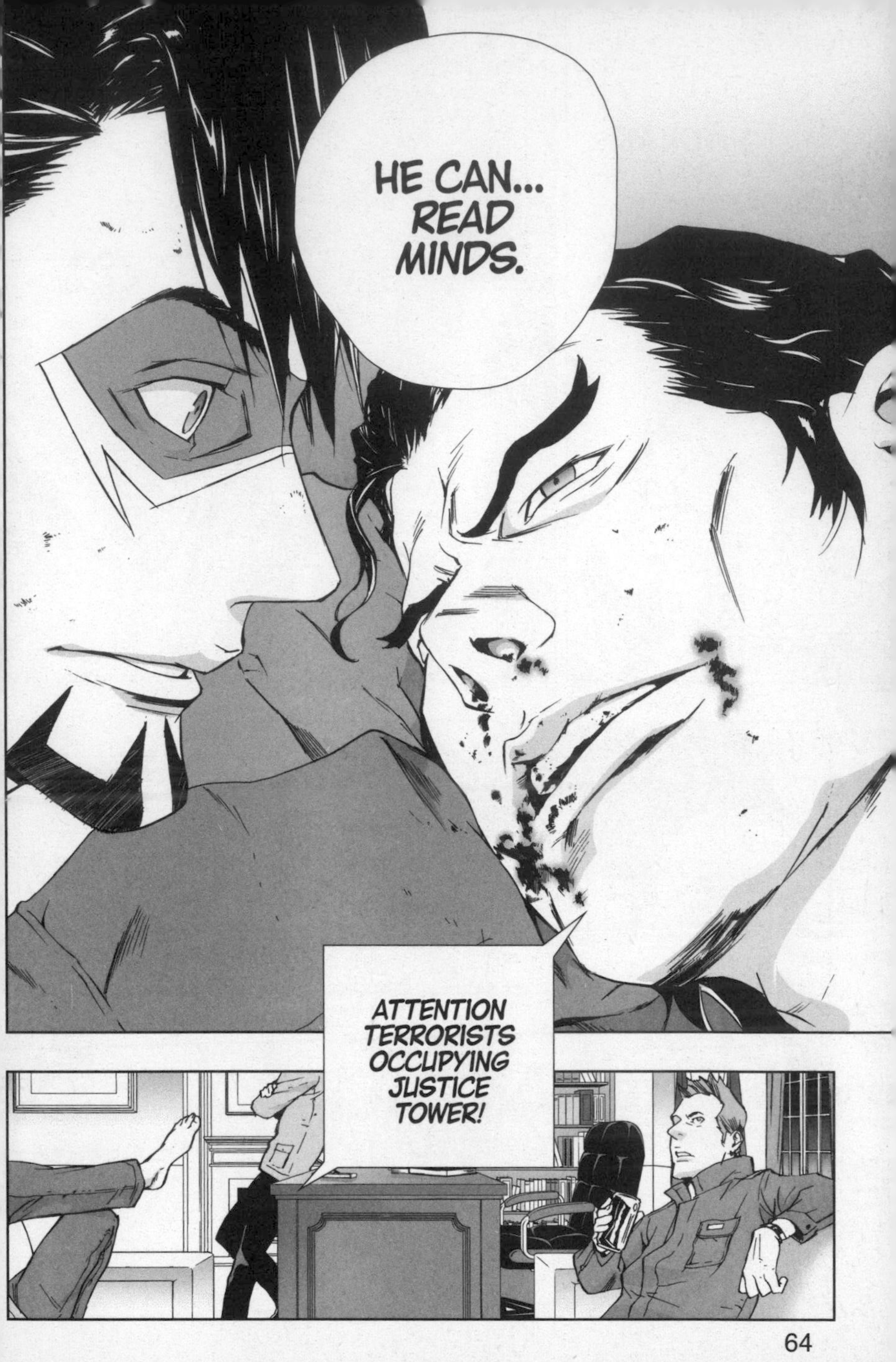
HE CAN... READ MINDS.
ATTENTION TERRORISTS OCCUPYING JUSTICE TOWER!

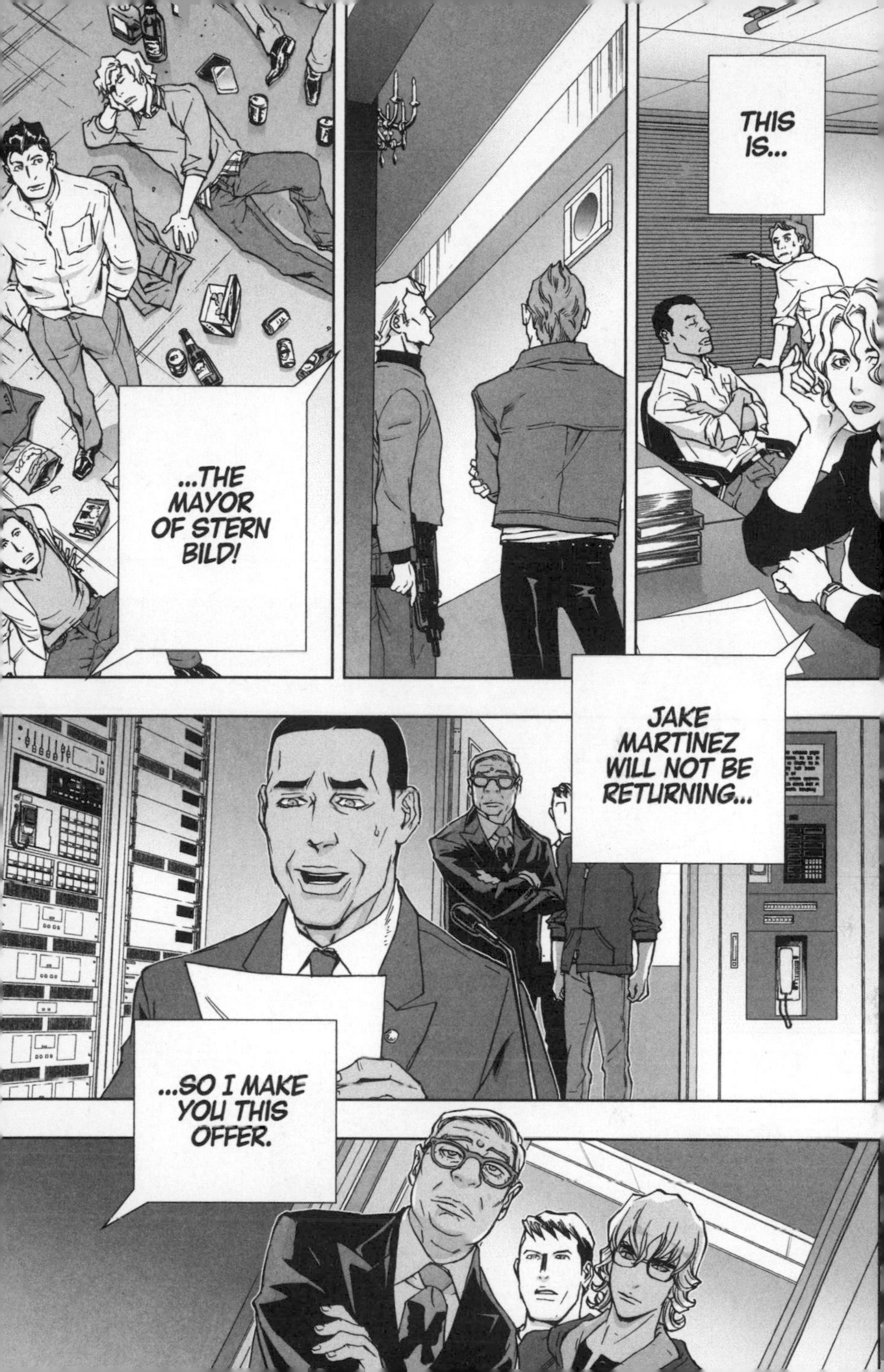
THIS IS...
...THE MAYOR OF STERN BILD!
JAKE MARTINEZ WILL NOT BE RETURNING...
...SO I MAKE YOU THIS OFFER.

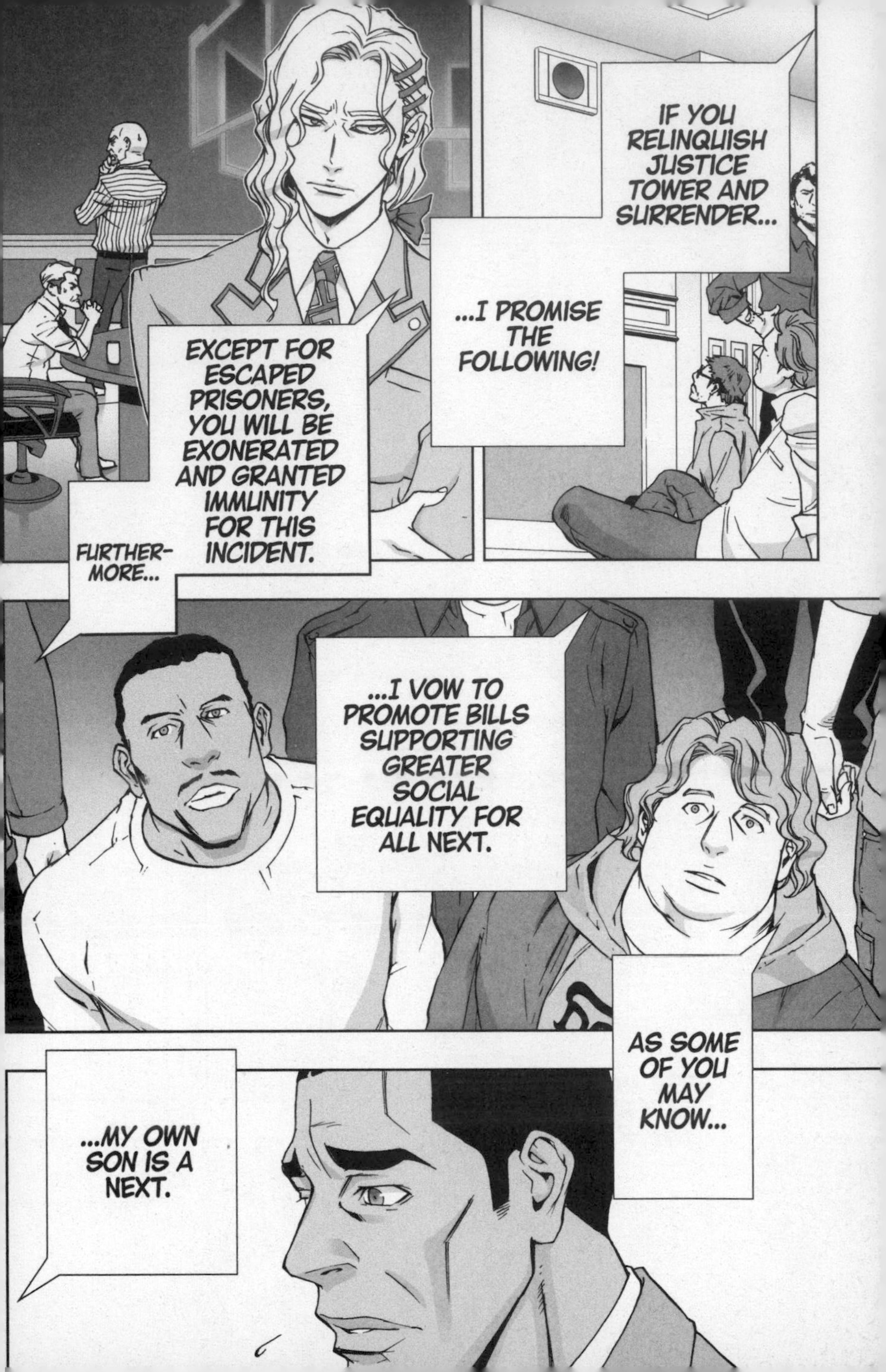
IF YOU RELINQUISH JUSTICE TOWER AND SURRENDER...
...I PROMISE THE FOLLOWING!
EXCEPT FOR ESCAPED PRISONERS, YOU WILL BE EXONERATED AND GRANTED IMMUNITY FOR THIS INCIDENT.
FURTHER-MORE...
...I VOW TO PROMOTE BILLS SUPPORTING GREATER SOCIAL EQUALITY FOR ALL NEXT.
AS SOME OF YOU MAY KNOW...
...MY OWN SON IS A NEXT.

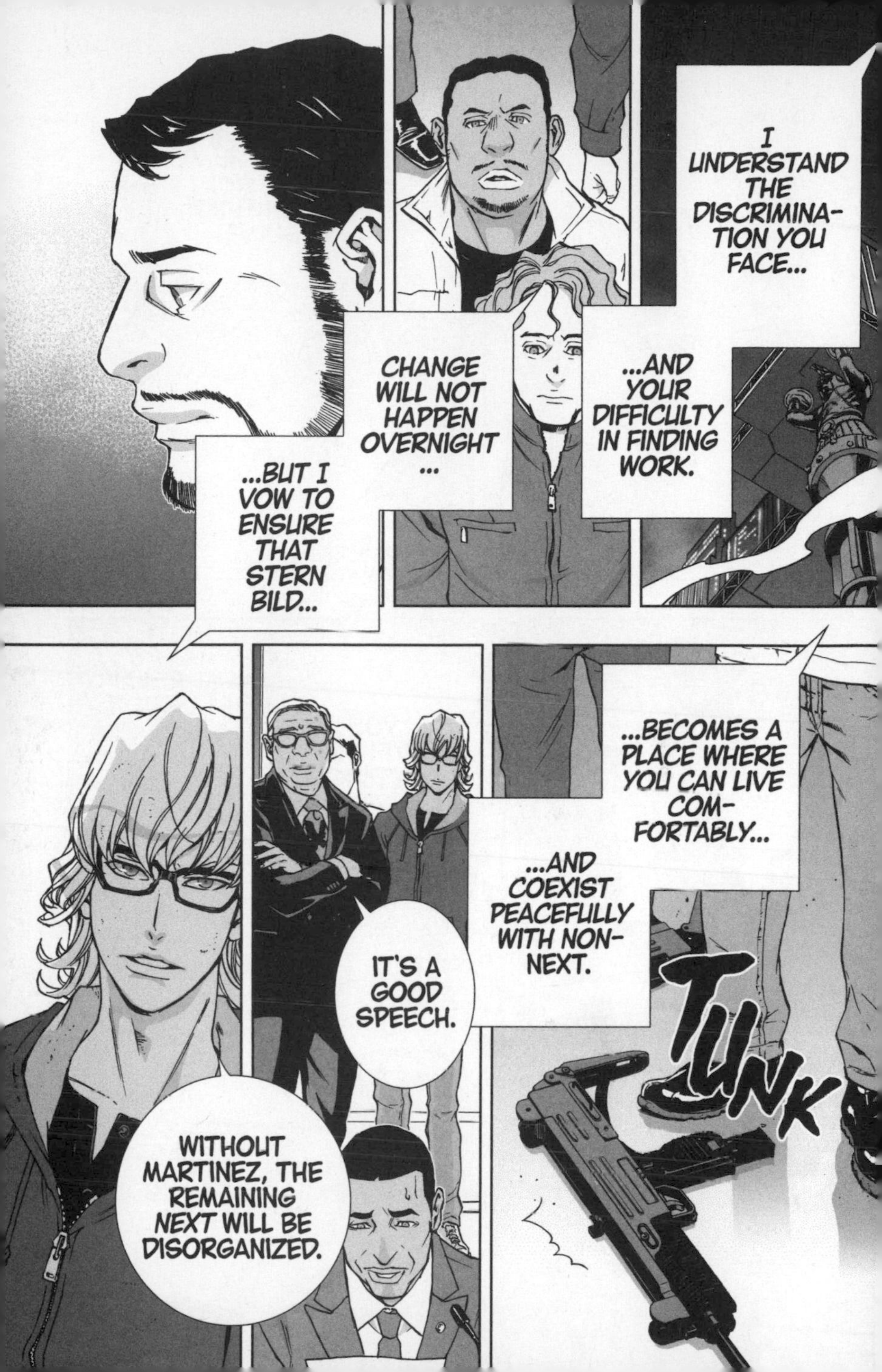
I UNDERSTAND THE DISCRIMINATION YOU FACE...
...AND YOUR DIFFICULTY IN FINDING WORK.
CHANGE WILL NOT HAPPEN OVERNIGHT...
...BUT I VOW TO ENSURE THAT STERN BILD...
...BECOMES A PLACE WHERE YOU CAN LIVE COMFORTABLY...
...AND COEXIST PEACEFULLY WITH NON-NEXT.
TUNK
IT'S A GOOD SPEECH.
WITHOUT MARTINEZ, THE REMAINING NEXT WILL BE DISORGANIZED.

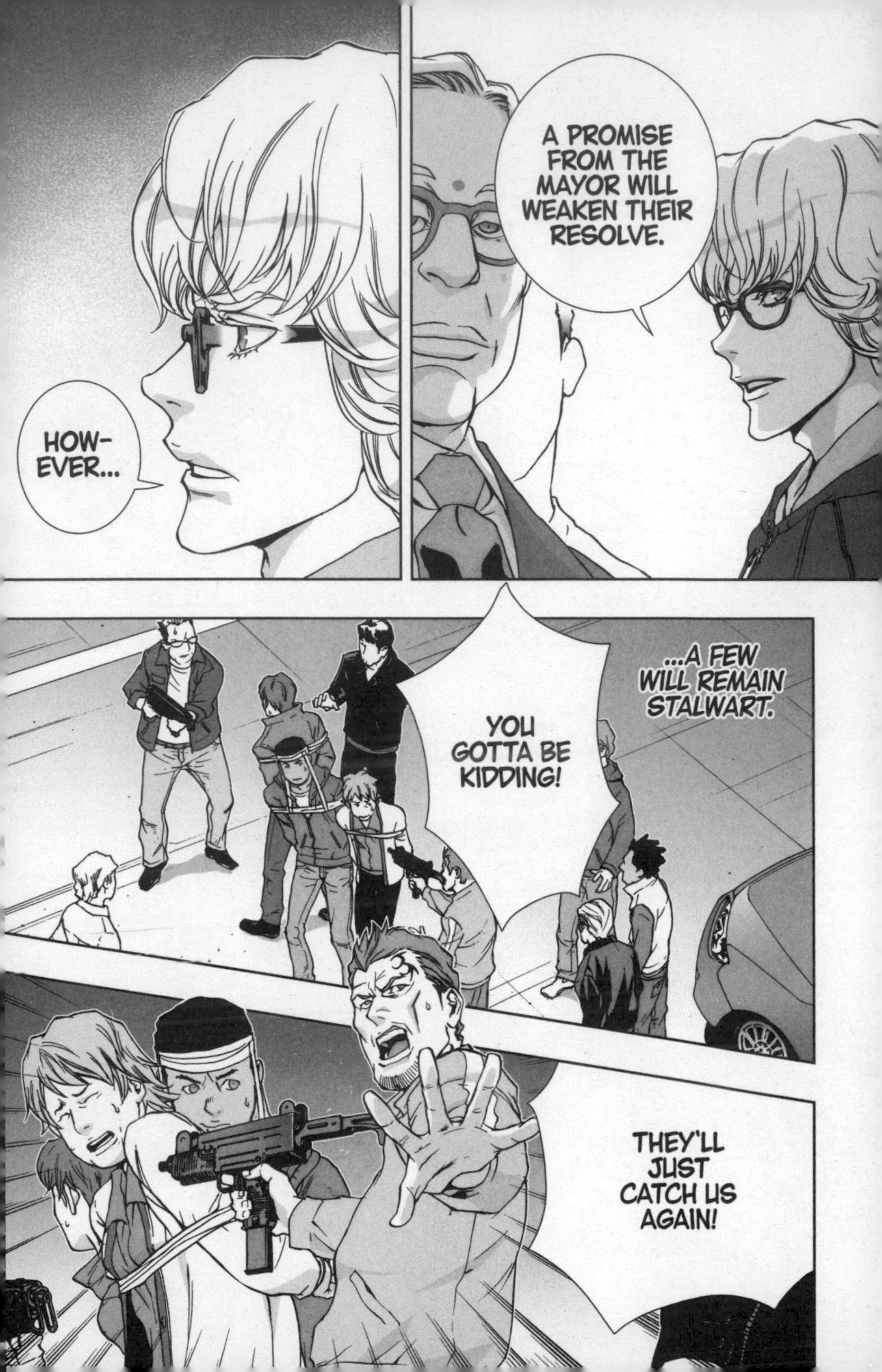
A PROMISE FROM THE MAYOR WILL WEAKEN THEIR RESOLVE.
HOW-EVER...
...A FEW WILL REMAIN STALWART.
YOU GOTTA BE KIDDING!
THEY'LL JUST CATCH US AGAIN!

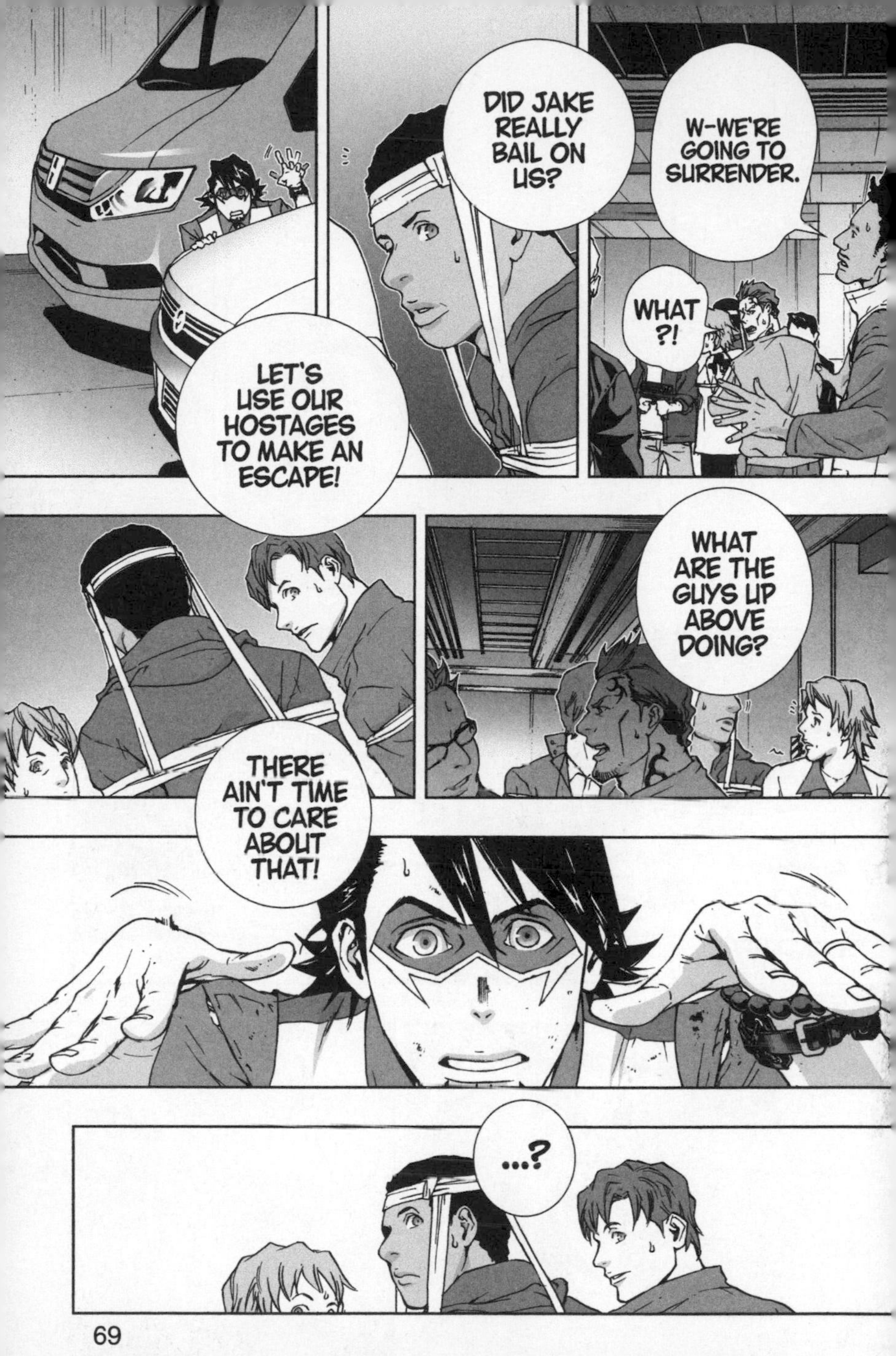
W-WE'RE GOING TO SURRENDER.
WHAT ?!
DID JAKE REALLY BAIL ON US?
LET'S USE OUR HOSTAGES TO MAKE AN ESCAPE!
WHAT ARE THE GUYS UP ABOVE DOING?
THERE AIN'T TIME TO CARE ABOUT THAT!
...?

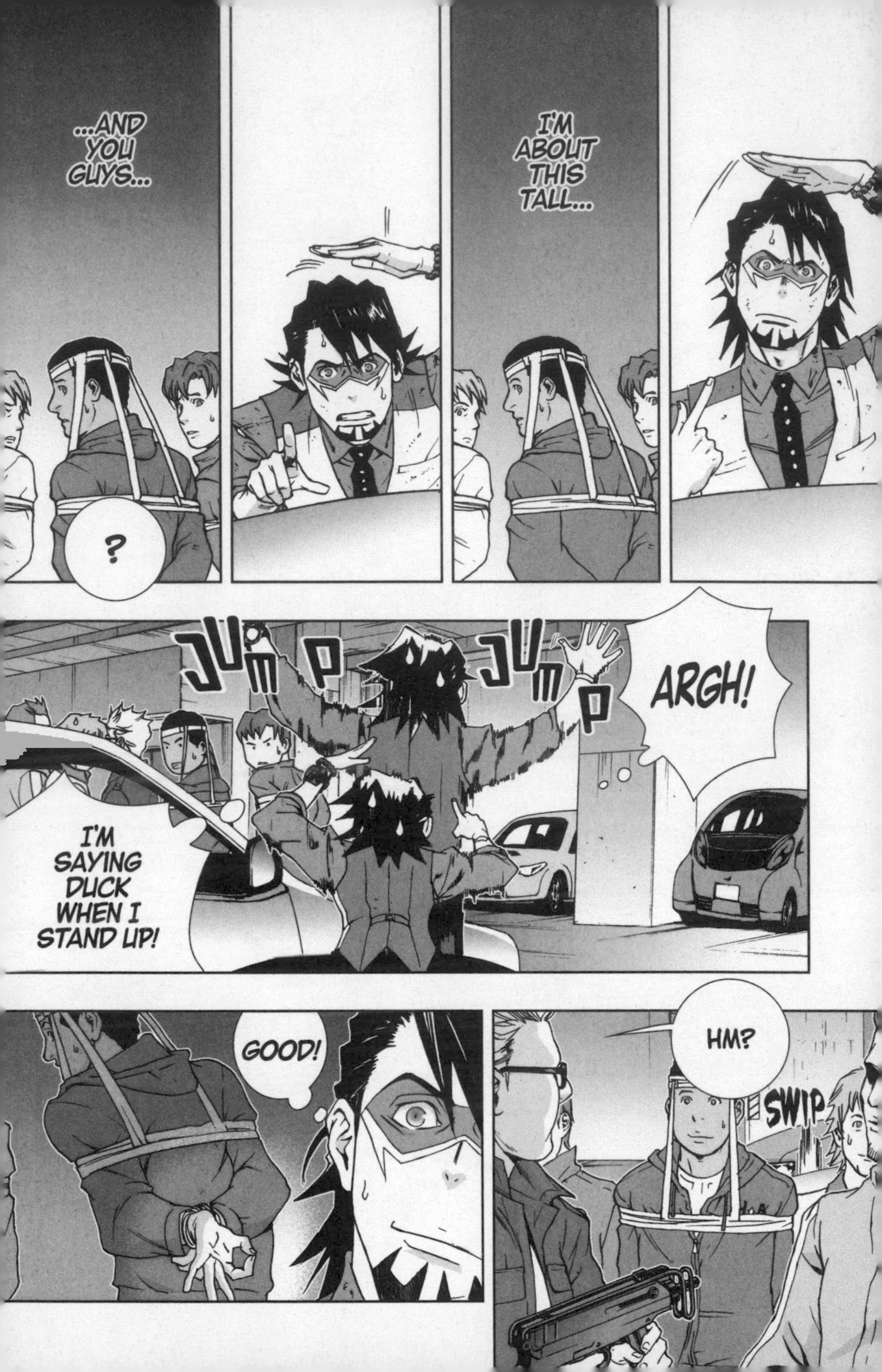
I'M ABOUT THIS TALL...
...AND YOU GUYS...
?
JUMP
JUMP
ARGH!
I'M SAYING DUCK WHEN I STAND UP!
HM?
SWIP
GOOD!

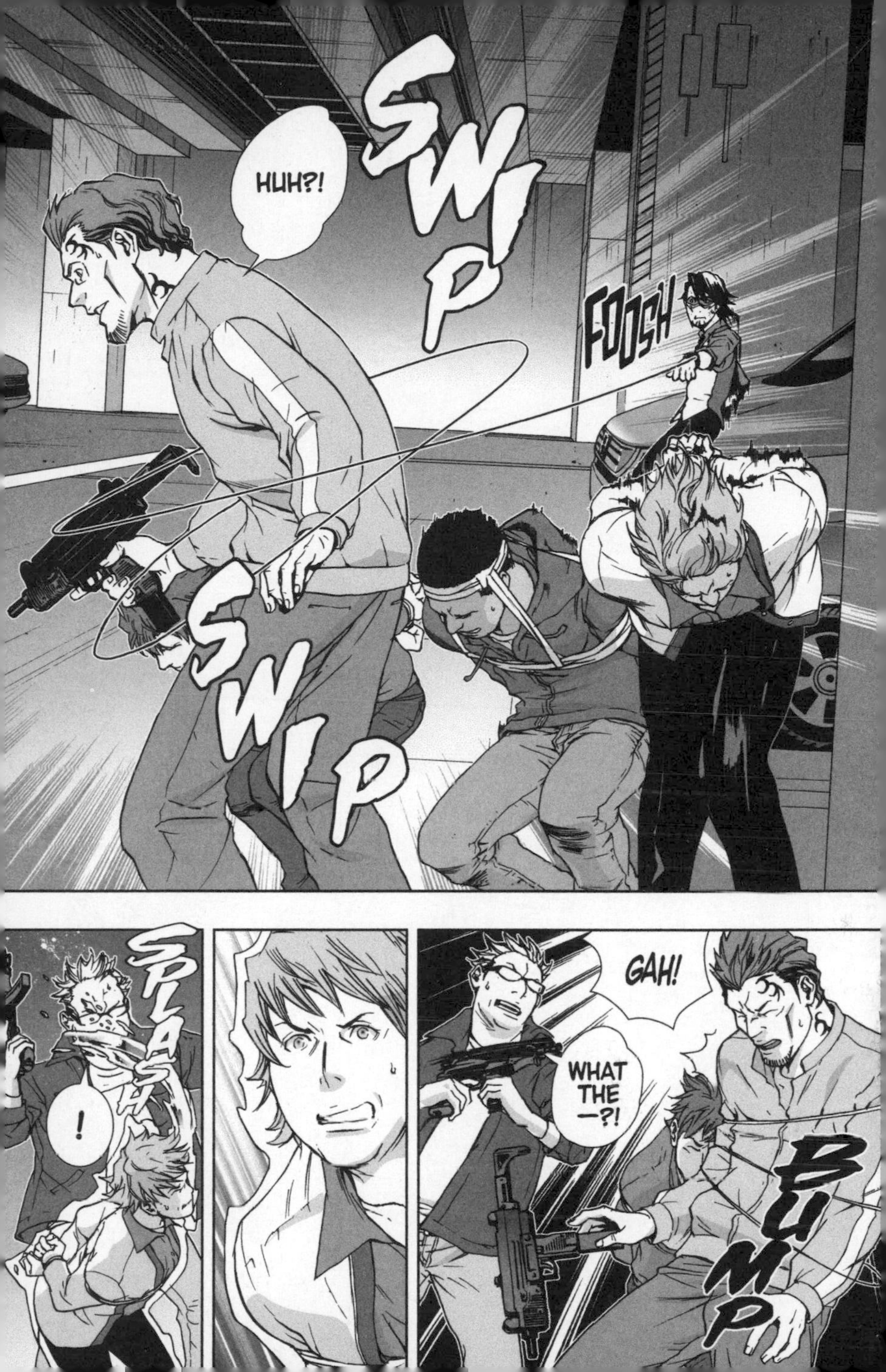
SWIP
HUH?!
FOOSH
SWIP
GAH!
WHAT THE —?!
BUMP
SPLASH
!

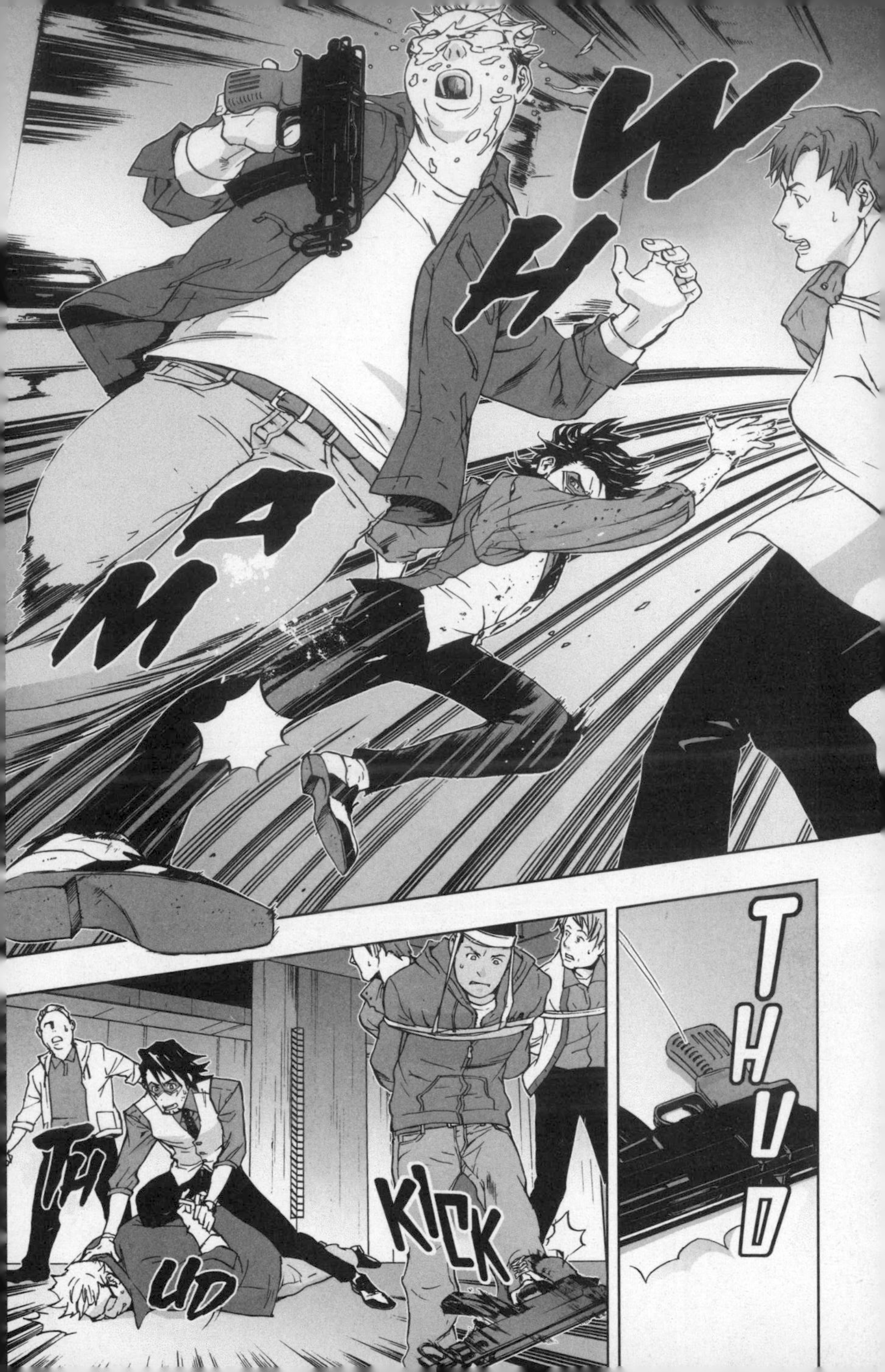
WHAM
THUD
KICK
THUD

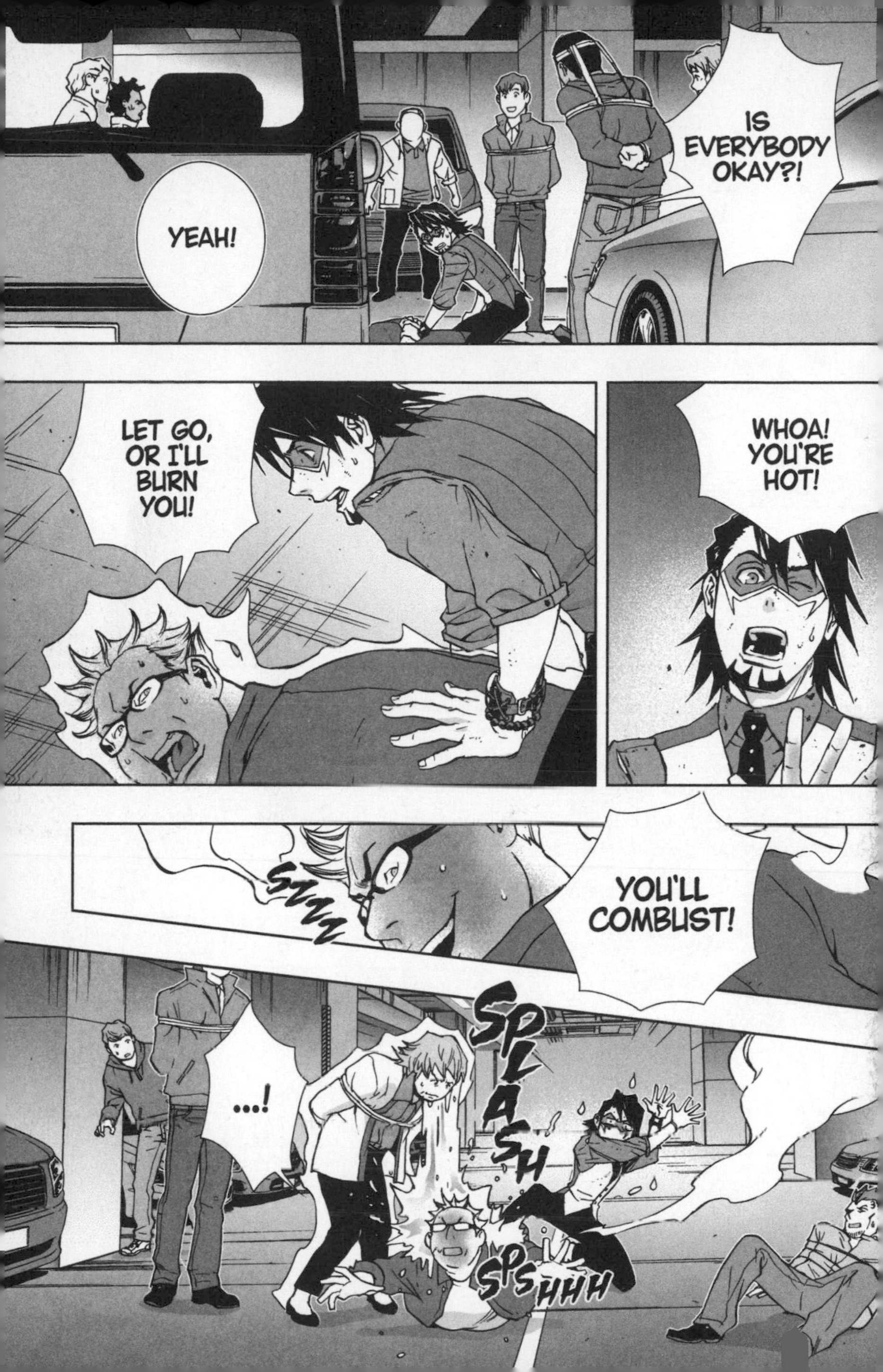
IS EVERYBODY OKAY?!
YEAH!
WHOA! YOU'RE HOT!
LET GO, OR I'LL BURN YOU!
YOU'LL COMBUST!
SZZZ
SPLASH
...!
SPSHHH

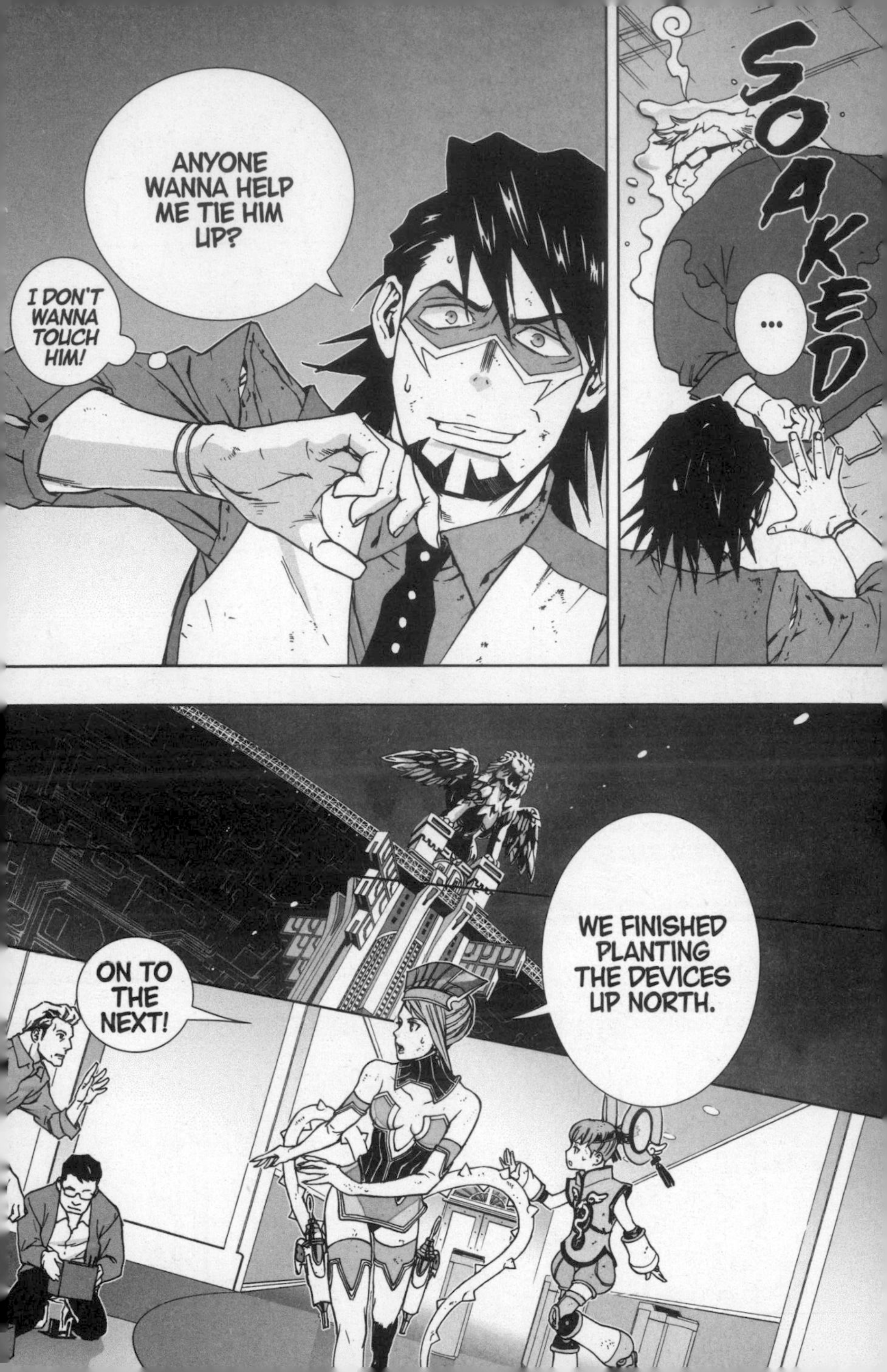
SOAKED
...
ANYONE WANNA HELP ME TIE HIM UP?
I DON'T WANNA TOUCH HIM!
WE FINISHED PLANTING THE DEVICES UP NORTH.
ON TO THE NEXT!

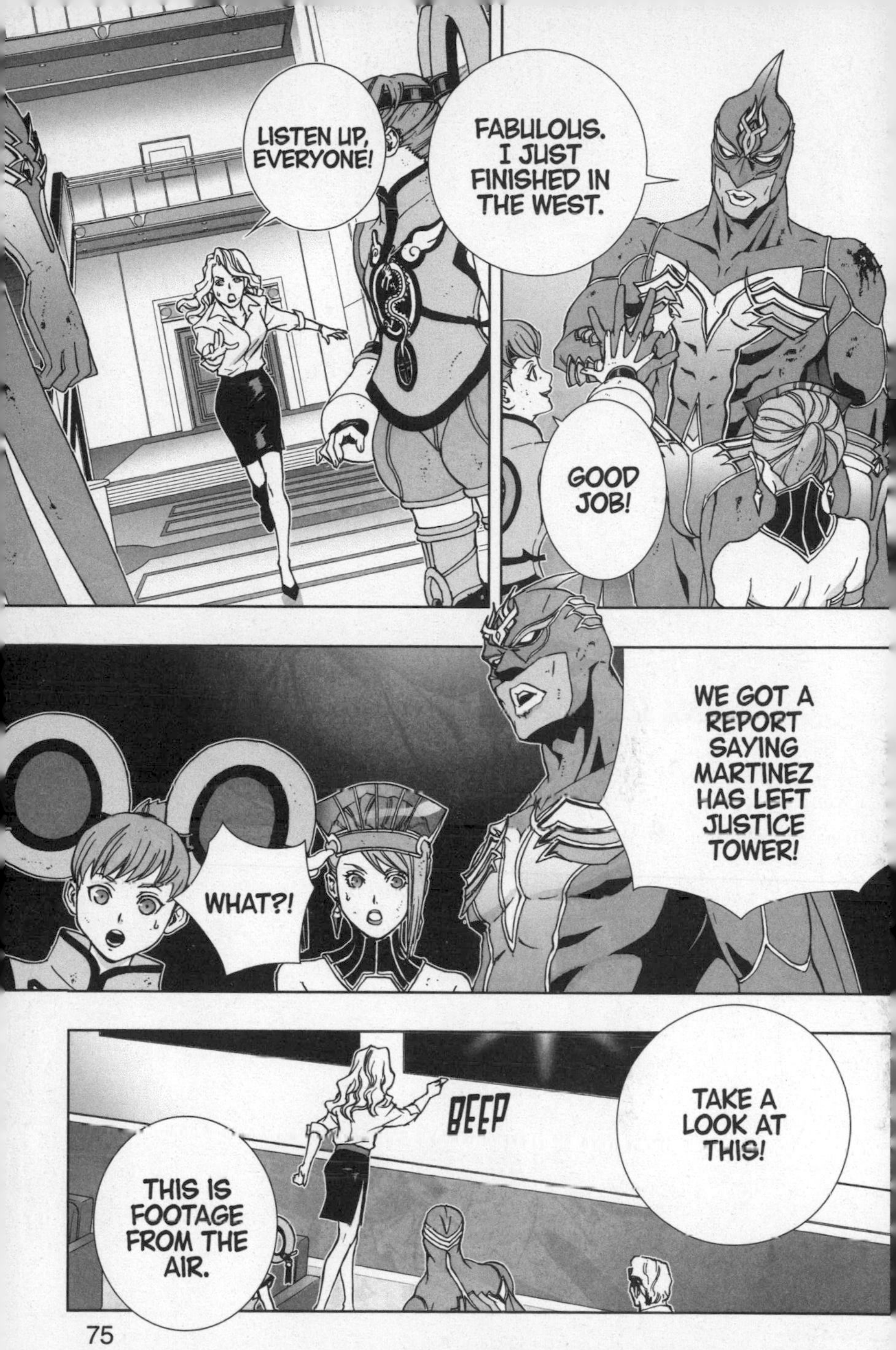
FABULOUS. I JUST FINISHED IN THE WEST.
GOOD JOB!
LISTEN UP, EVERYONE!
WE GOT A REPORT SAYING MARTINEZ HAS LEFT JUSTICE TOWER!
WHAT?!
TAKE A LOOK AT THIS!
BEEP
THIS IS FOOTAGE FROM THE AIR.

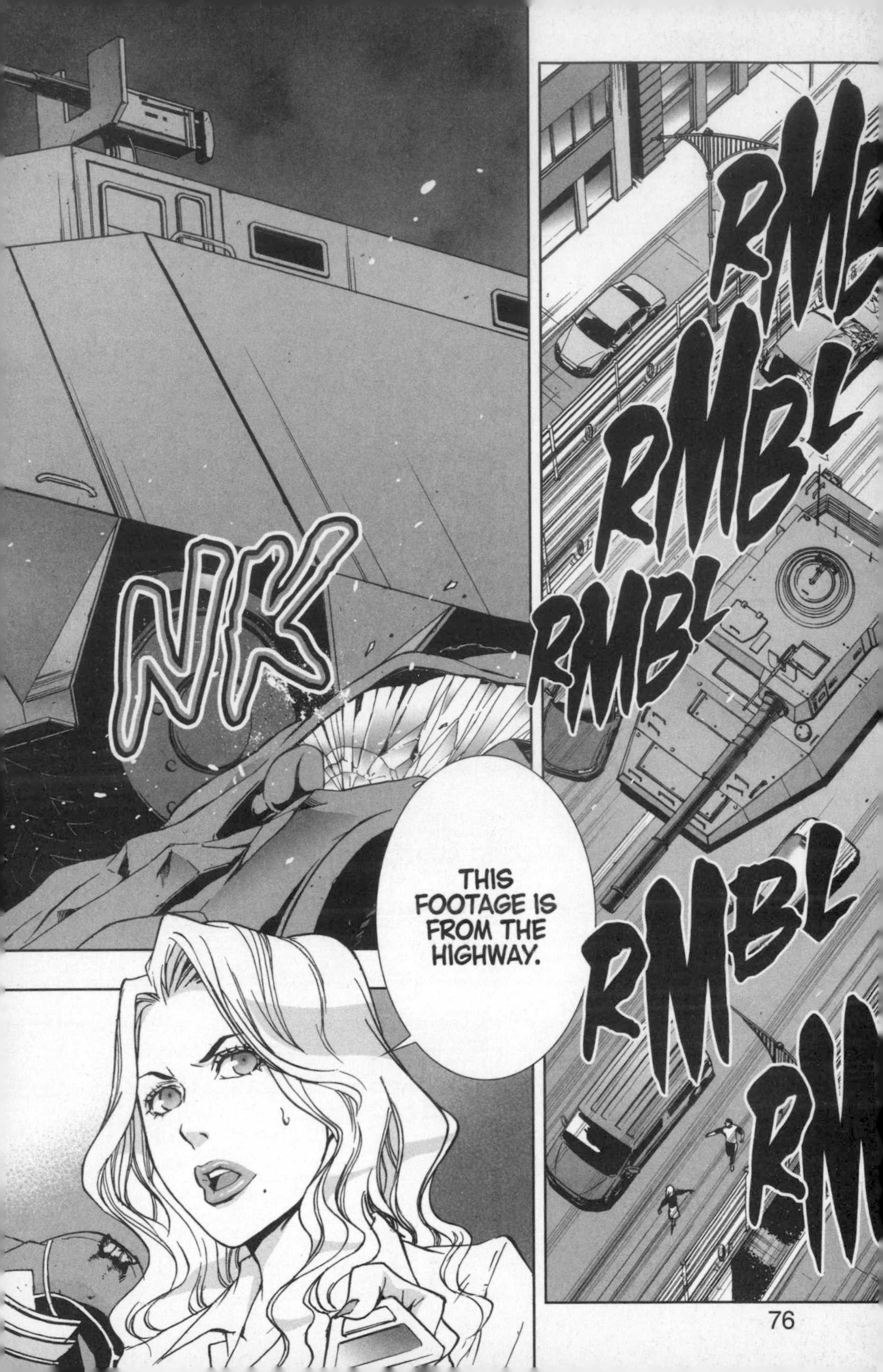
RMBL
RMBL
RMBL
NIK
THIS FOOTAGE IS FROM THE HIGHWAY.

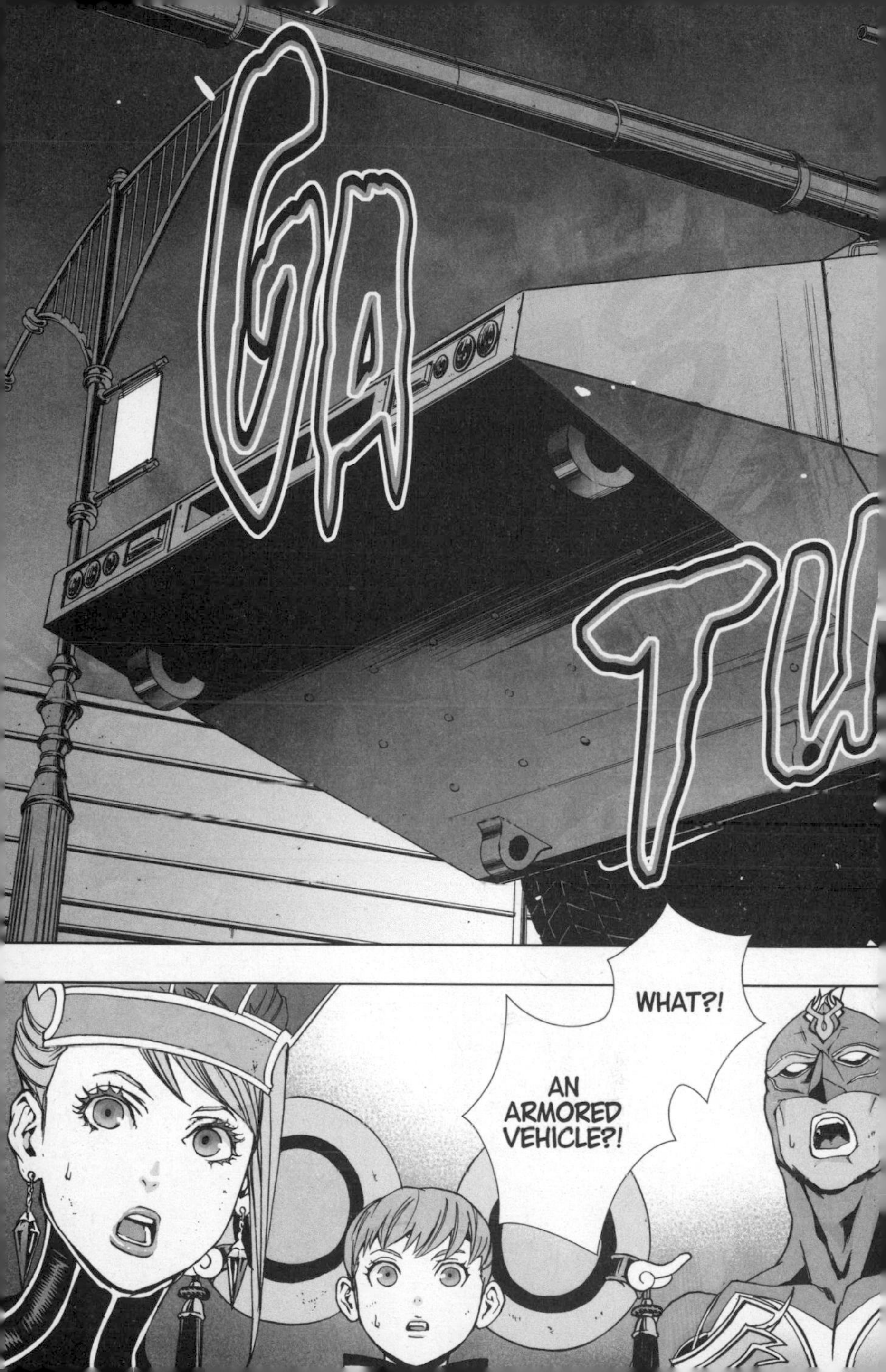
GA
WHAT?!
AN ARMORED VEHICLE?!

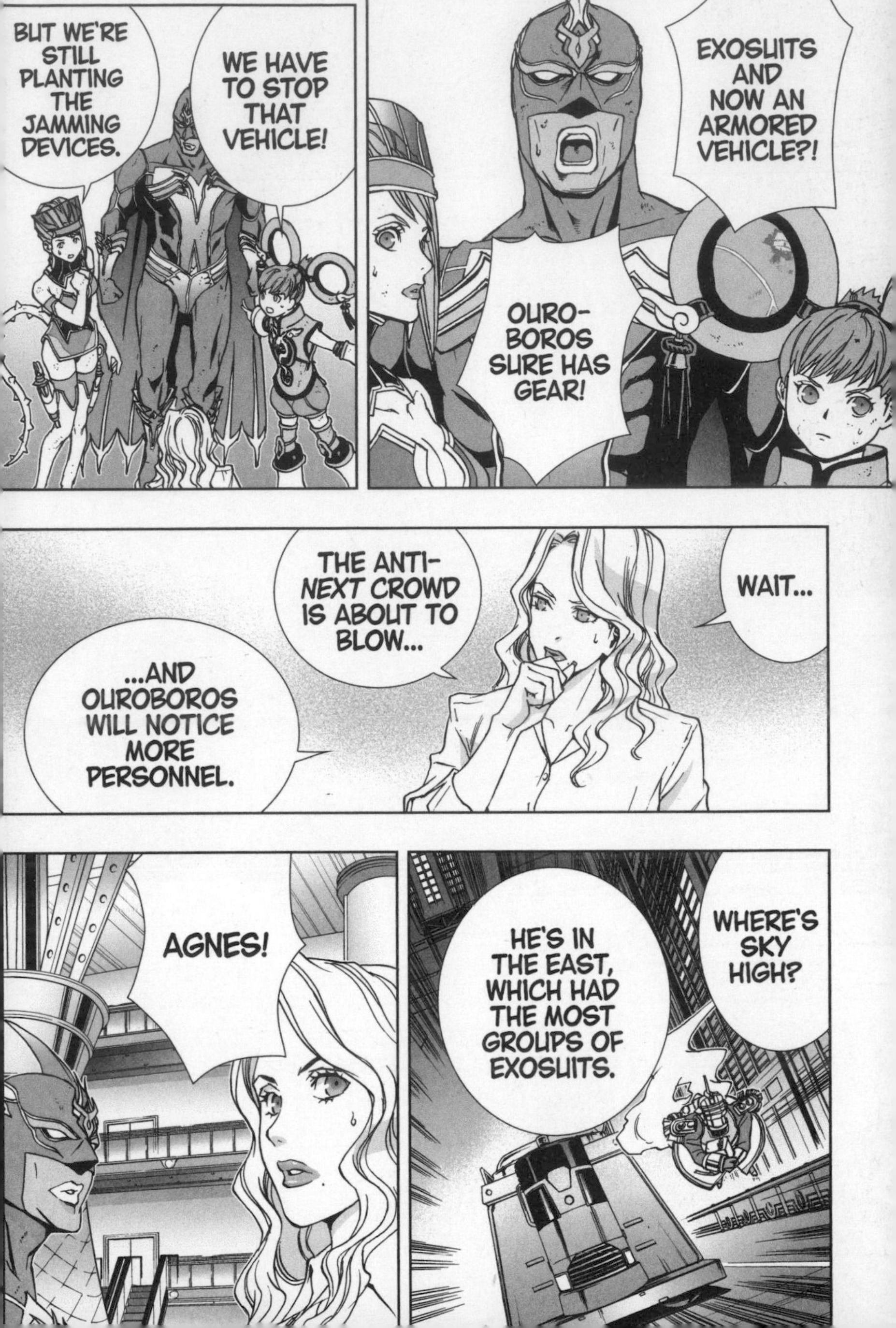
EXOSUITS AND NOW AN ARMORED VEHICLE?!
OURO-BOROS SURE HAS GEAR!
WE HAVE TO STOP THAT VEHICLE!
BUT WE'RE STILL PLANTING THE JAMMING DEVICES.
WAIT...
THE ANTI-*NEXT* CROWD IS ABOUT TO BLOW...
...AND OUROBOROS WILL NOTICE MORE PERSONNEL.
WHERE'S SKY HIGH?
HE'S IN THE EAST, WHICH HAD THE MOST GROUPS OF EXOSUITS.
AGNES!

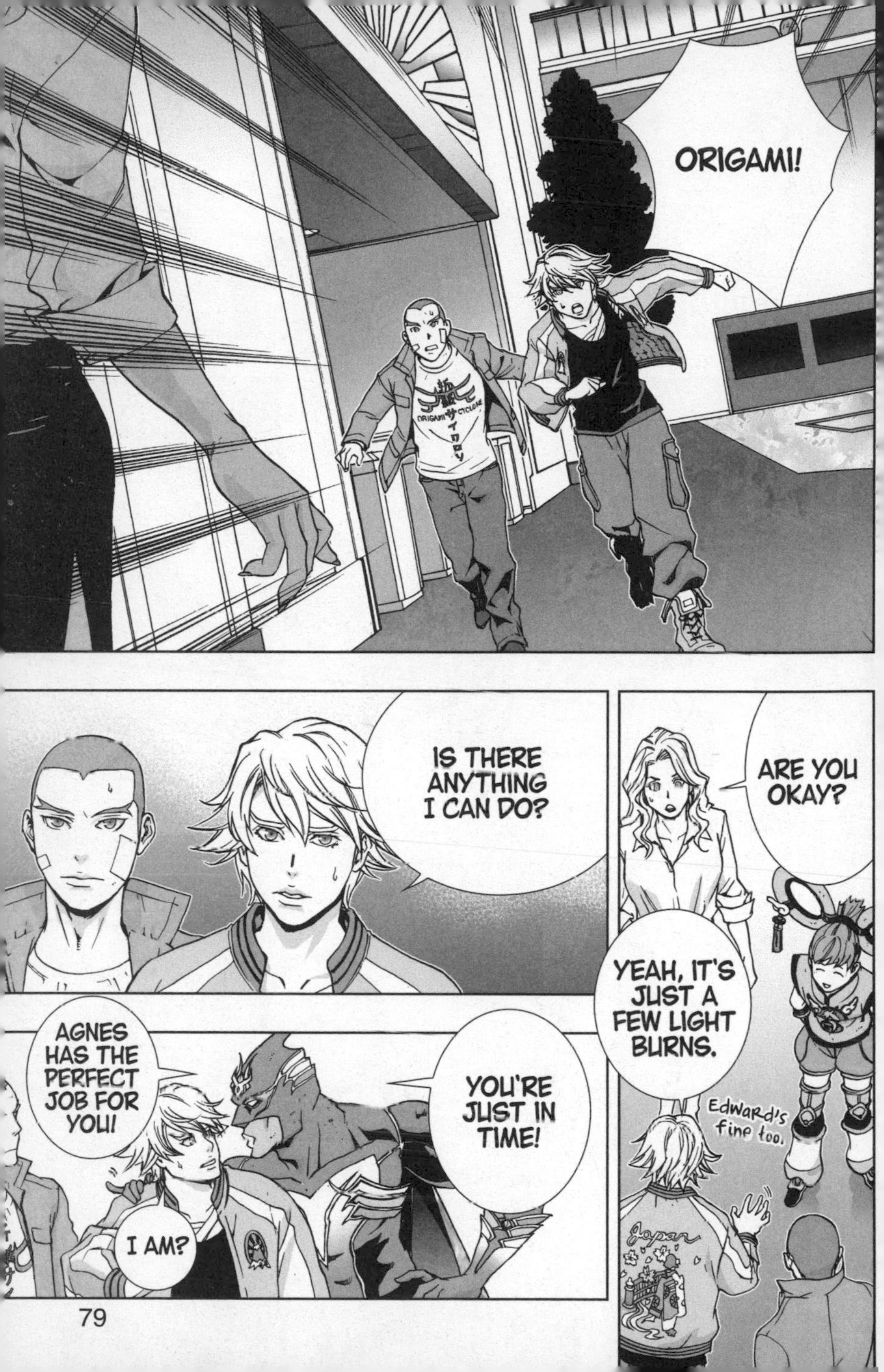
ORIGAMI!
ARE YOU OKAY?
YEAH, IT'S JUST A FEW LIGHT BURNS.
Edward's fine too.
IS THERE ANYTHING I CAN DO?
YOU'RE JUST IN TIME!
AGNES HAS THE PERFECT JOB FOR YOU!
I AM?

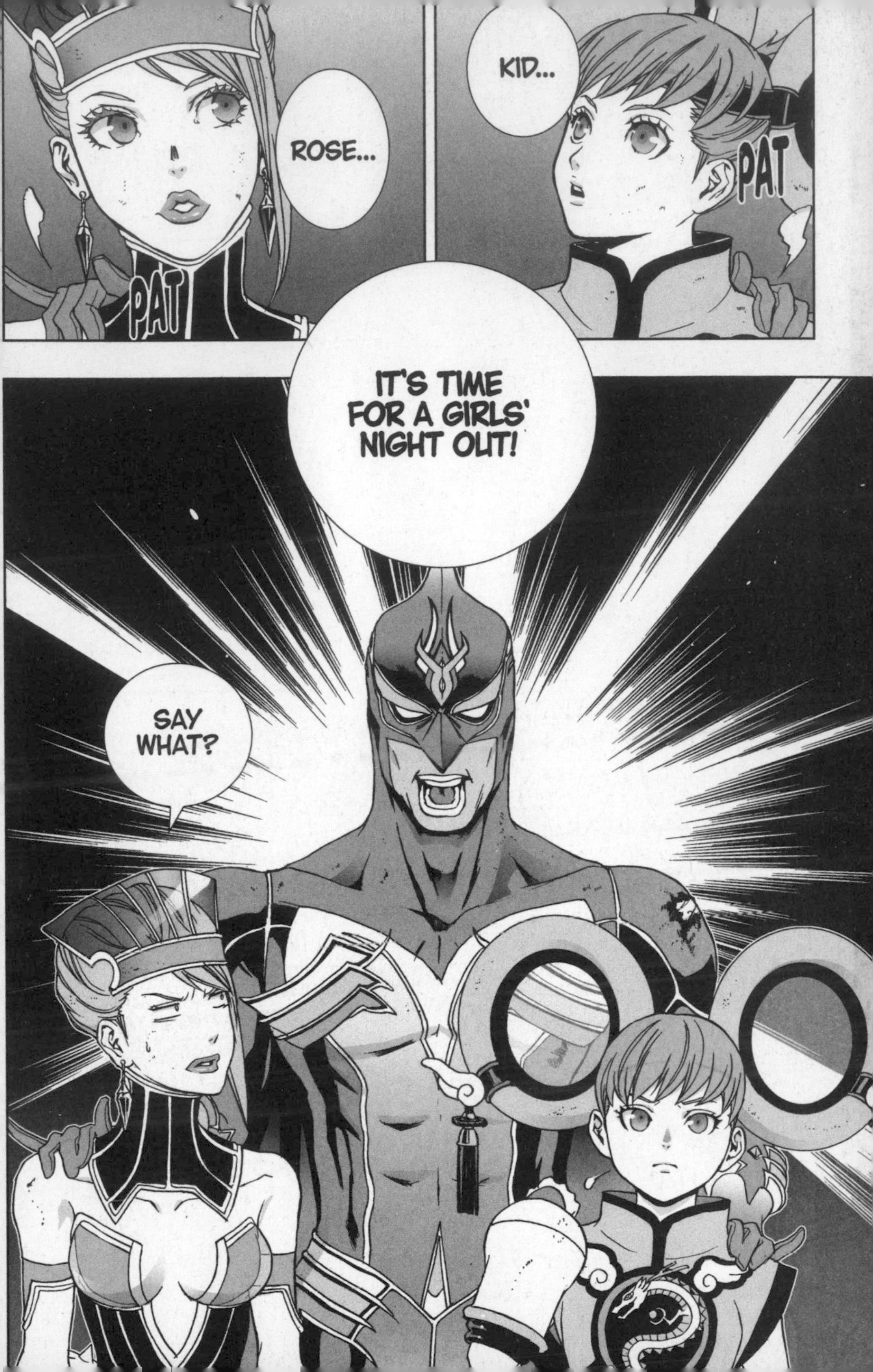
KID...
PAT
ROSE...
PAT
IT'S TIME FOR A GIRLS' NIGHT OUT!
SAY WHAT?

TIGER & BUNNY

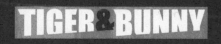

TIGER & BUNNY

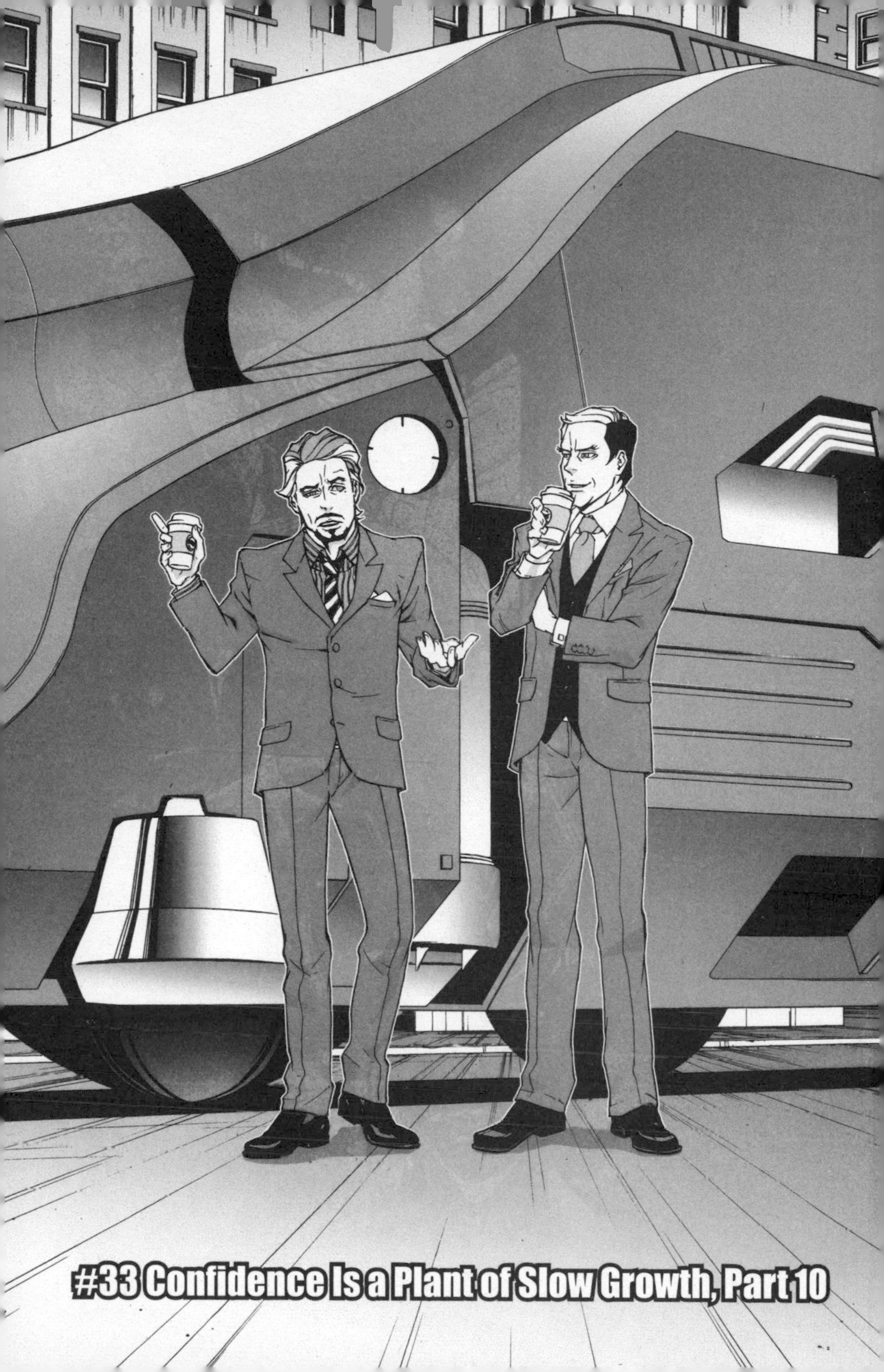

#33 Confidence Is a Plant of Slow Growth, Part 10

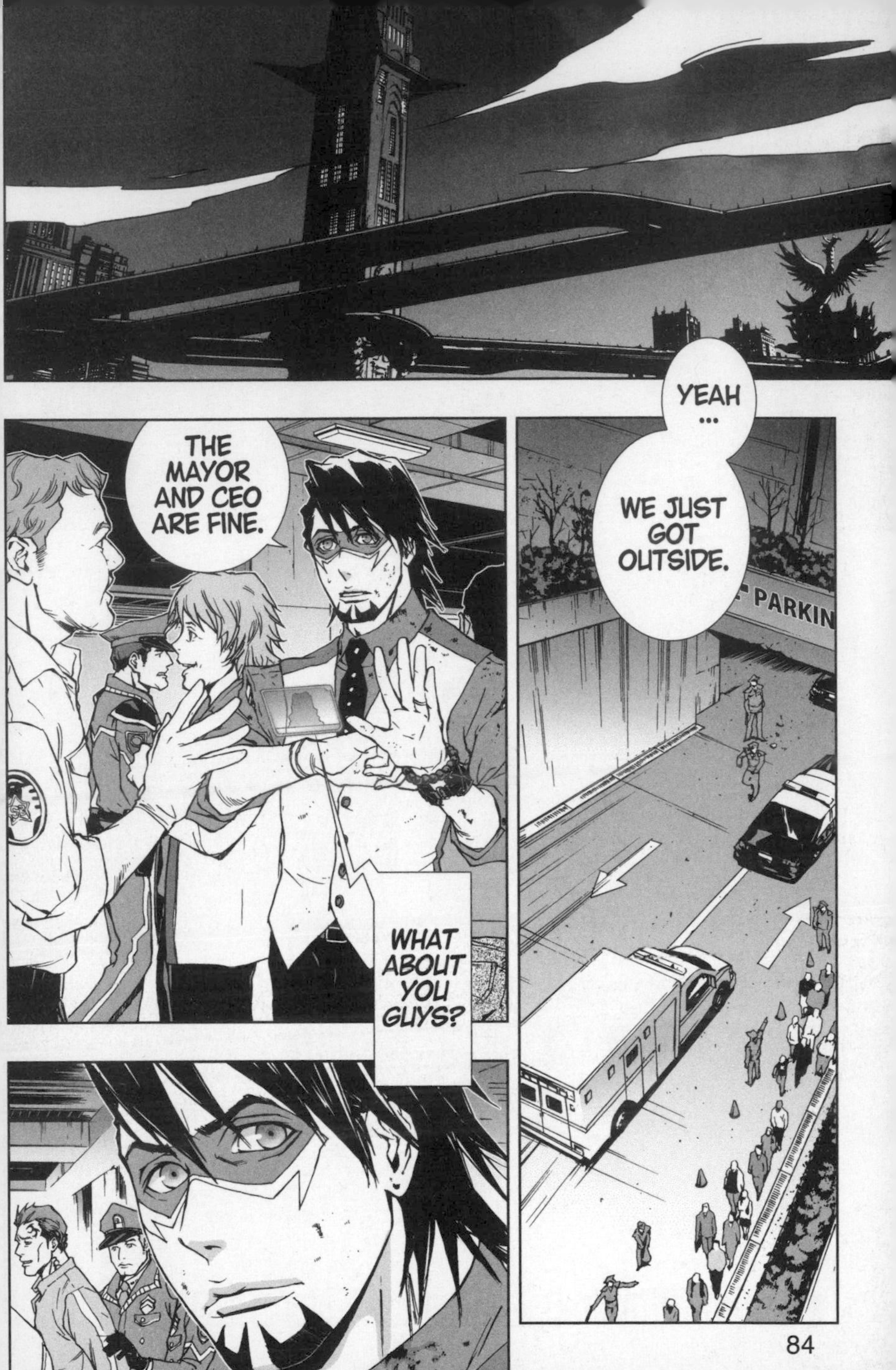
YEAH ...
WE JUST GOT OUTSIDE.
PARKIN
THE MAYOR AND CEO ARE FINE.
WHAT ABOUT YOU GUYS?

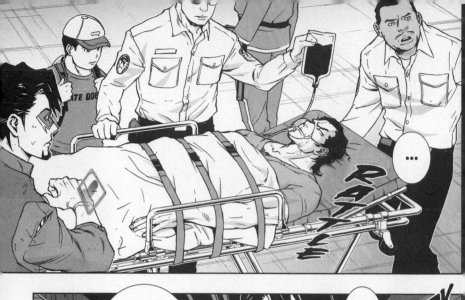

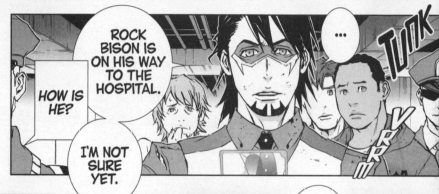

...
RATTLE
TUNK
...
VRRM
ROCK BISON IS ON HIS WAY TO THE HOSPITAL.
HOW IS HE?
I'M NOT SURE YET.
AND MARTINEZ?
FIRE EMBLEM, BLUE ROSE AND DRAGON KID ARE PURSUING THE ARMORED VEHICLE.
WILL THEY BE ALL RIGHT?

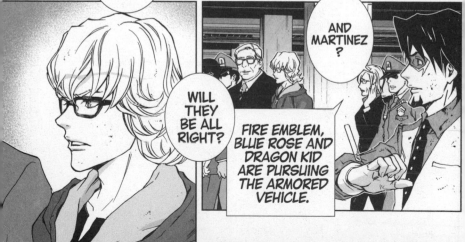

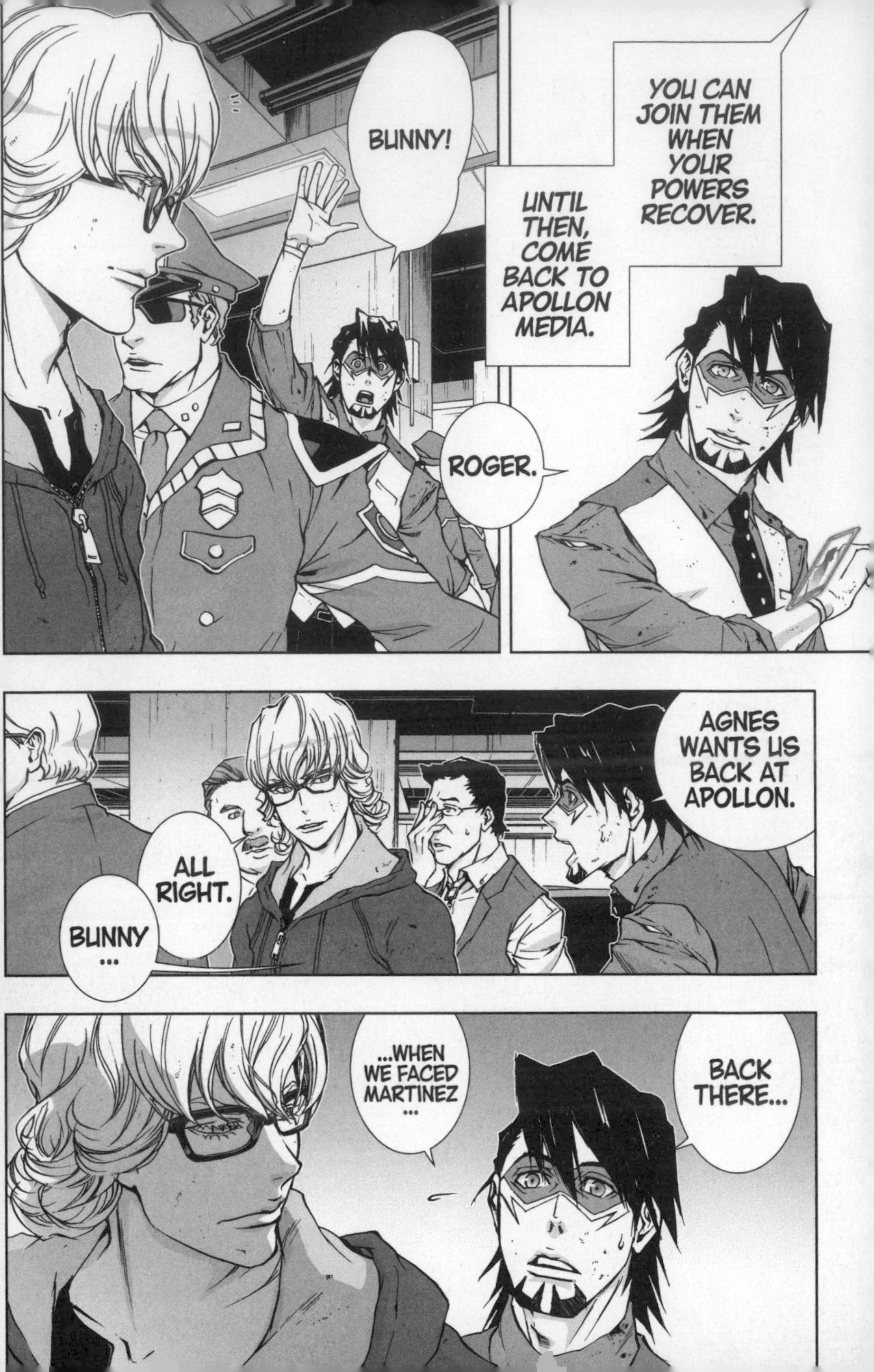
YOU CAN JOIN THEM WHEN YOUR POWERS RECOVER.
UNTIL THEN, COME BACK TO APOLLON MEDIA.
ROGER.
BUNNY!
AGNES WANTS US BACK AT APOLLON.
ALL RIGHT.
BUNNY ...
BACK THERE...
...WHEN WE FACED MARTINEZ ...

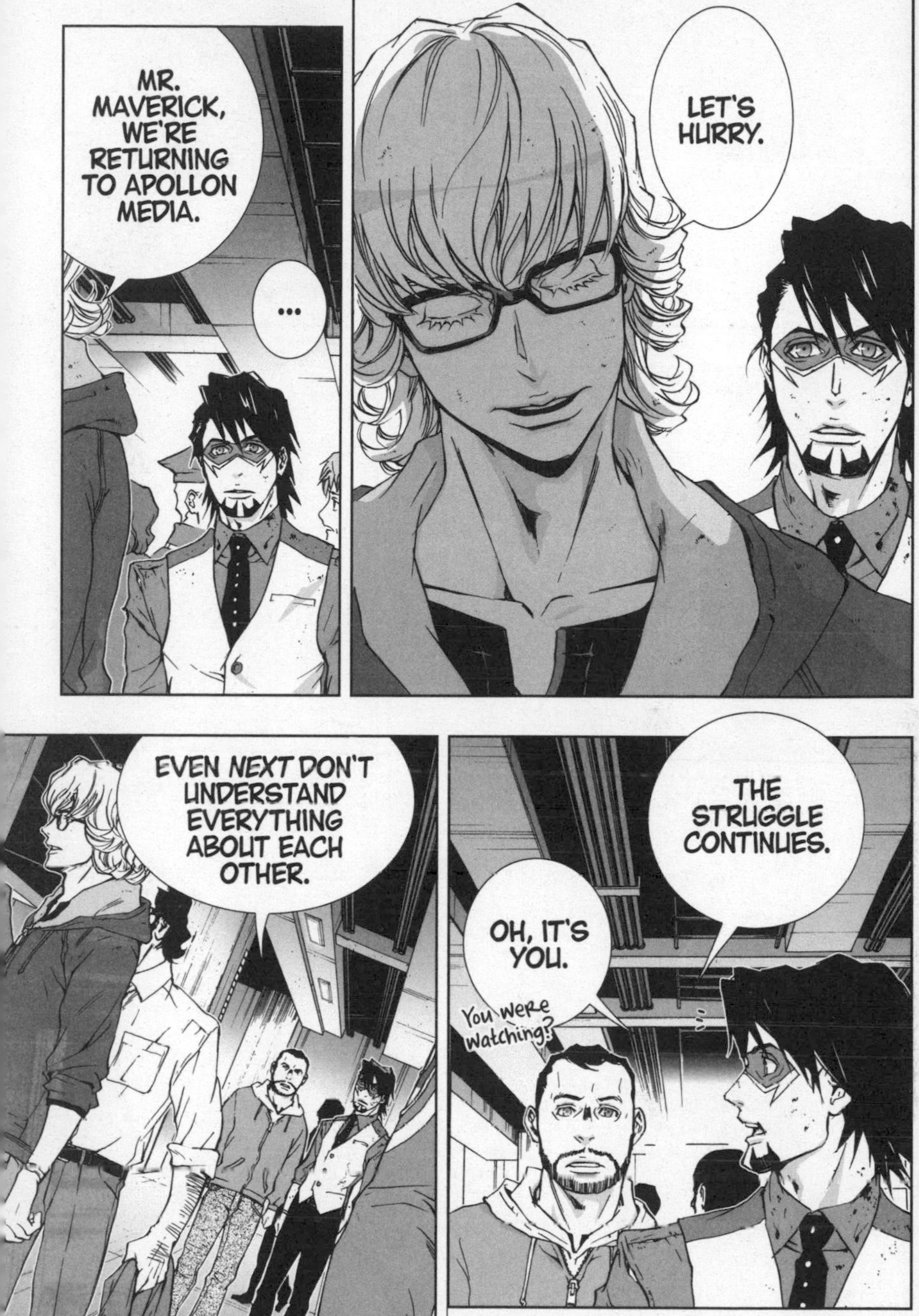
LET'S HURRY.
MR. MAVERICK, WE'RE RETURNING TO APOLLON MEDIA.
...
THE STRUGGLE CONTINUES.
OH, IT'S YOU.
You were watching?
EVEN *NEXT* DON'T UNDERSTAND EVERYTHING ABOUT EACH OTHER.

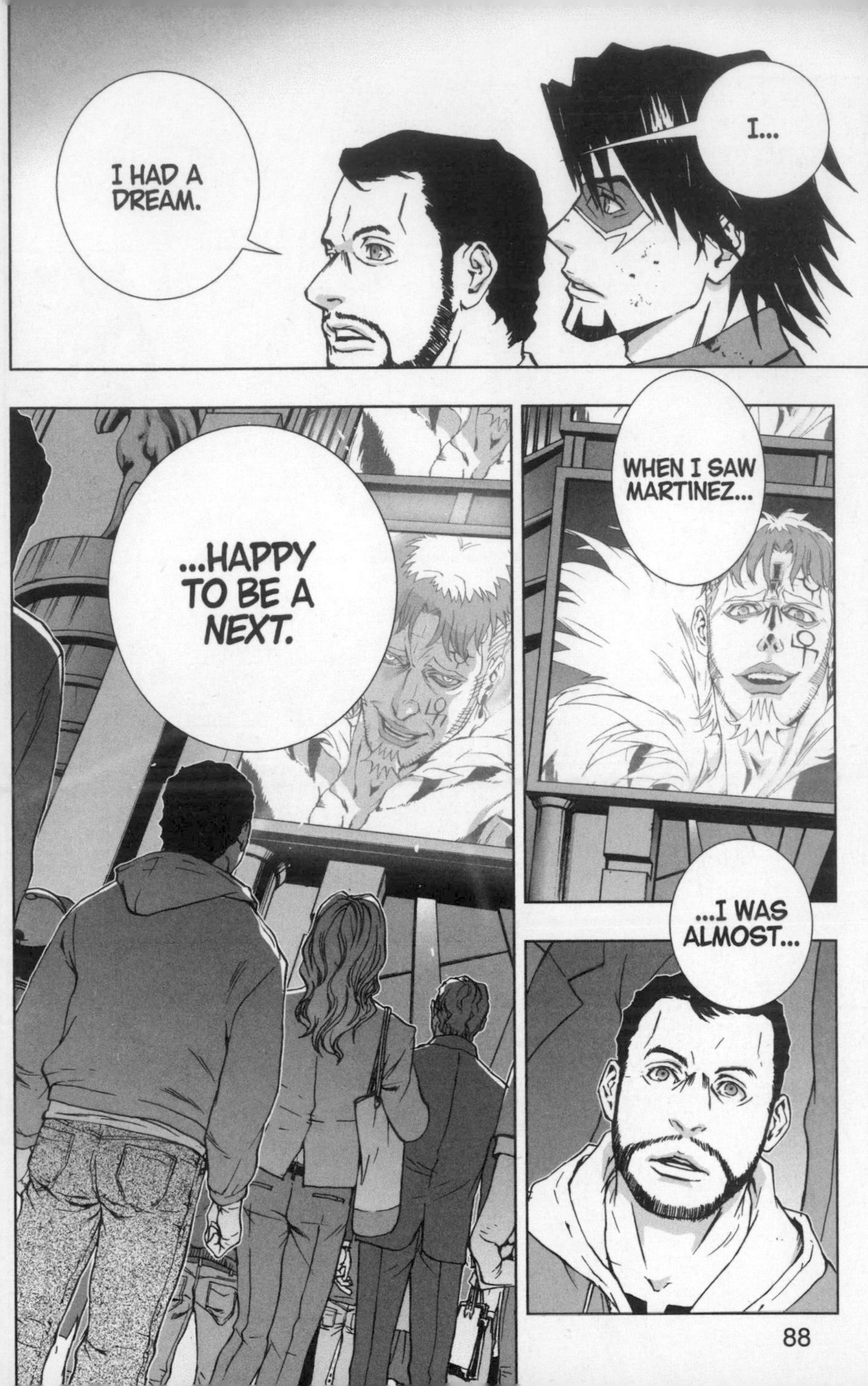
I...
I HAD A DREAM.
WHEN I SAW MARTINEZ...
...I WAS ALMOST...
...HAPPY TO BE A NEXT.

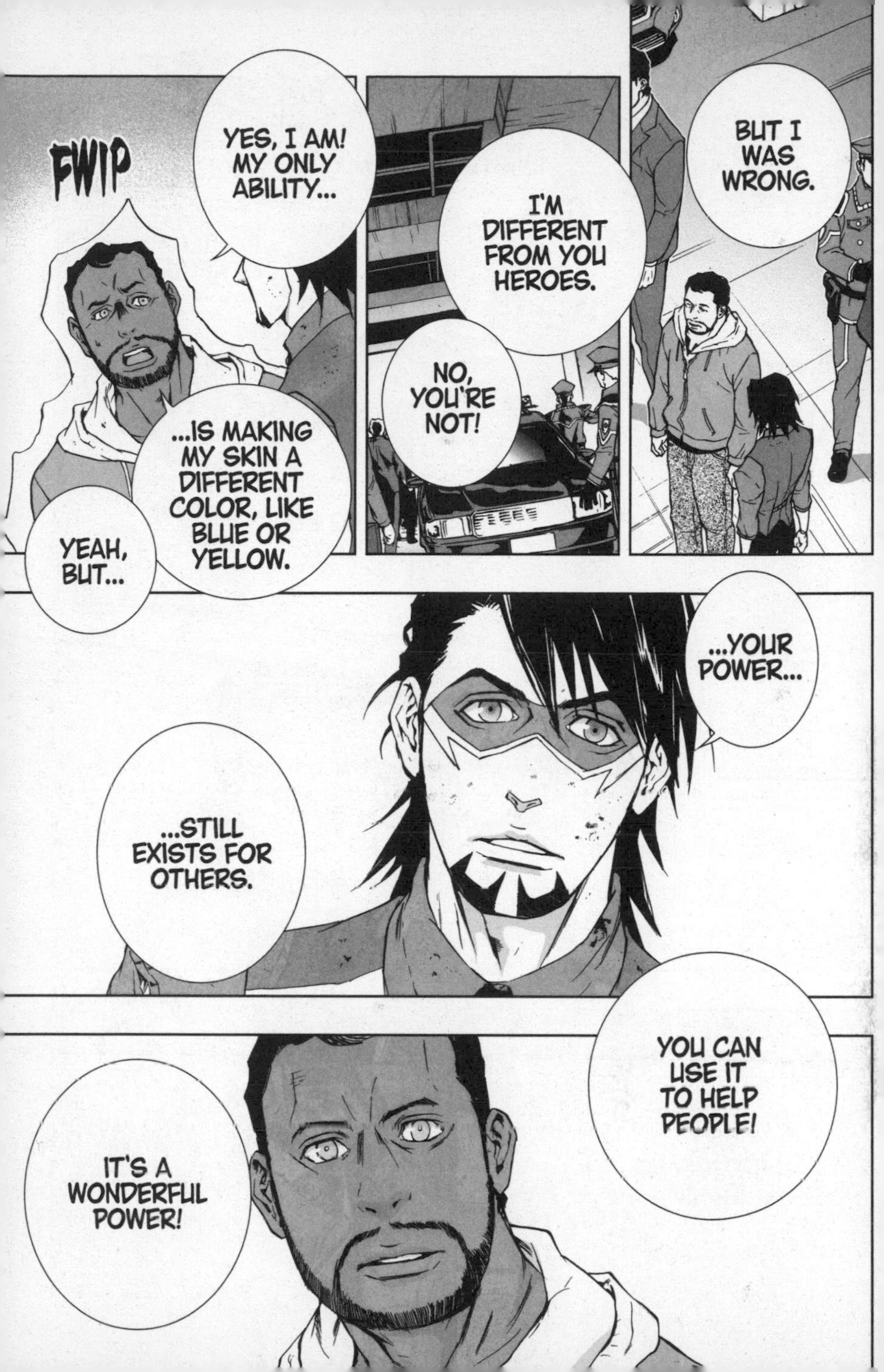
BUT I WAS WRONG.
I'M DIFFERENT FROM YOU HEROES.
NO, YOU'RE NOT!
YES, I AM! MY ONLY ABILITY...
FWIP
...IS MAKING MY SKIN A DIFFERENT COLOR, LIKE BLUE OR YELLOW.
YEAH, BUT...
...YOUR POWER...
...STILL EXISTS FOR OTHERS.
YOU CAN USE IT TO HELP PEOPLE!
IT'S A WONDERFUL POWER!

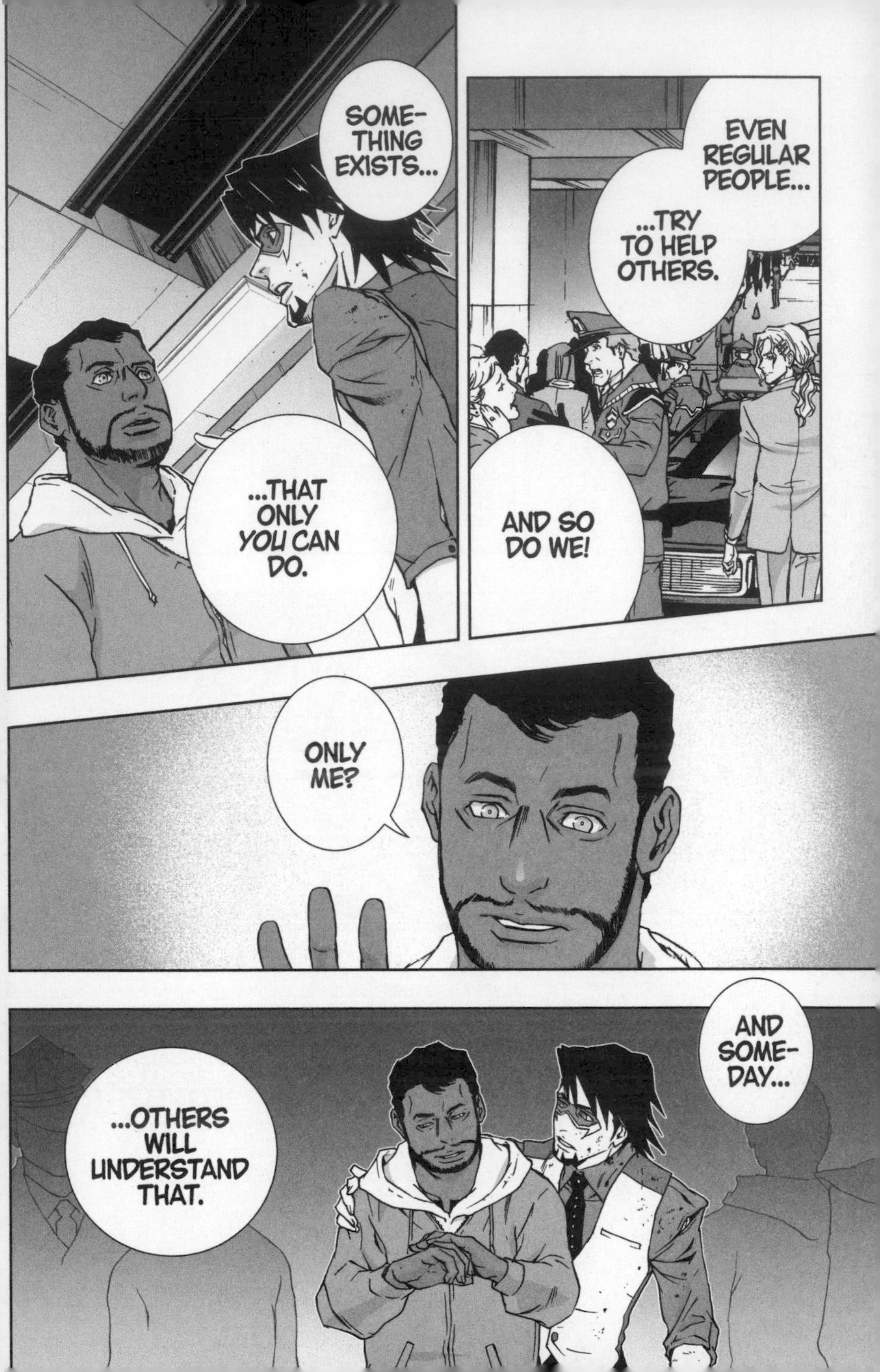
EVEN REGULAR PEOPLE...
...TRY TO HELP OTHERS.
AND SO DO WE!
SOME-THING EXISTS...
...THAT ONLY YOU CAN DO.
ONLY ME?
AND SOME-DAY...
...OTHERS WILL UNDERSTAND THAT.

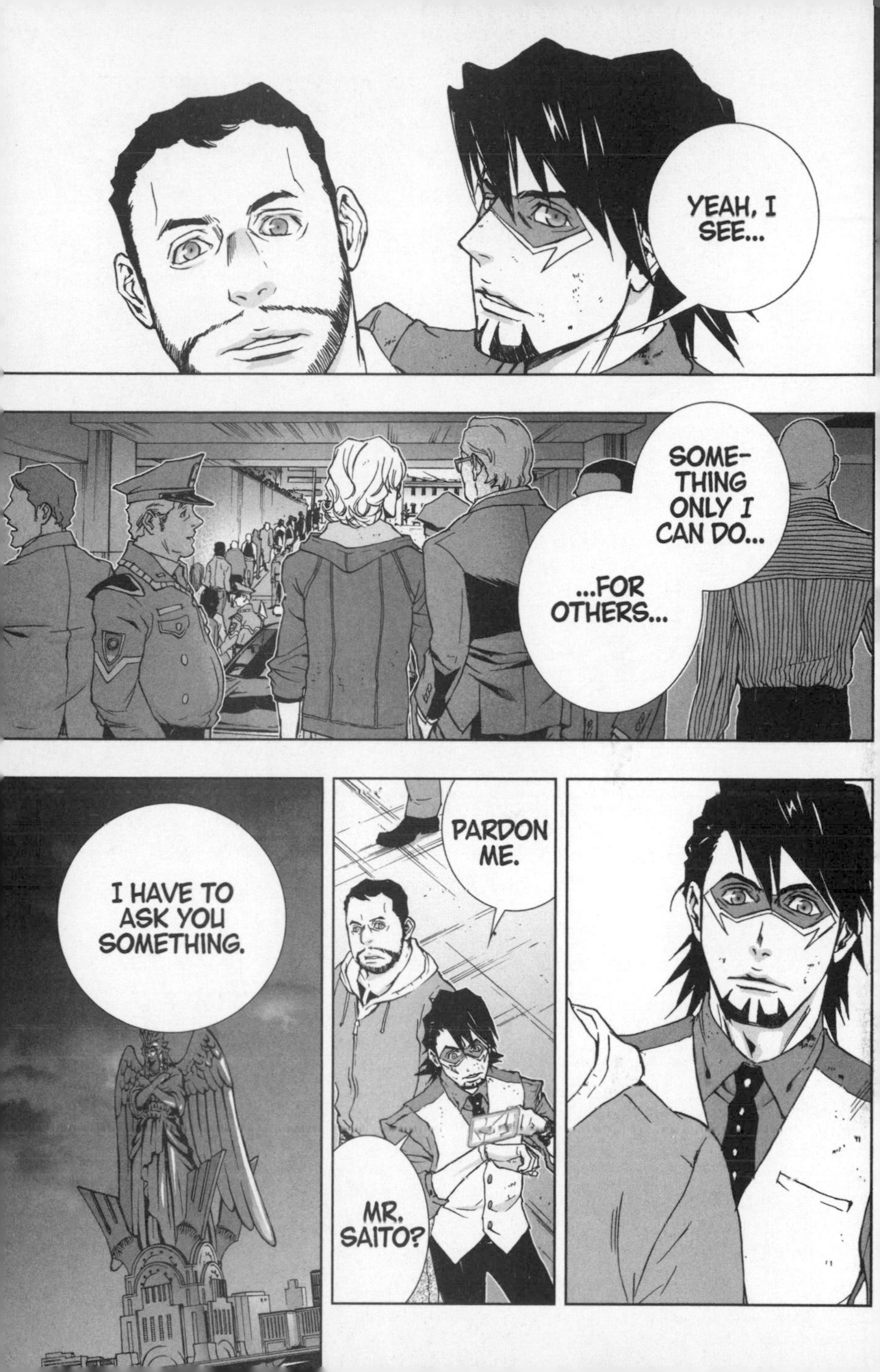
YEAH, I SEE...
SOME-THING ONLY I CAN DO...
...FOR OTHERS...
PARDON ME.
MR. SAITO?
I HAVE TO ASK YOU SOMETHING.

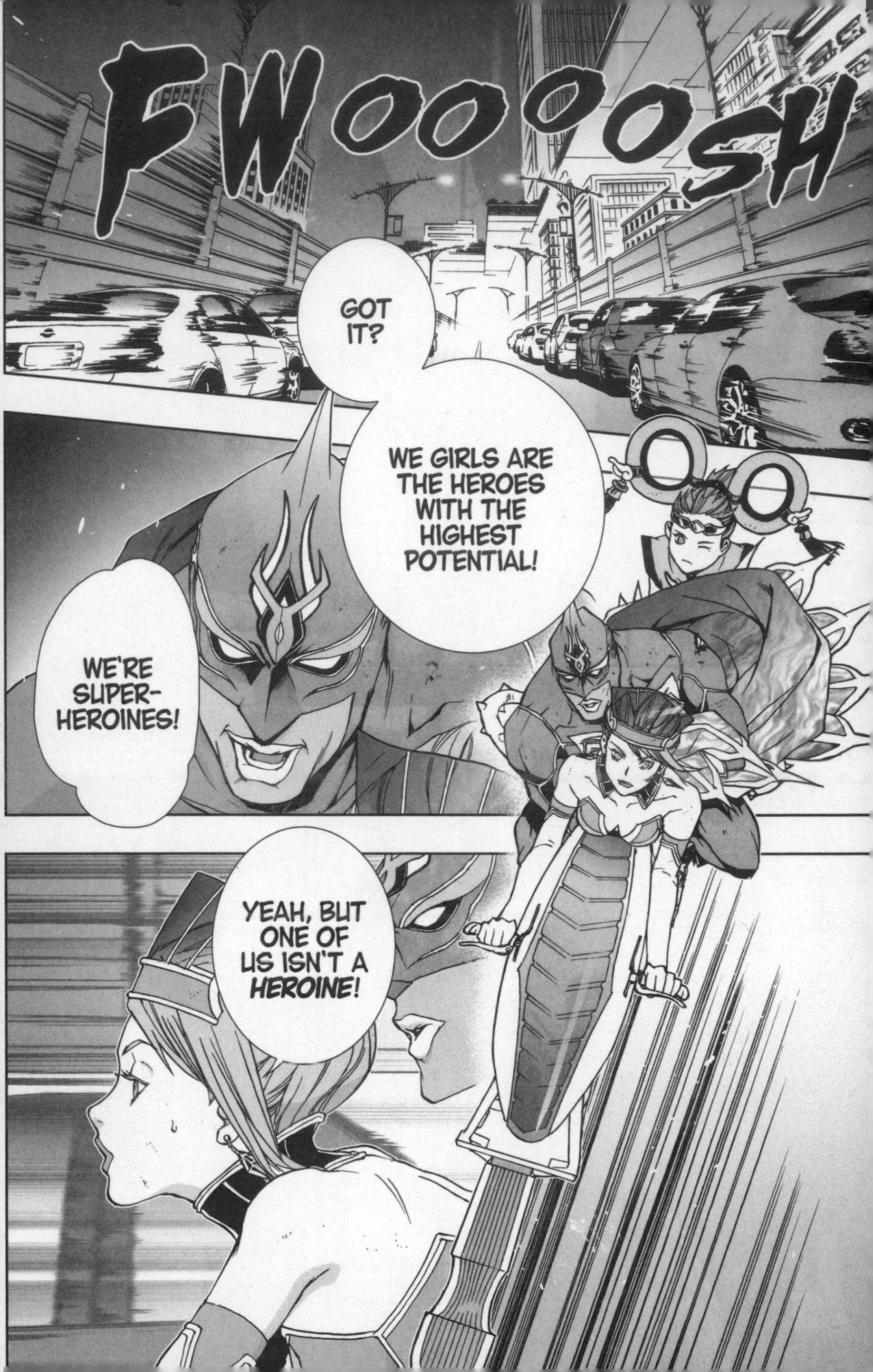
FWOOOOSH
GOT IT?
WE GIRLS ARE THE HEROES WITH THE HIGHEST POTENTIAL!
WE'RE SUPER-HEROINES!
YEAH, BUT ONE OF US ISN'T A HEROINE!

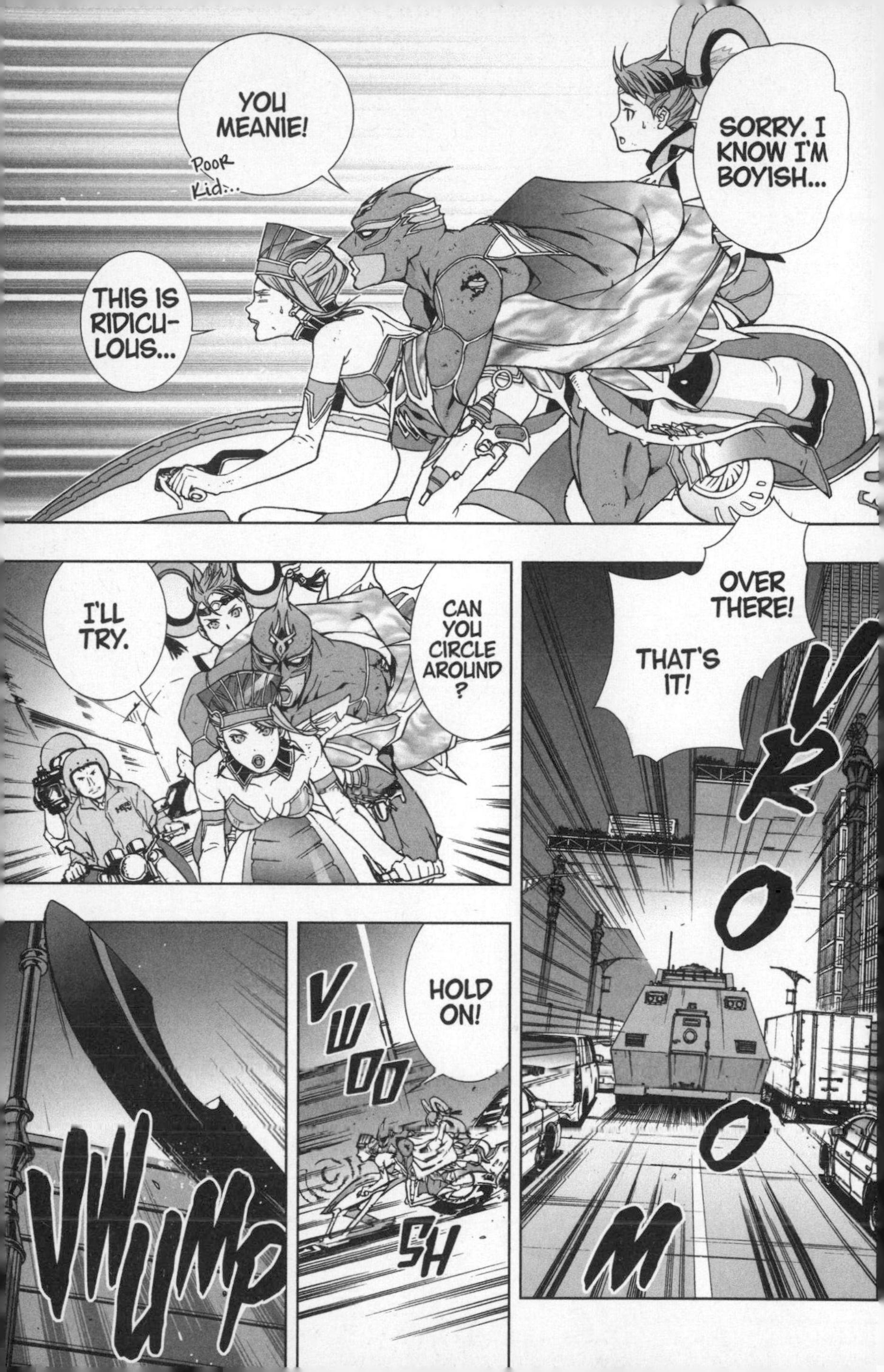
SORRY. I KNOW I'M BOYISH...
YOU MEANIE!
Poor Kid...
THIS IS RIDICU-LOUS...
OVER THERE!
THAT'S IT!
VROOOM
CAN YOU CIRCLE AROUND?
I'LL TRY.
HOLD ON!
VWOOSH
VWUMP

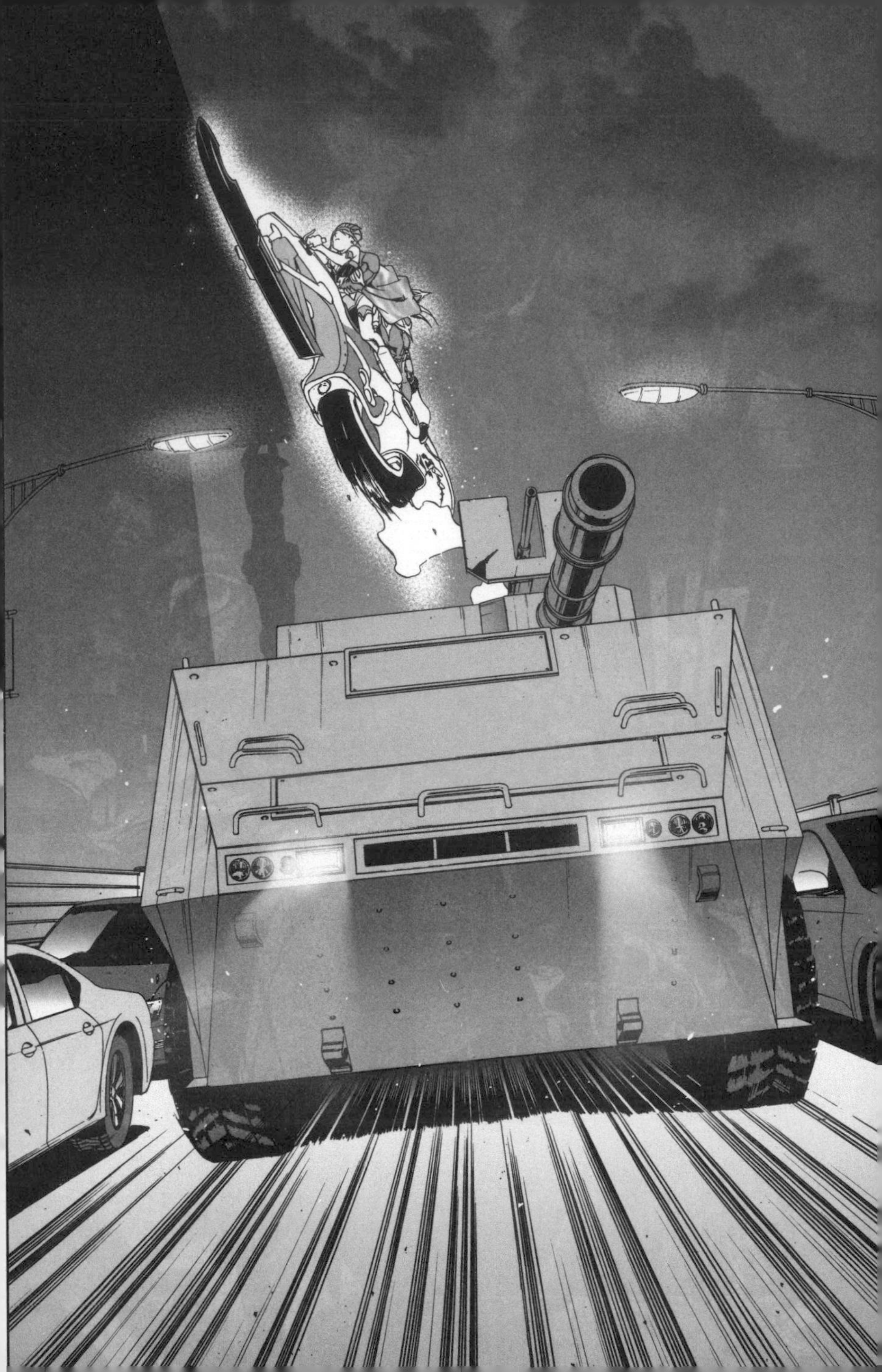

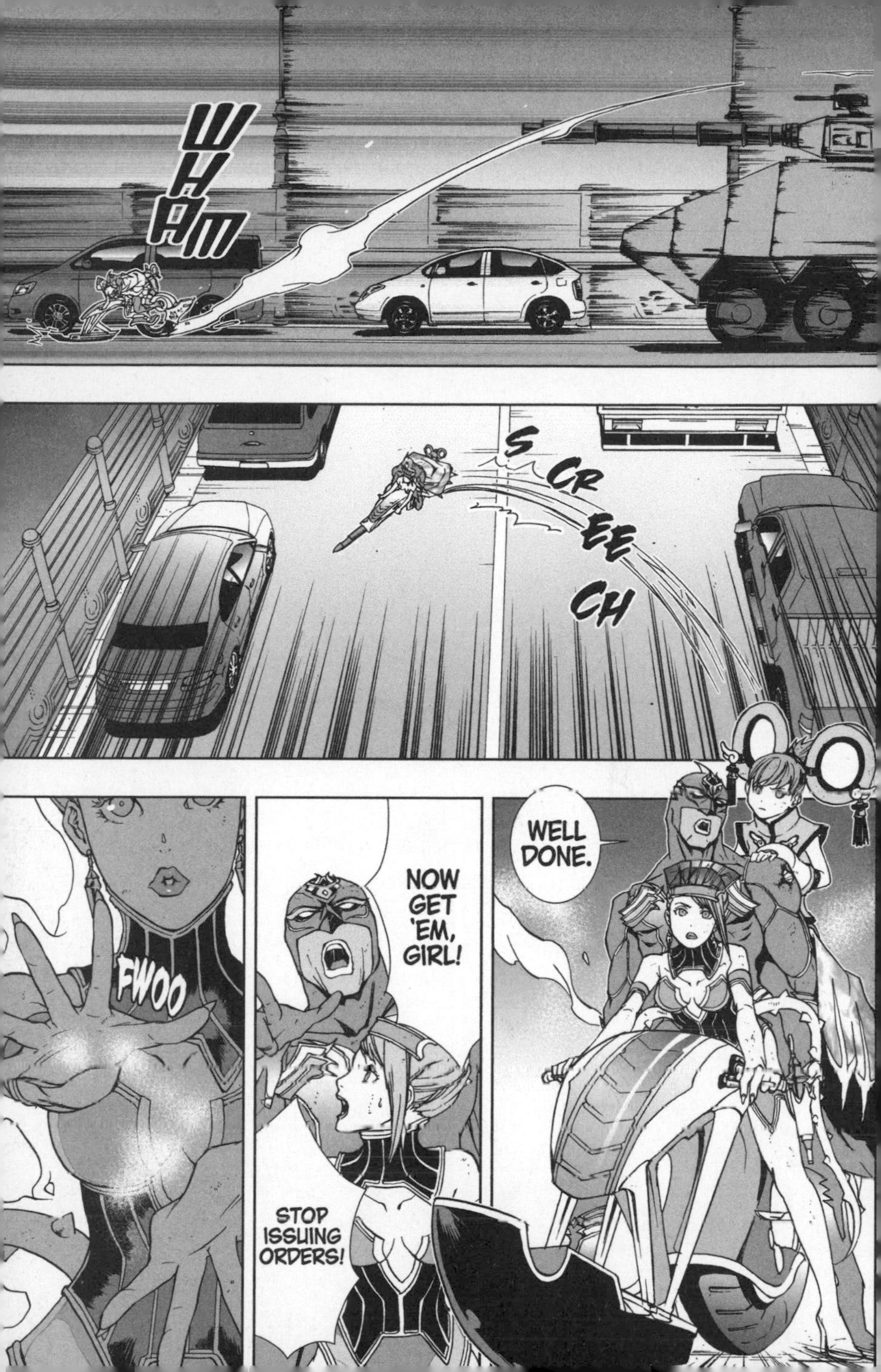
WHAM
SCREECH
WELL DONE.
NOW GET 'EM, GIRL!
STOP ISSUING ORDERS!
FWOO

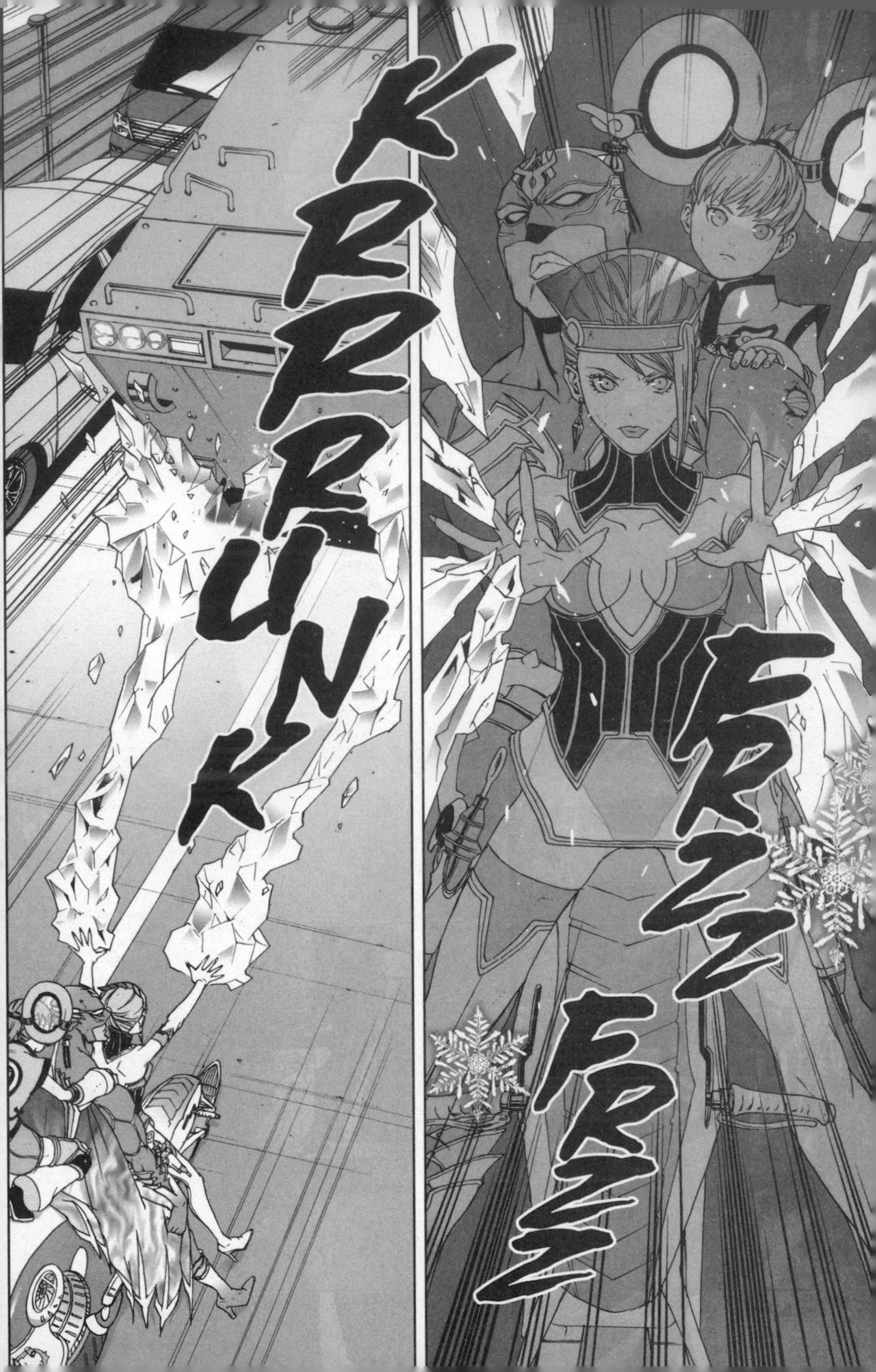
FRZZ
FRZZ
KRRRUNK

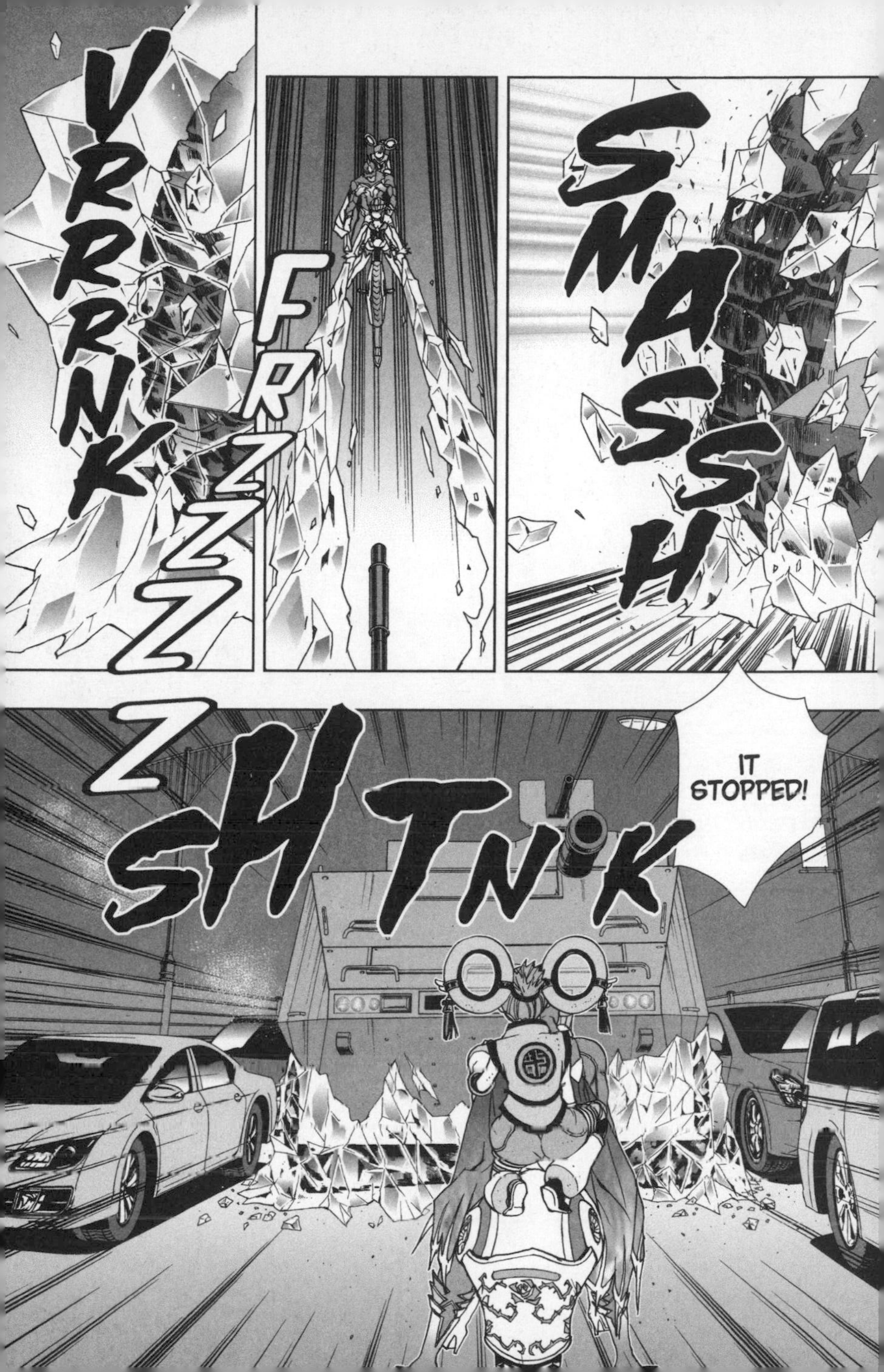
SMASSH
FRZZZZ
VRRRNK
IT STOPPED!
SHTNIK

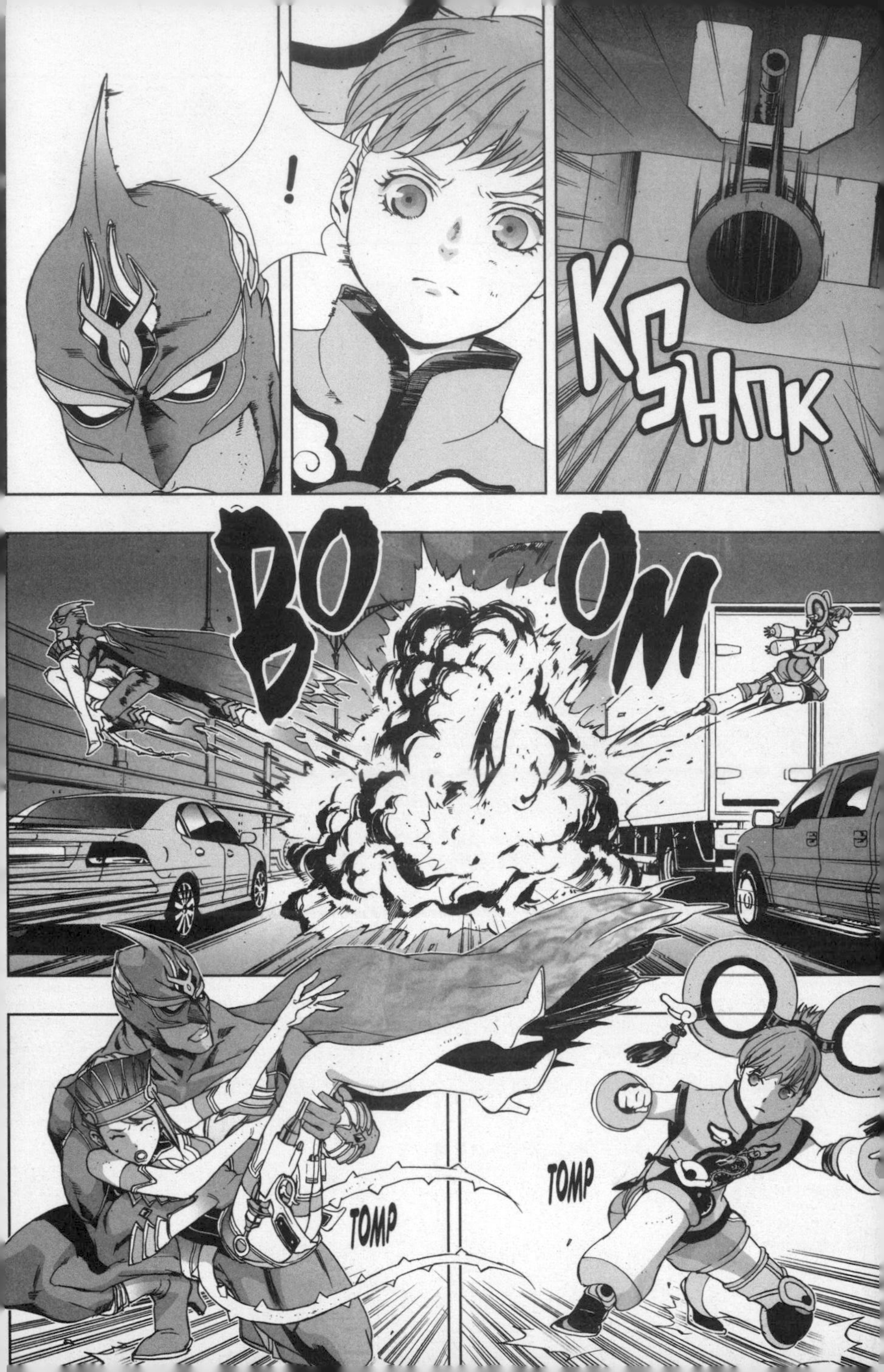
KSHNK
!
BOOM
TOMP
TOMP

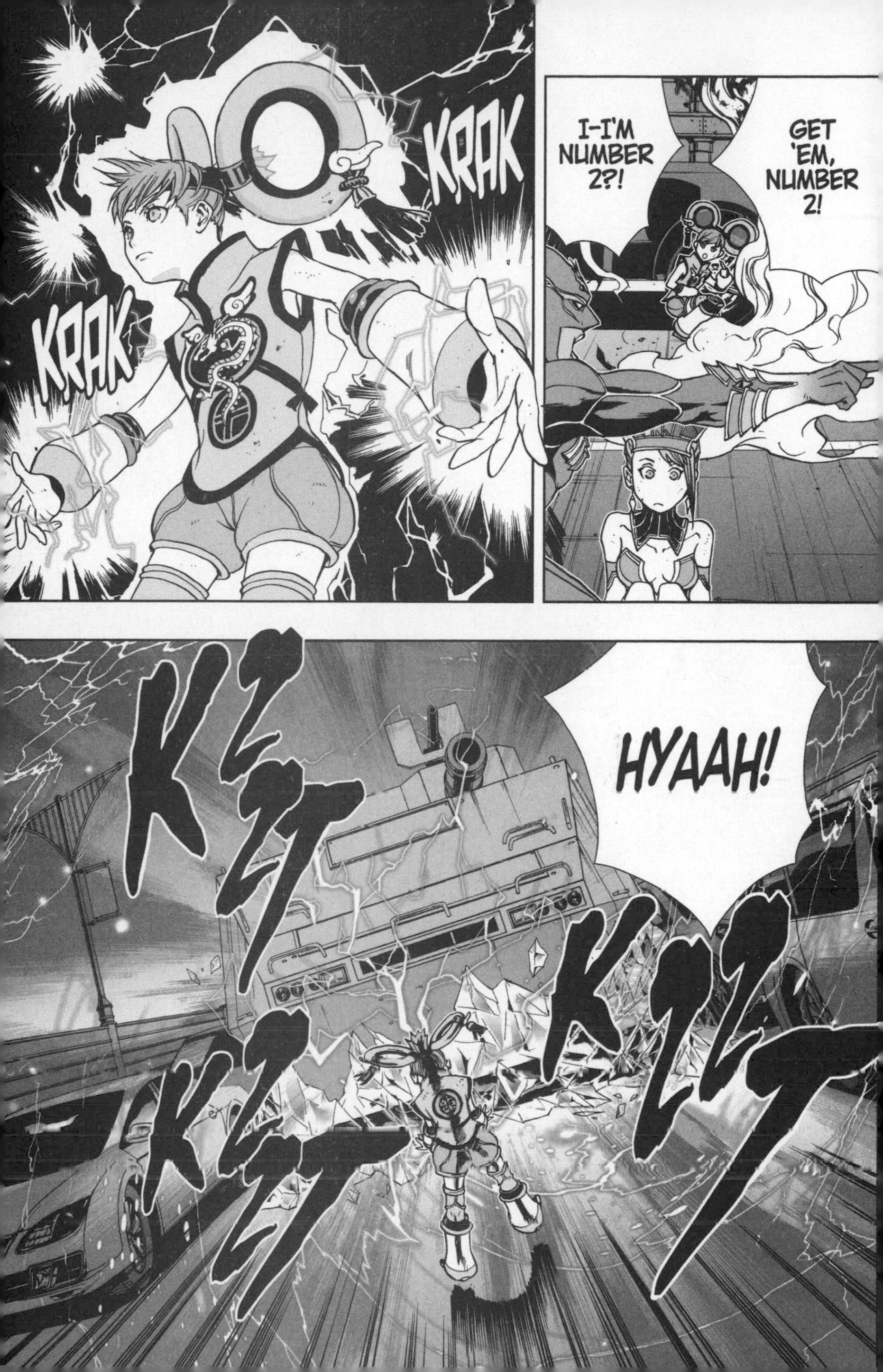
GET 'EM, NUMBER 2!
I-I'M NUMBER 2?!
KRAK
KRAK
HYAAH!

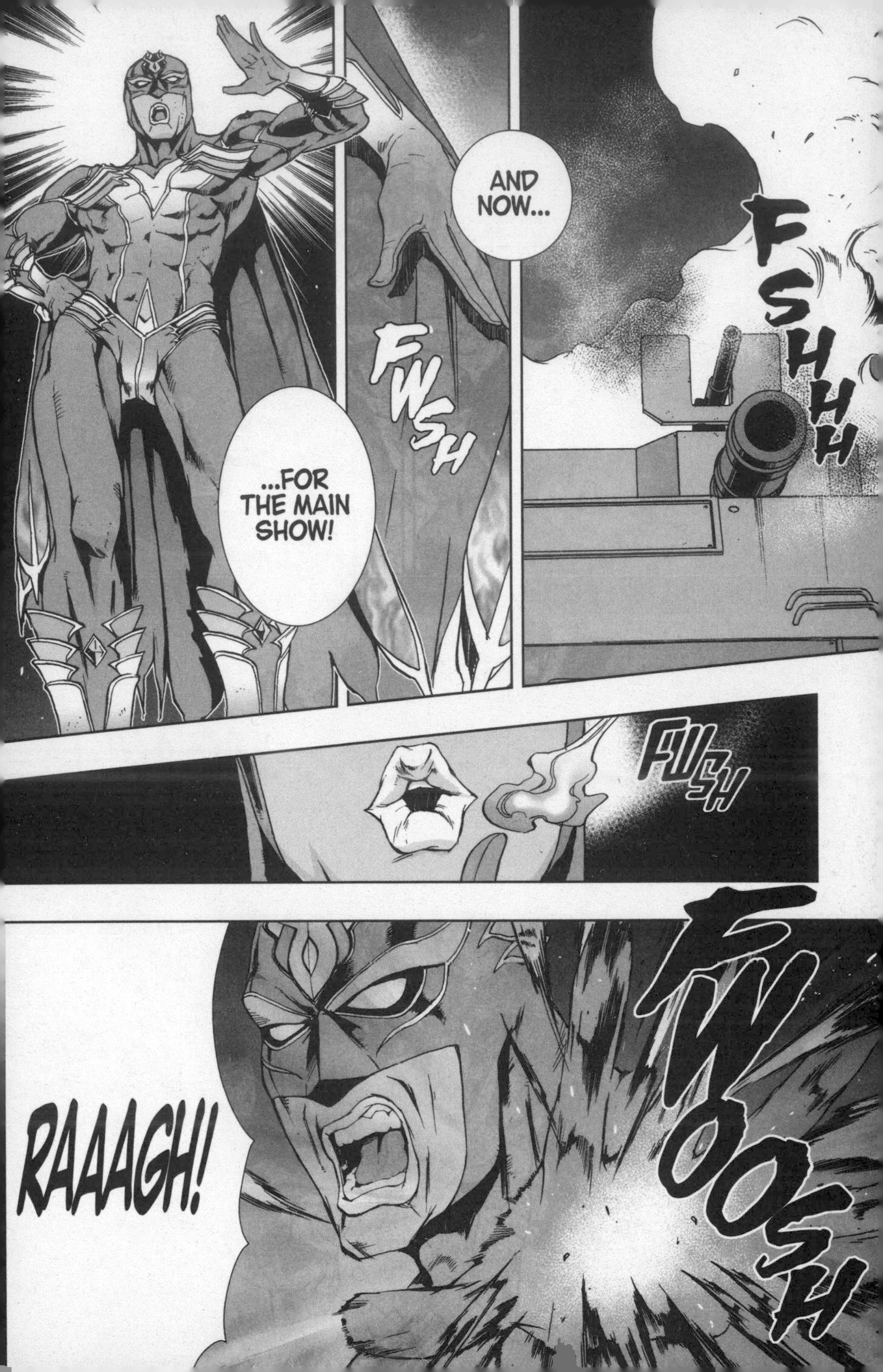
FSHHH
AND NOW...
FWSH
...FOR THE MAIN SHOW!
FWSH
FWOOSH
RAAAGH!

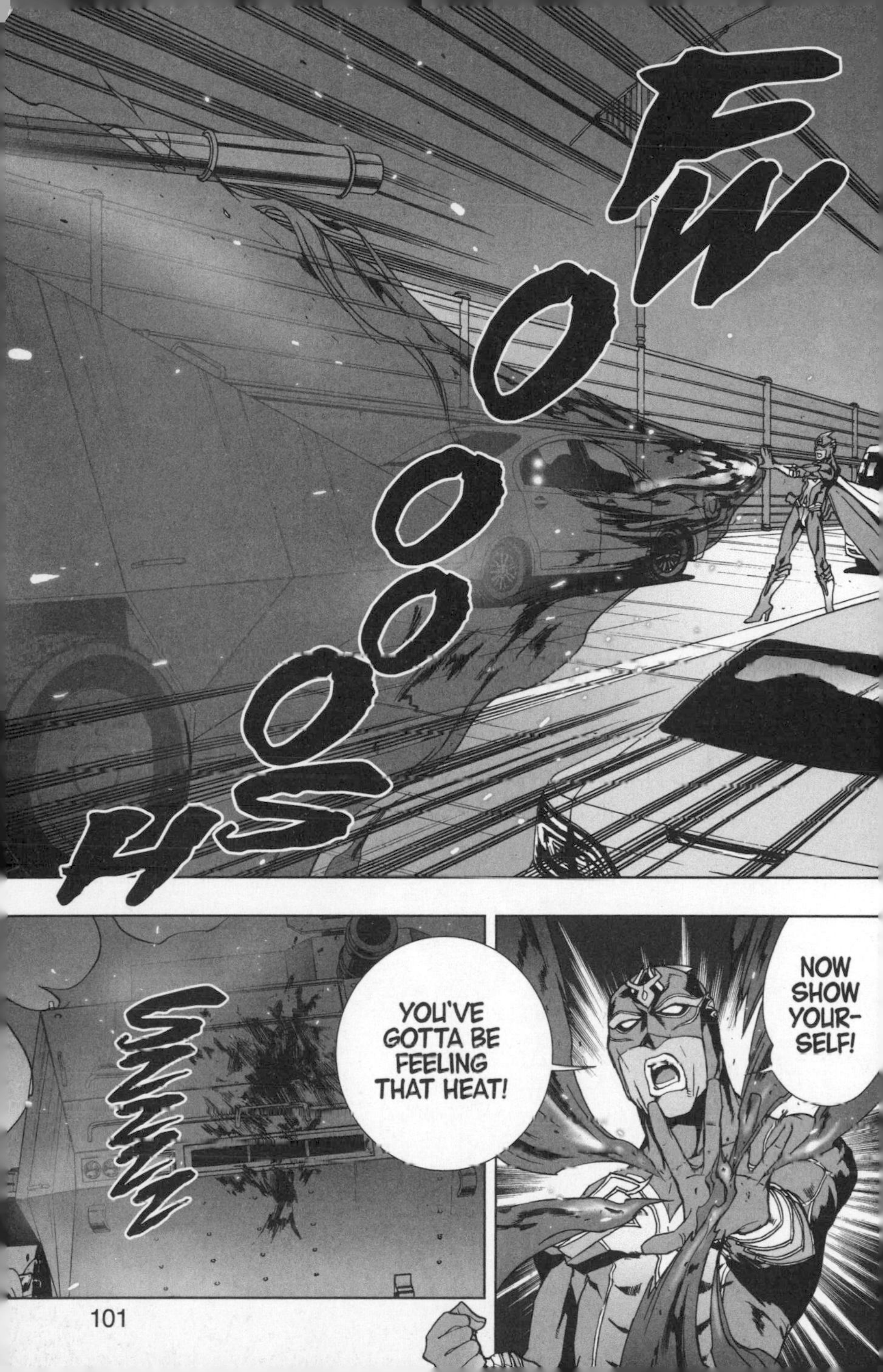
FWOOOOOSH
NOW SHOW YOURSELF!
YOU'VE GOTTA BE FEELING THAT HEAT!
SNNNNN

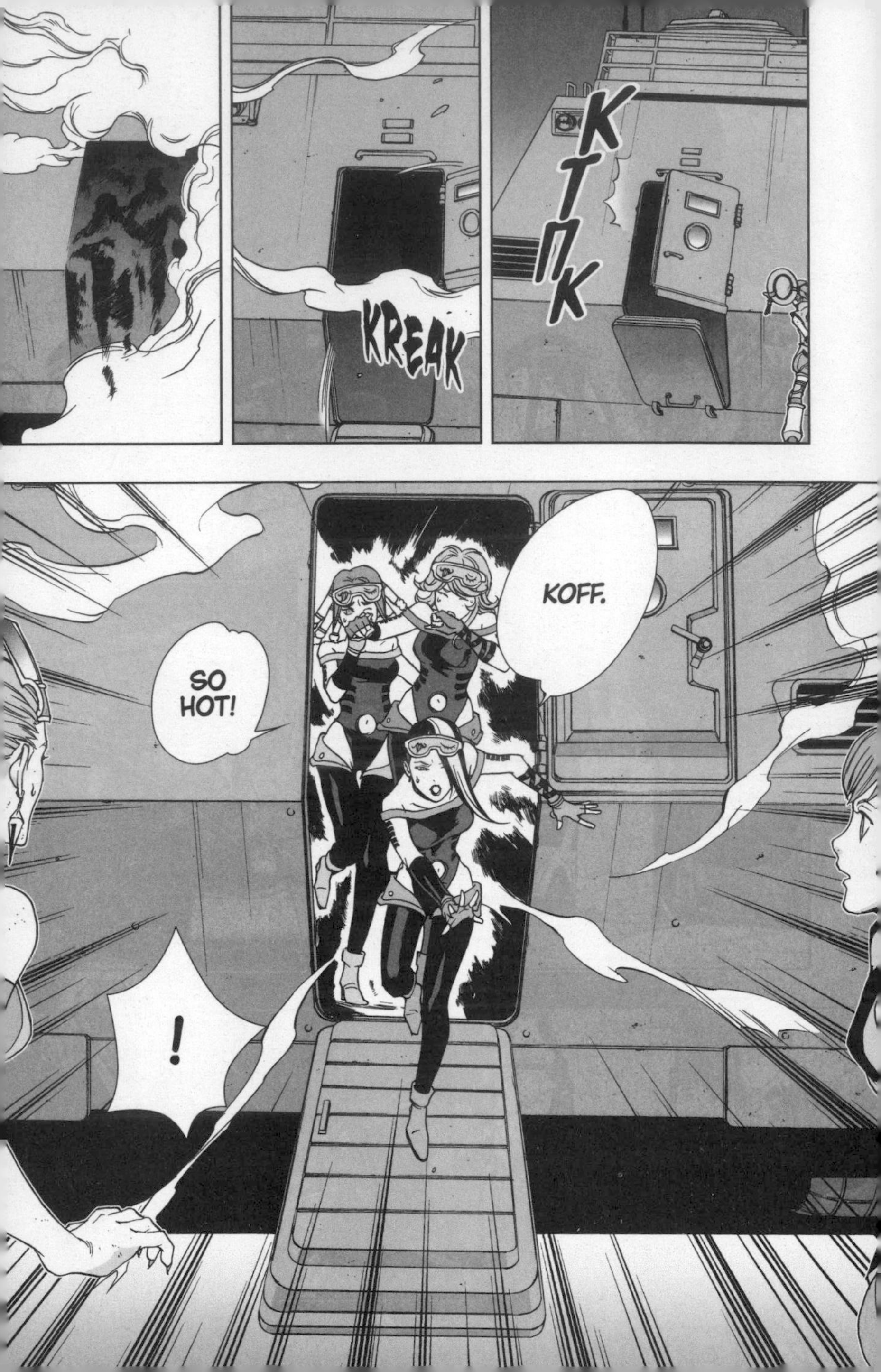
KTINK
KREAK
KOFF.
SO HOT!
!

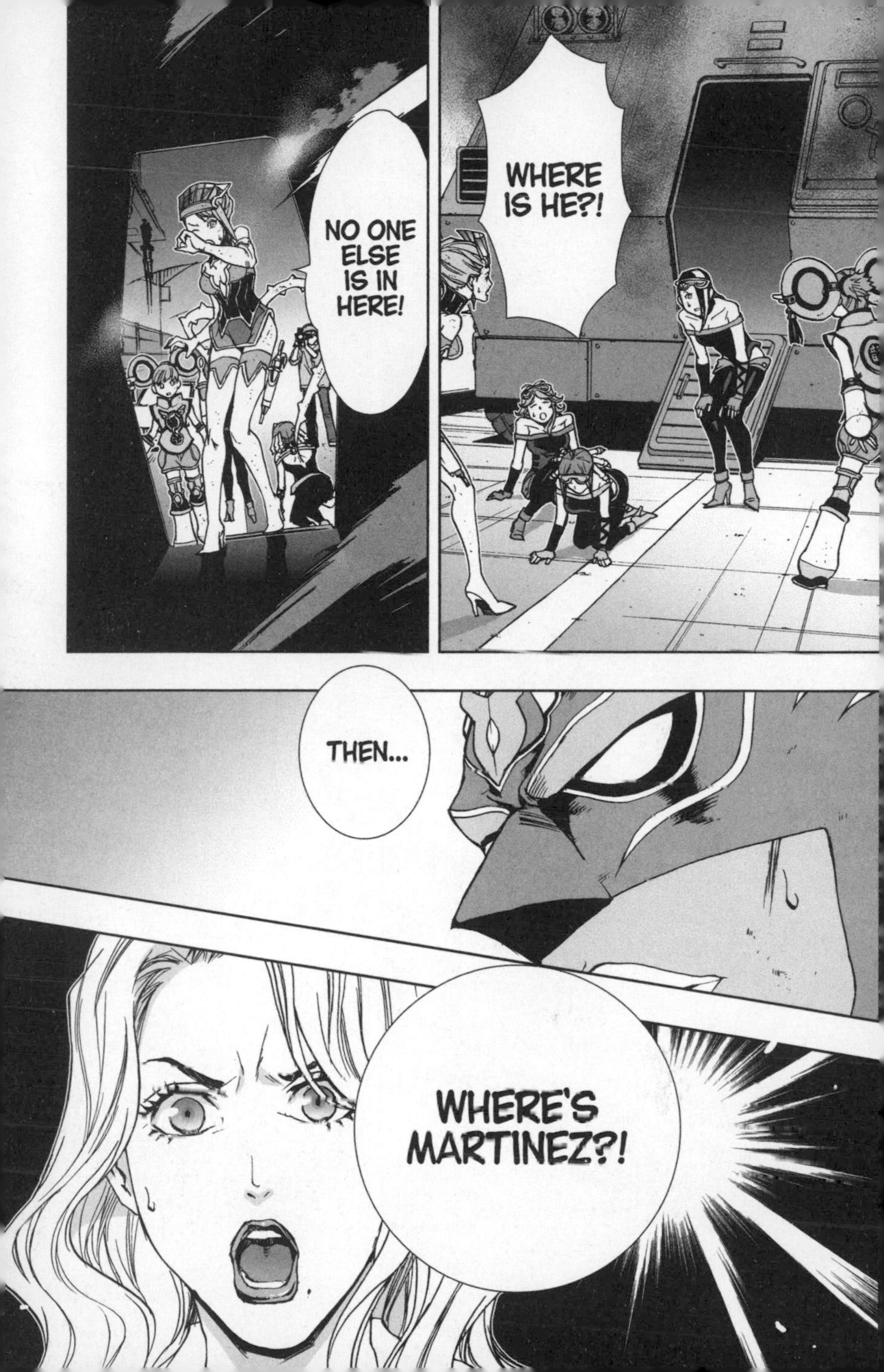
WHERE IS HE?!
NO ONE ELSE IS IN HERE!
THEN...
WHERE'S MARTINEZ?!

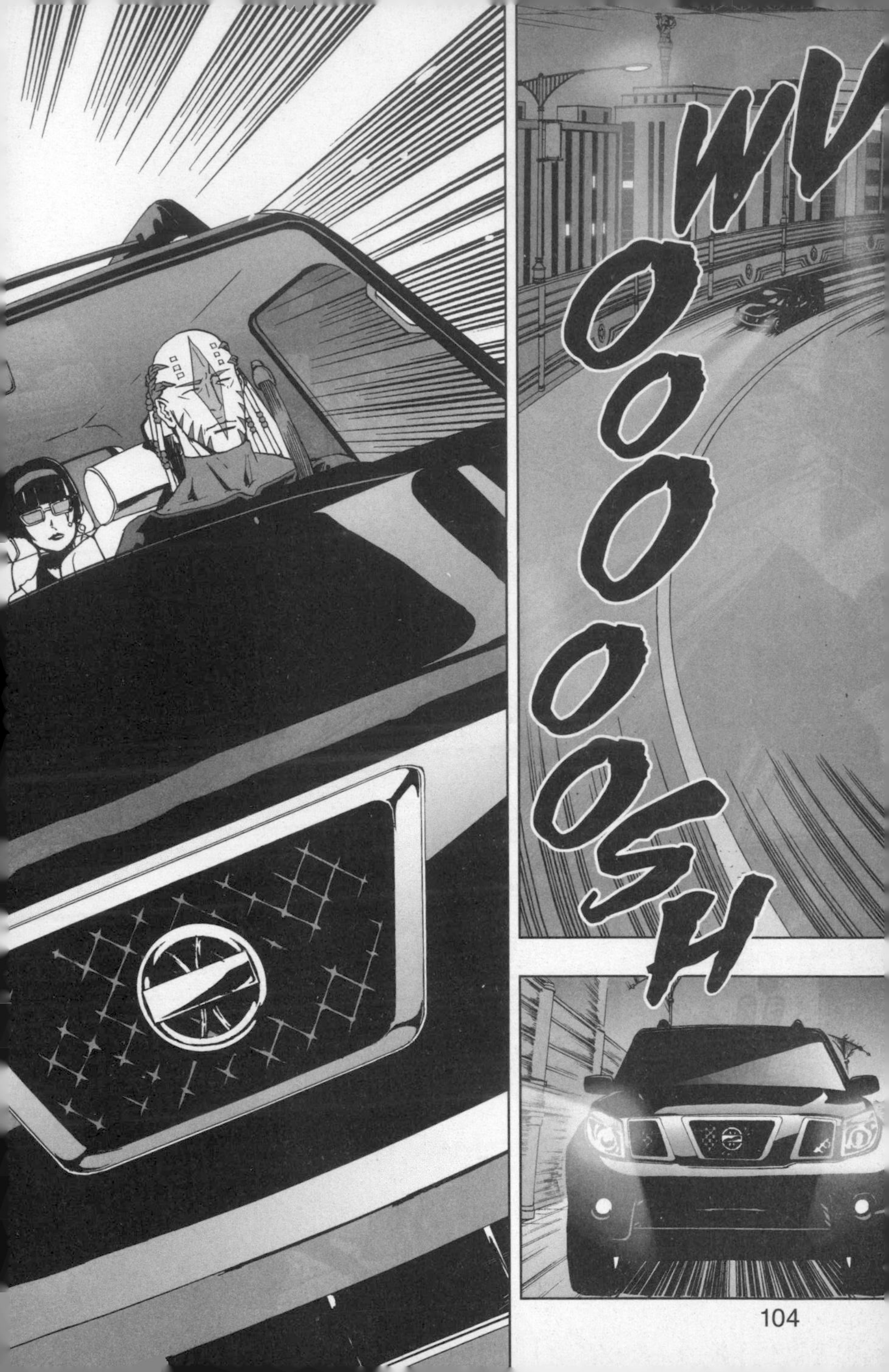
WVOOOOOSH

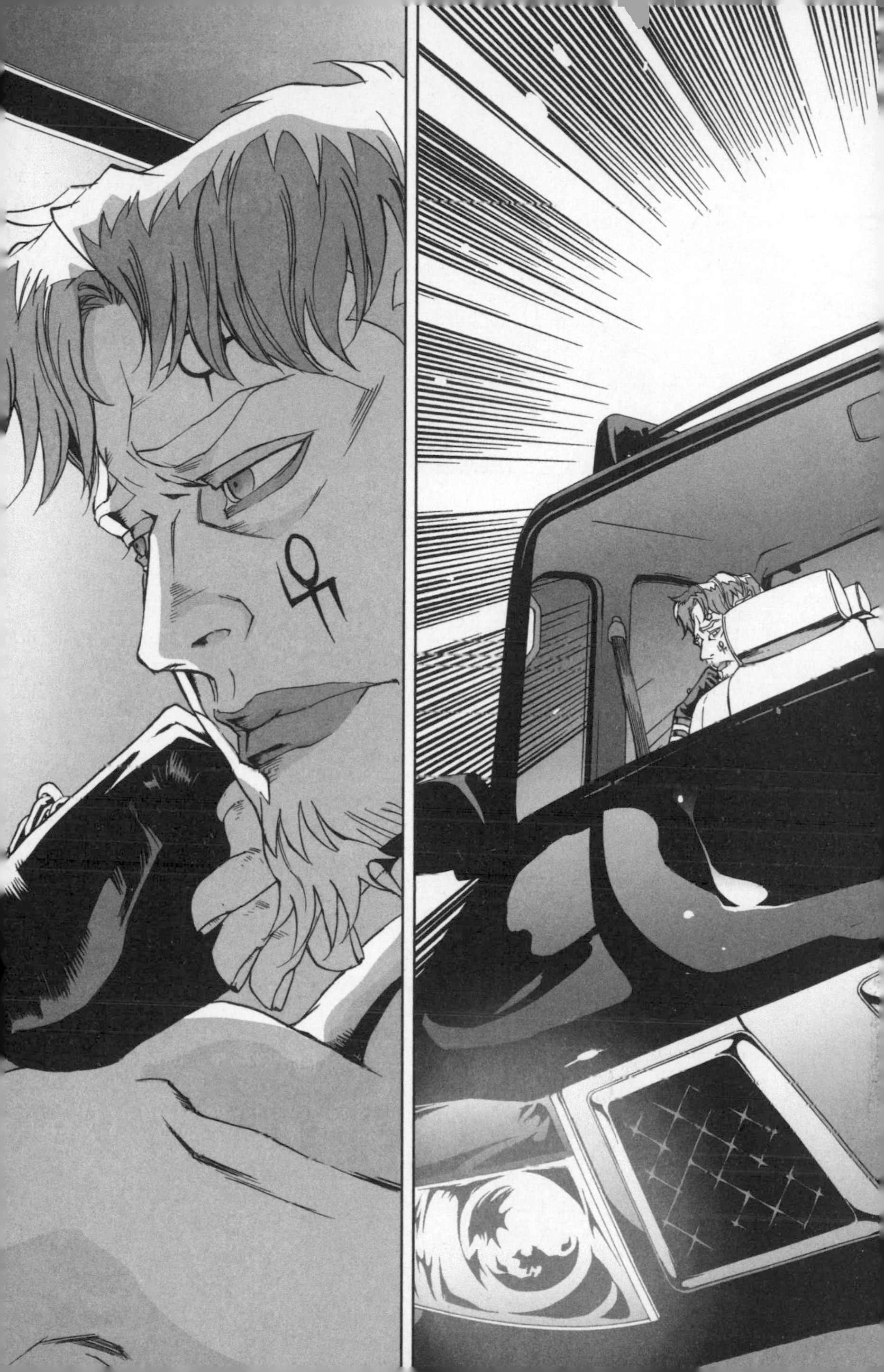

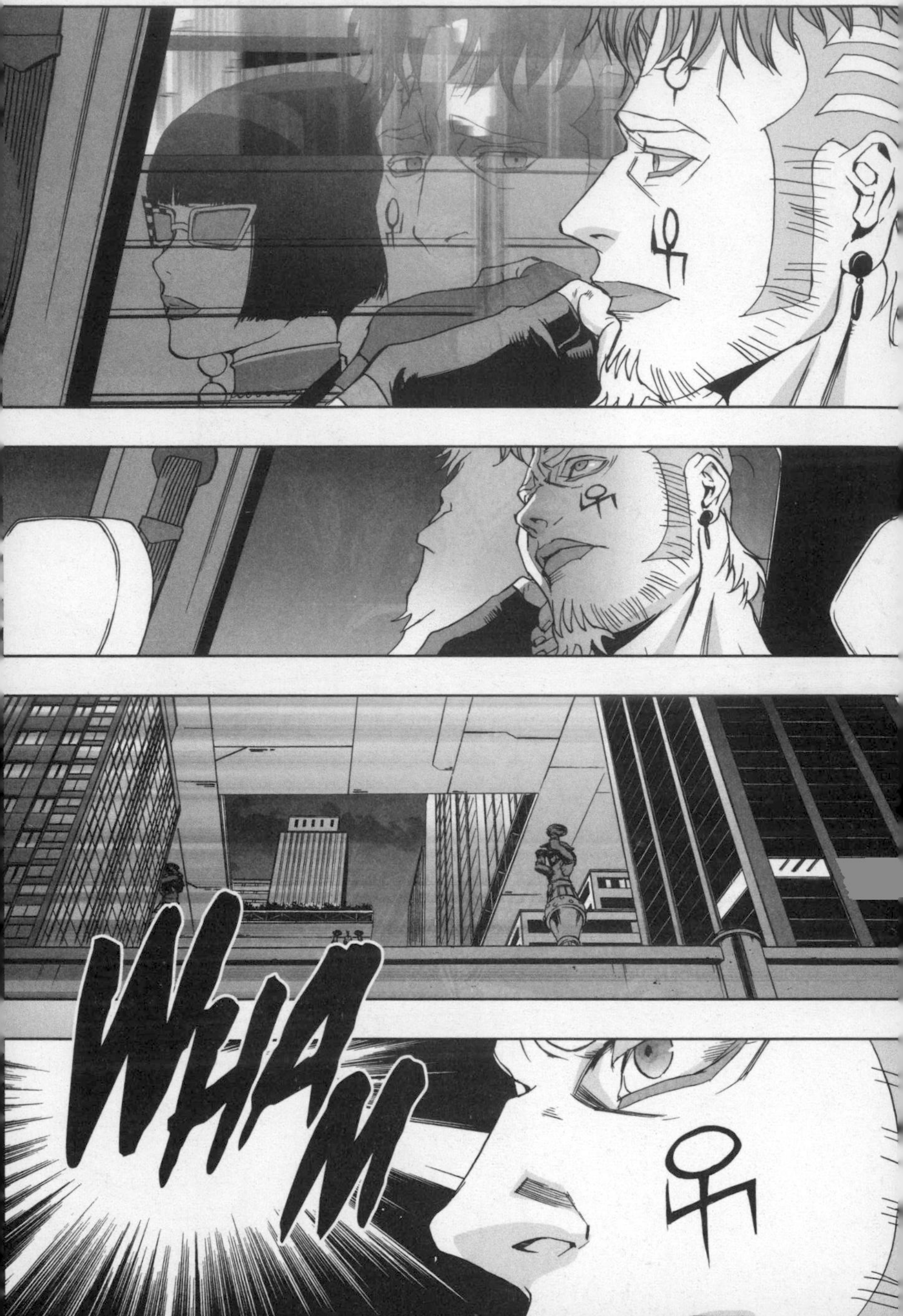
WHAM

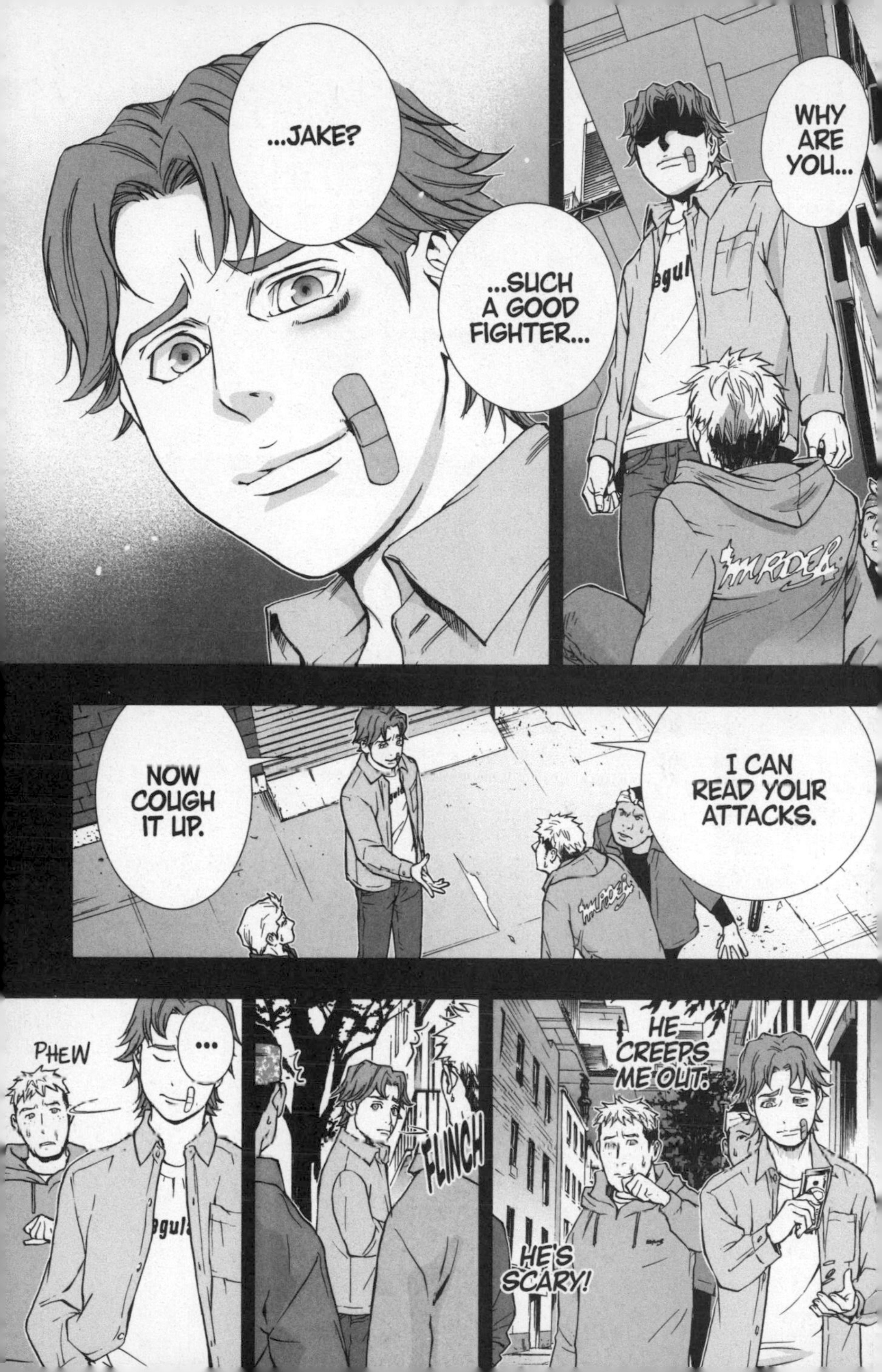
WHY ARE YOU...
...SUCH A GOOD FIGHTER...
...JAKE?
I CAN READ YOUR ATTACKS.
NOW COUGH IT UP.
HE CREEPS ME OUT.
HE'S SCARY!
FLINCH
PHEW
...

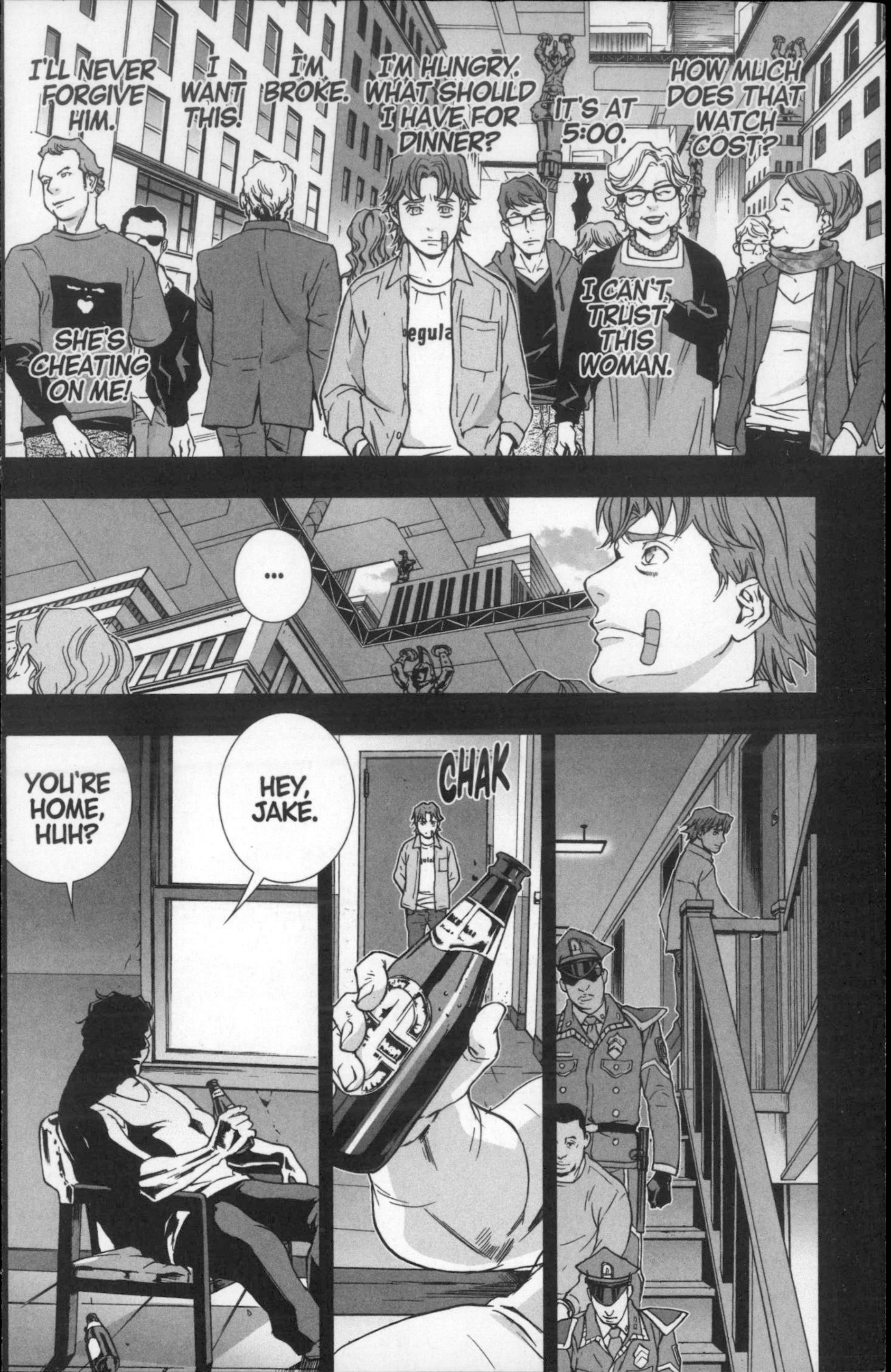
HOW MUCH DOES THAT WATCH COST?
IT'S AT 5:00.
I'M HUNGRY. WHAT SHOULD I HAVE FOR DINNER?
I CAN'T TRUST THIS WOMAN.
I'M BROKE.
I WANT THIS!
I'LL NEVER FORGIVE HIM.
SHE'S CHEATING ON ME!
...
CHAK
HEY, JAKE.
YOU'RE HOME, HUH?

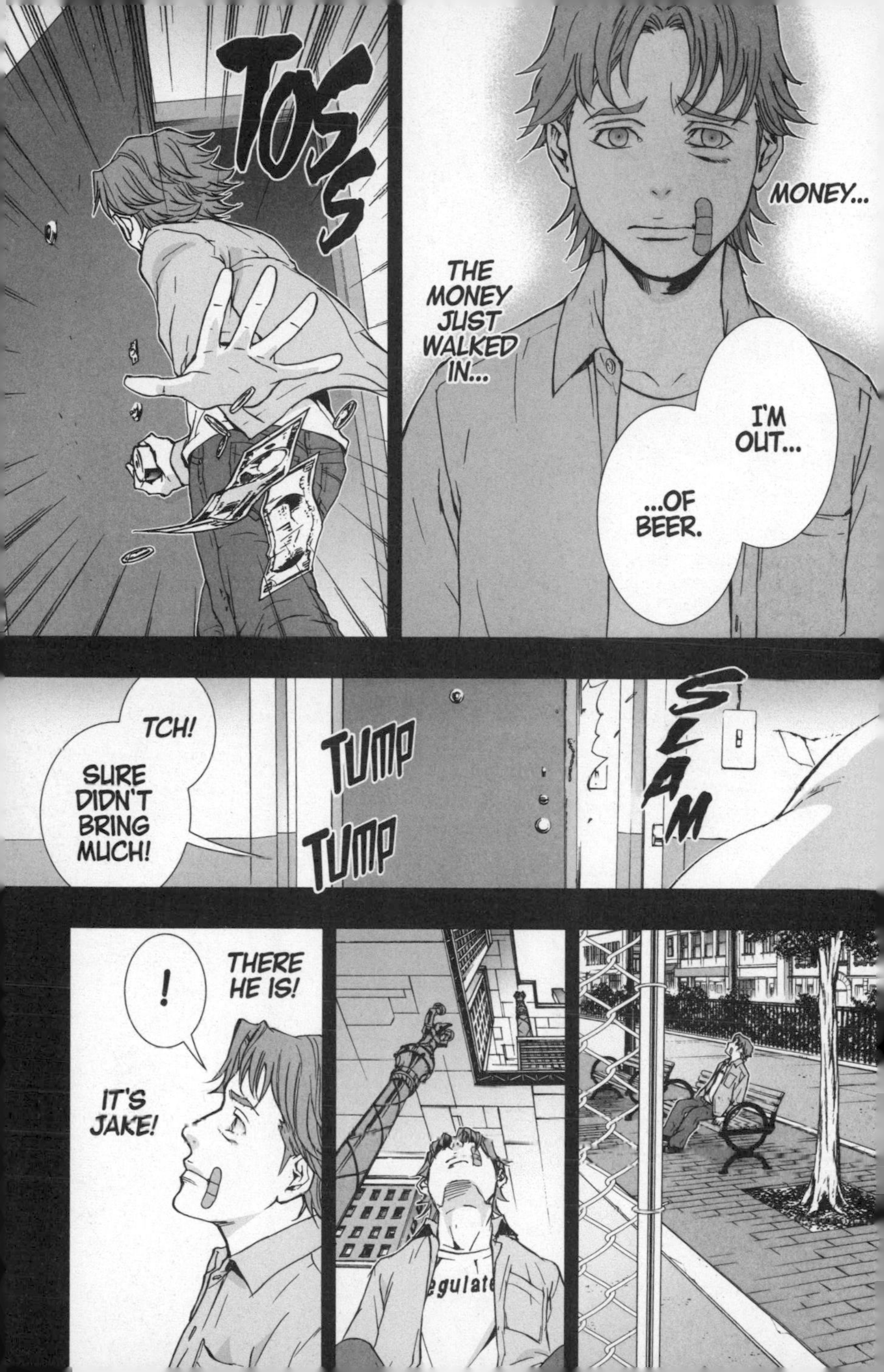
MONEY...
THE MONEY JUST WALKED IN...
I'M OUT...
...OF BEER.
TOSS
SLAM
TUMP
TUMP
TCH!
SURE DIDN'T BRING MUCH!
egulate
THERE HE IS!
!
IT'S JAKE!

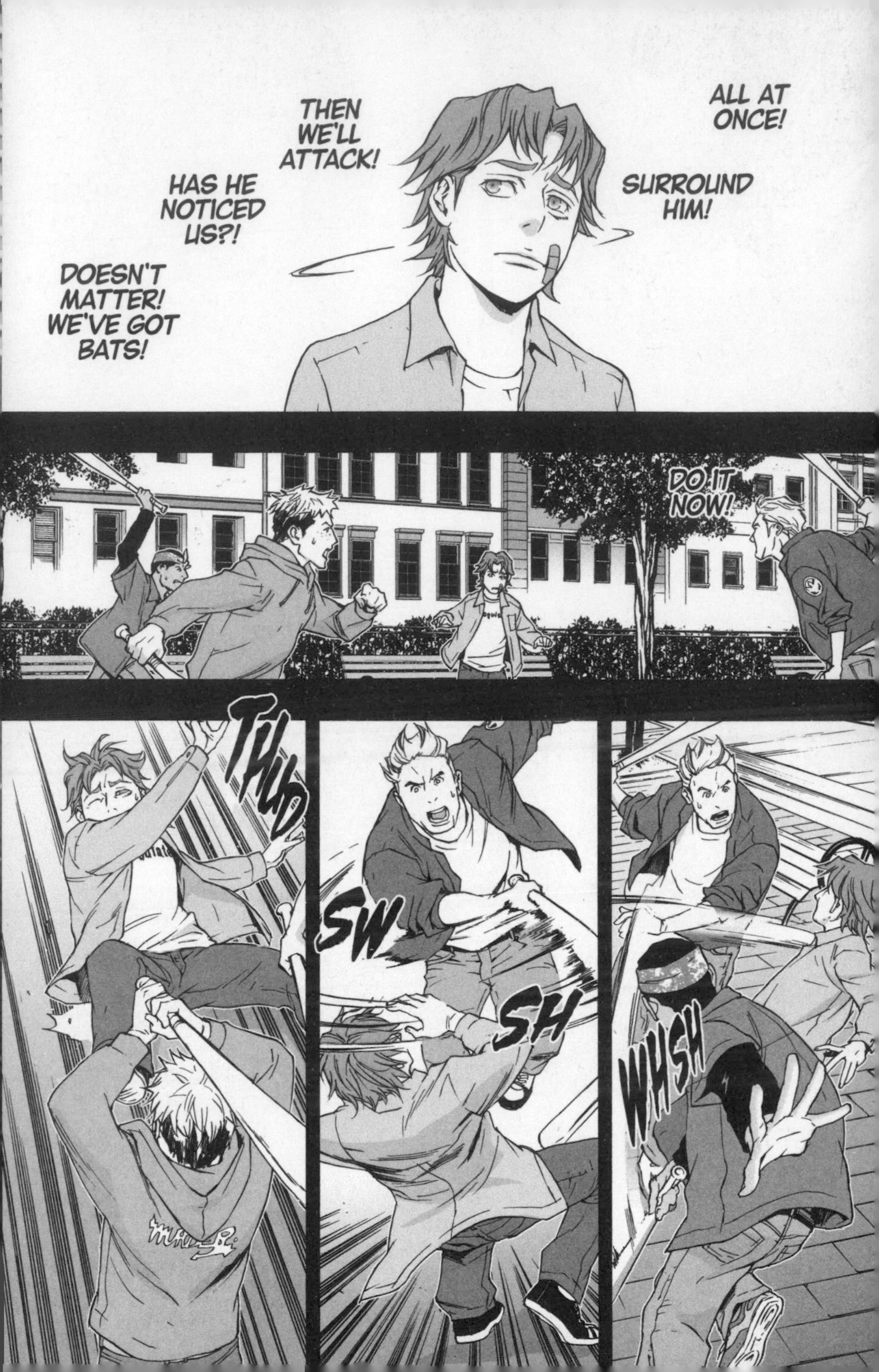
ALL AT ONCE!
SURROUND HIM!
THEN WE'LL ATTACK!
HAS HE NOTICED US?!
DOESN'T MATTER! WE'VE GOT BATS!
DO IT NOW!
WHSH
SW
SH
THUD

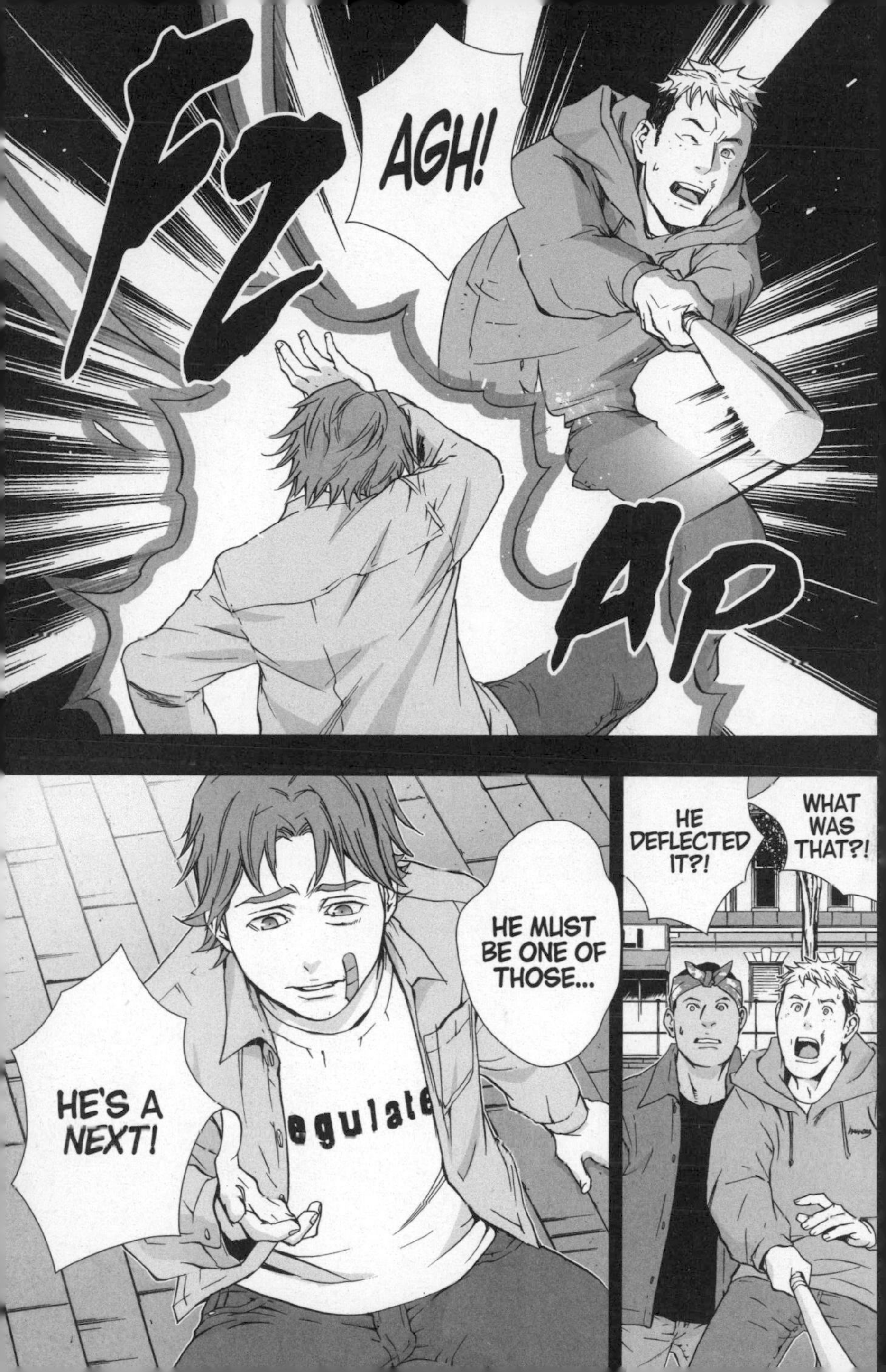
AGH!
WHAT WAS THAT?!
HE DEFLECTED IT?!
HE MUST BE ONE OF THOSE...
HE'S A NEXT!

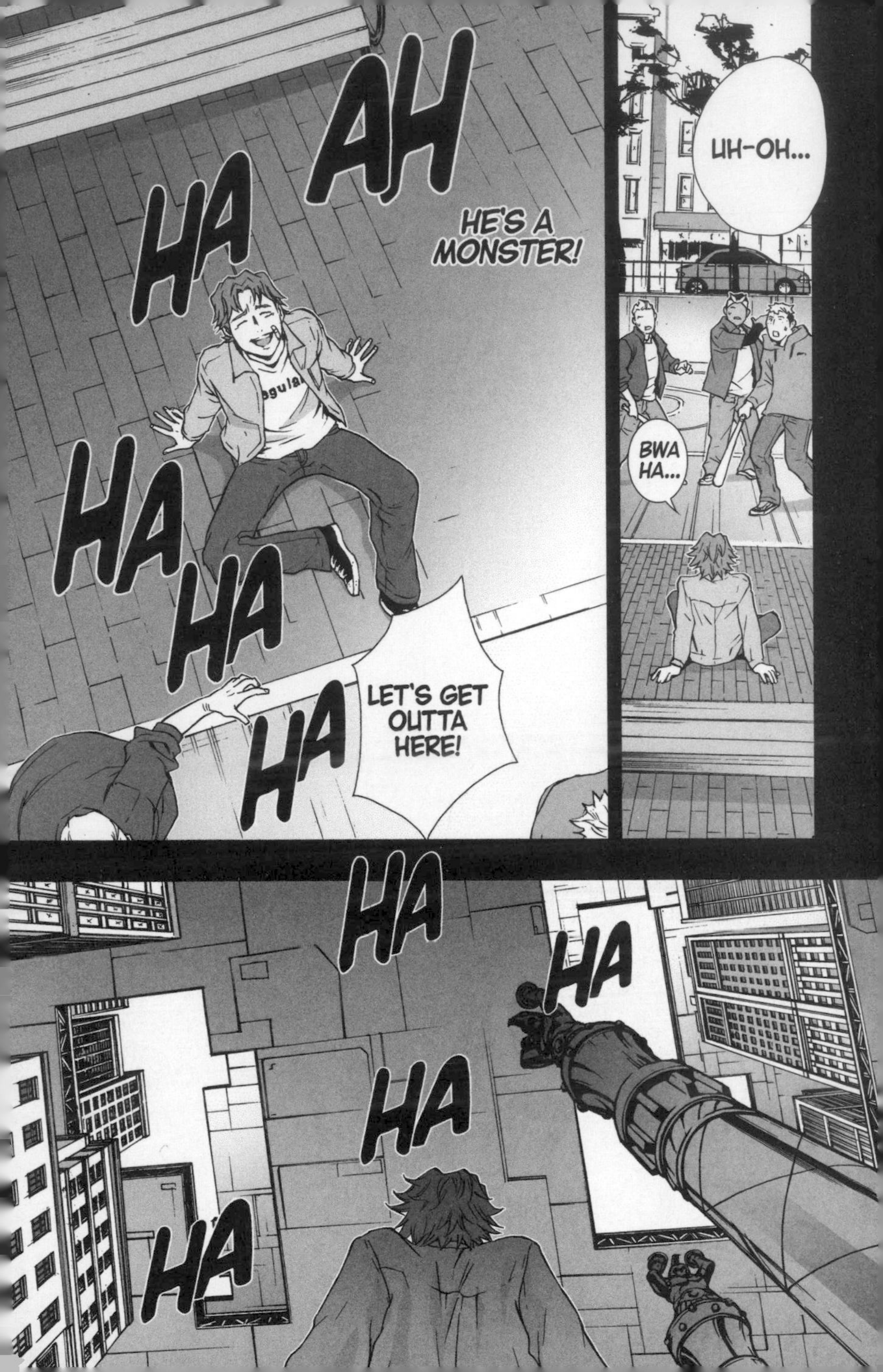
UH-OH...
BWA HA...
AH
HE'S A MONSTER!
HA
HA
HA
LET'S GET OUTTA HERE!
HA
HA
HA
HA
HA

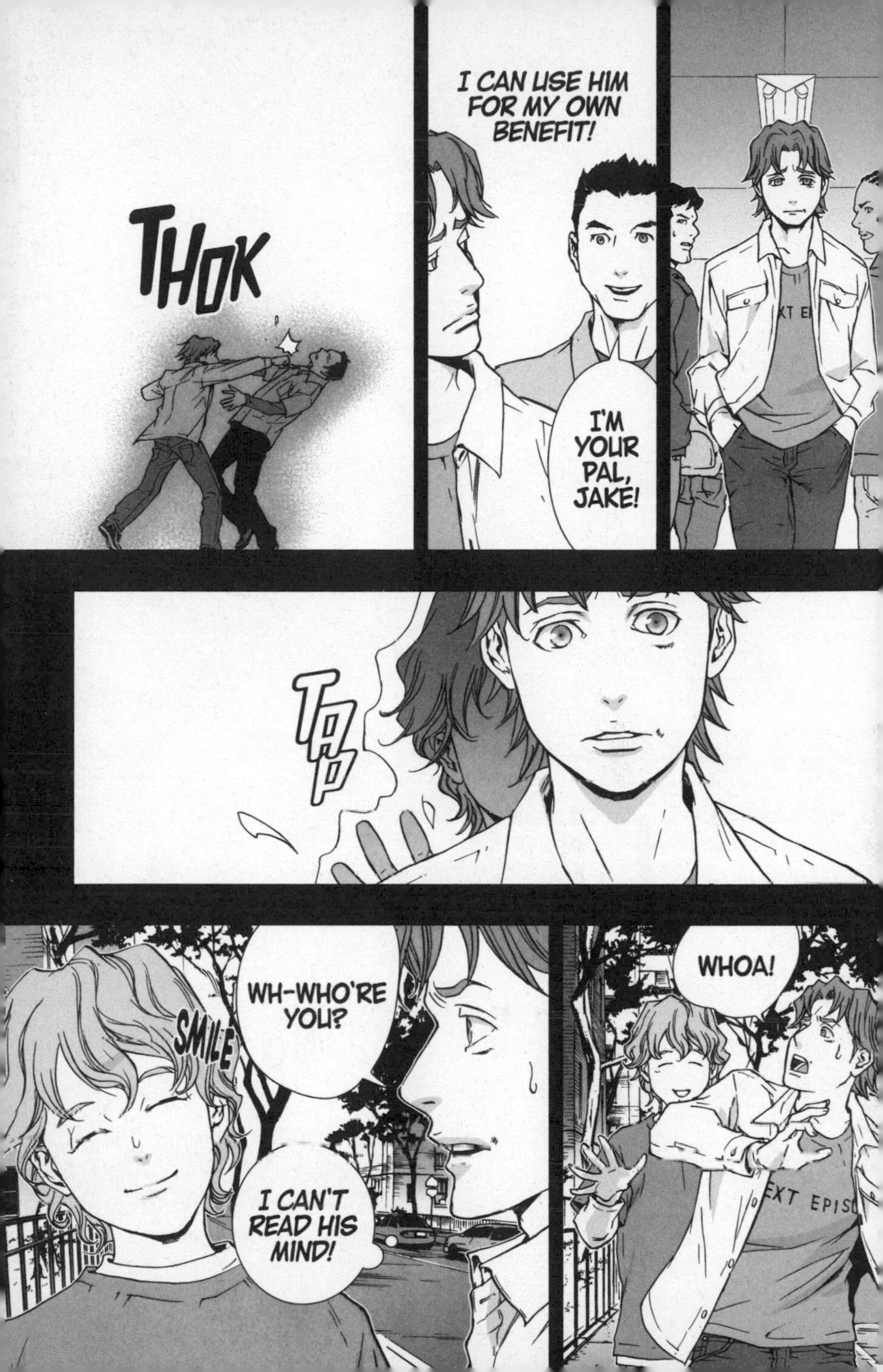
I CAN USE HIM FOR MY OWN BENEFIT!
I'M YOUR PAL, JAKE!
THOK
TAP
WHOA!
WH-WHO'RE YOU?
SMILE
I CAN'T READ HIS MIND!

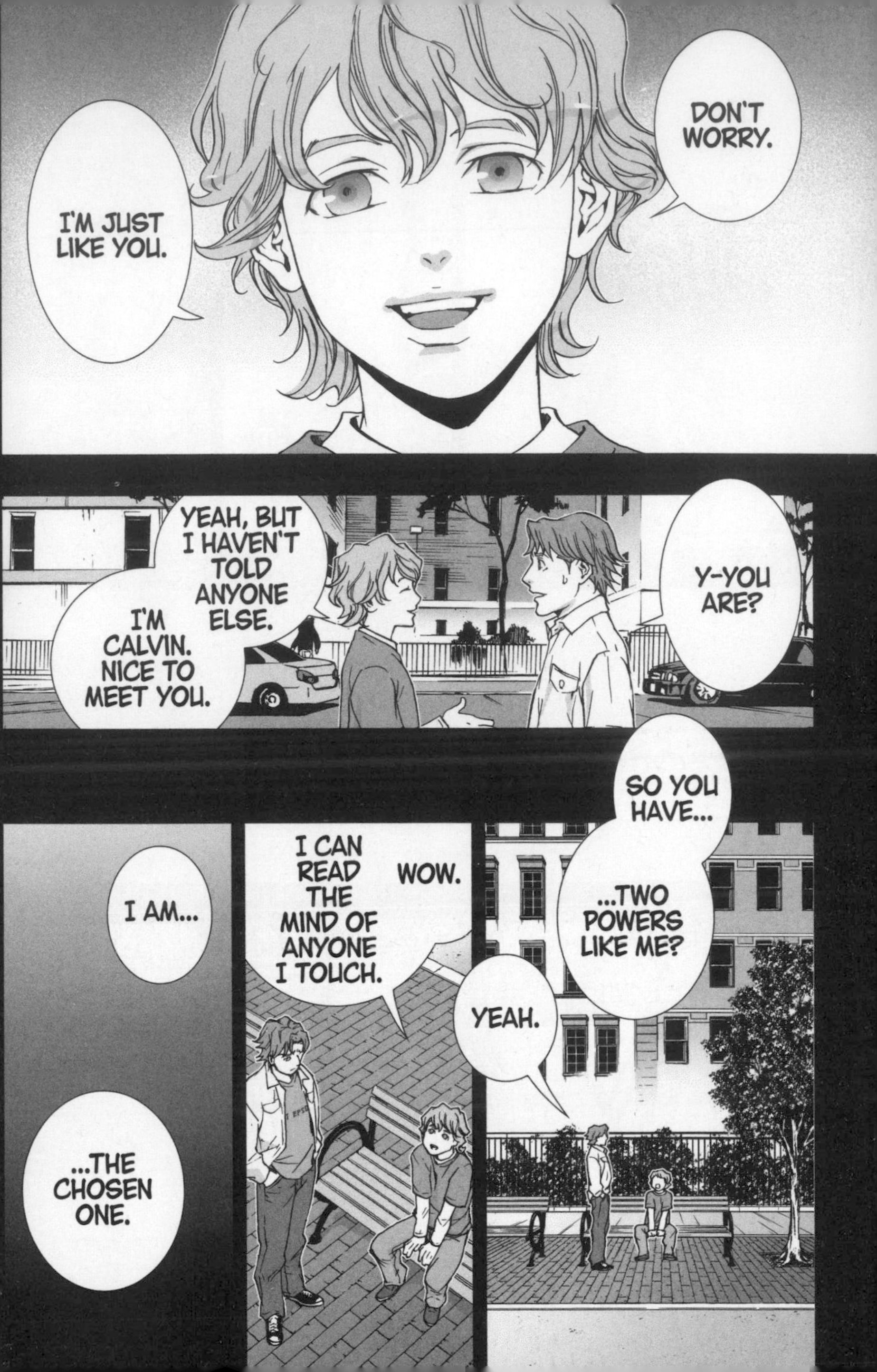
DON'T WORRY.
I'M JUST LIKE YOU.
Y-YOU ARE?
YEAH, BUT I HAVEN'T TOLD ANYONE ELSE.
I'M CALVIN. NICE TO MEET YOU.
SO YOU HAVE...
...TWO POWERS LIKE ME?
YEAH.
WOW.
I CAN READ THE MIND OF ANYONE I TOUCH.
I AM...
...THE CHOSEN ONE.

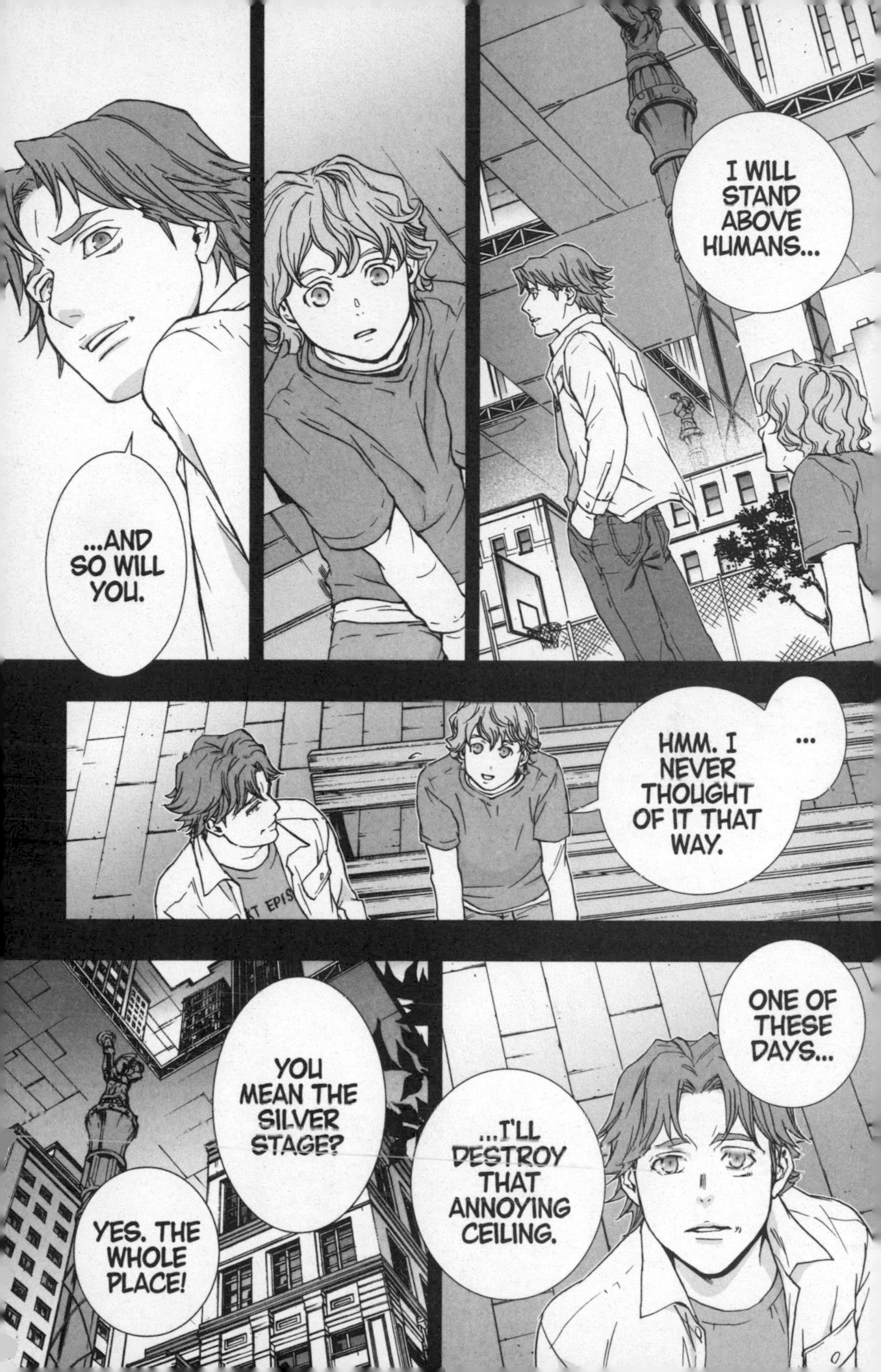
I WILL STAND ABOVE HUMANS...
...AND SO WILL YOU.
...
HMM. I NEVER THOUGHT OF IT THAT WAY.
ONE OF THESE DAYS...
...I'LL DESTROY THAT ANNOYING CEILING.
YOU MEAN THE SILVER STAGE?
YES. THE WHOLE PLACE!

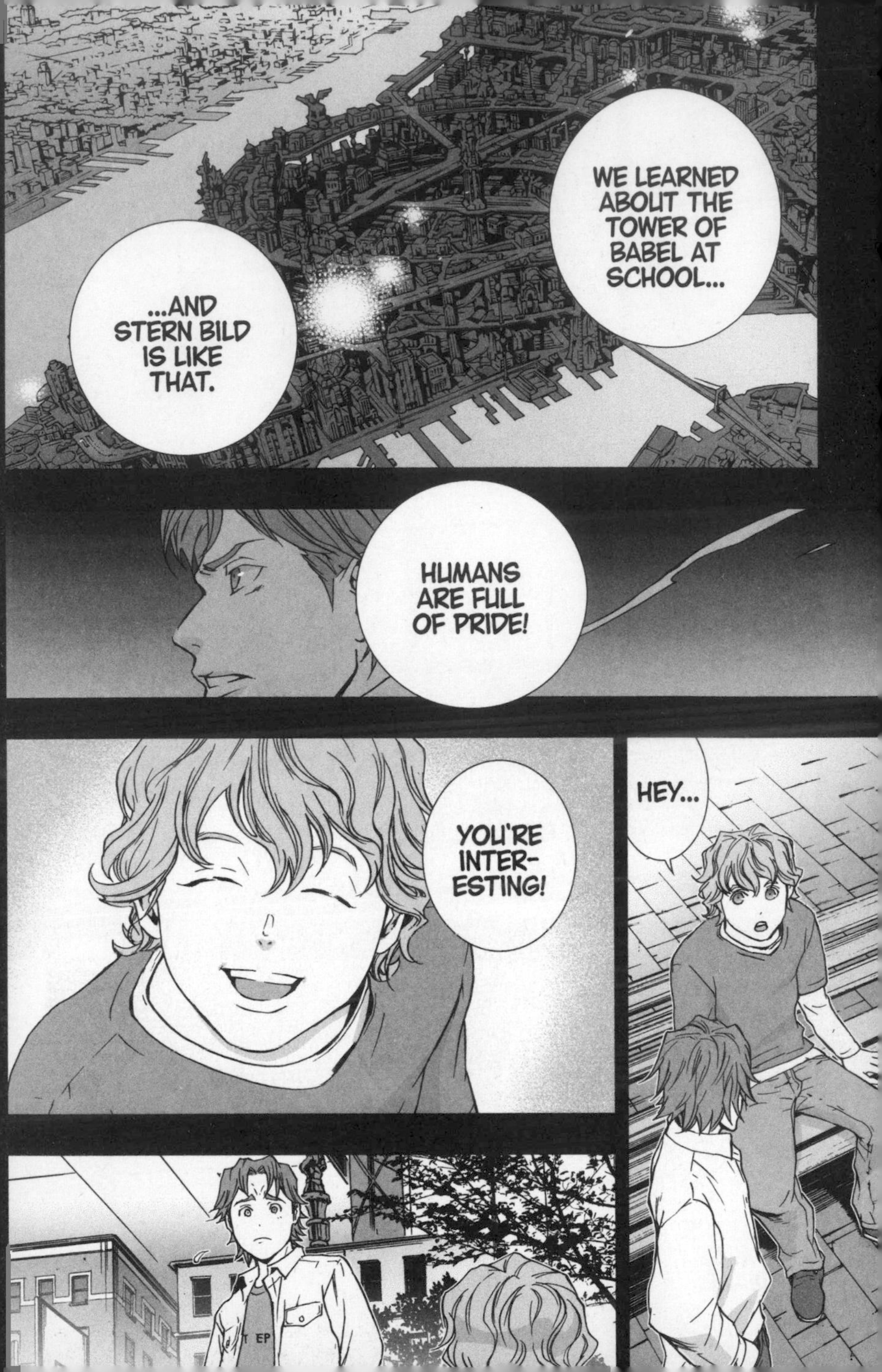
WE LEARNED ABOUT THE TOWER OF BABEL AT SCHOOL...
...AND STERN BILD IS LIKE THAT.
HUMANS ARE FULL OF PRIDE!
HEY...
YOU'RE INTER-ESTING!

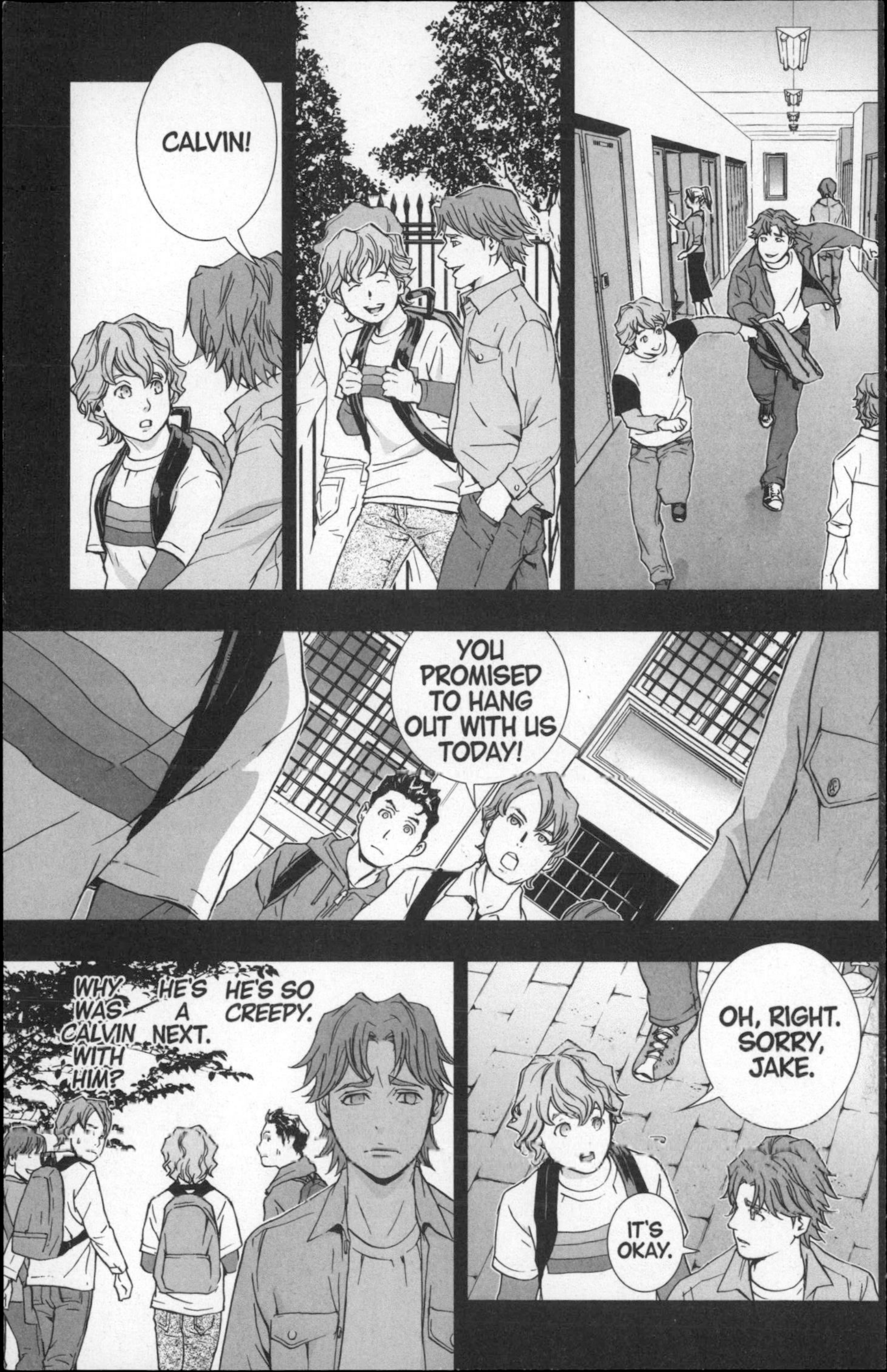
CALVIN!
YOU PROMISED TO HANG OUT WITH US TODAY!
OH, RIGHT. SORRY, JAKE.
IT'S OKAY.
HE'S SO CREEPY.
HE'S A NEXT.
WHY WAS CALVIN WITH HIM?

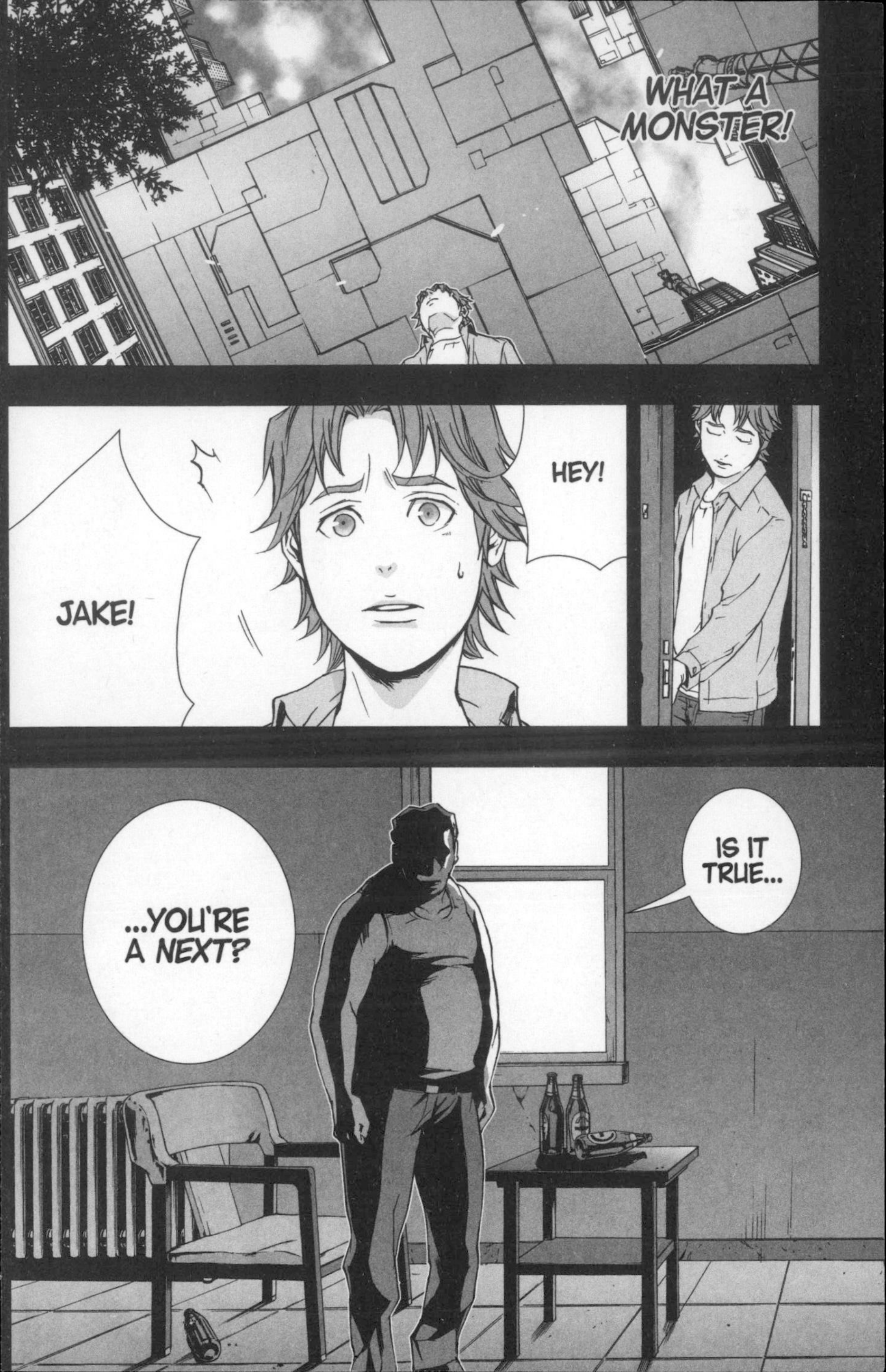
WHAT A MONSTER!
HEY!
JAKE!
IS IT TRUE...
...YOU'RE A NEXT?

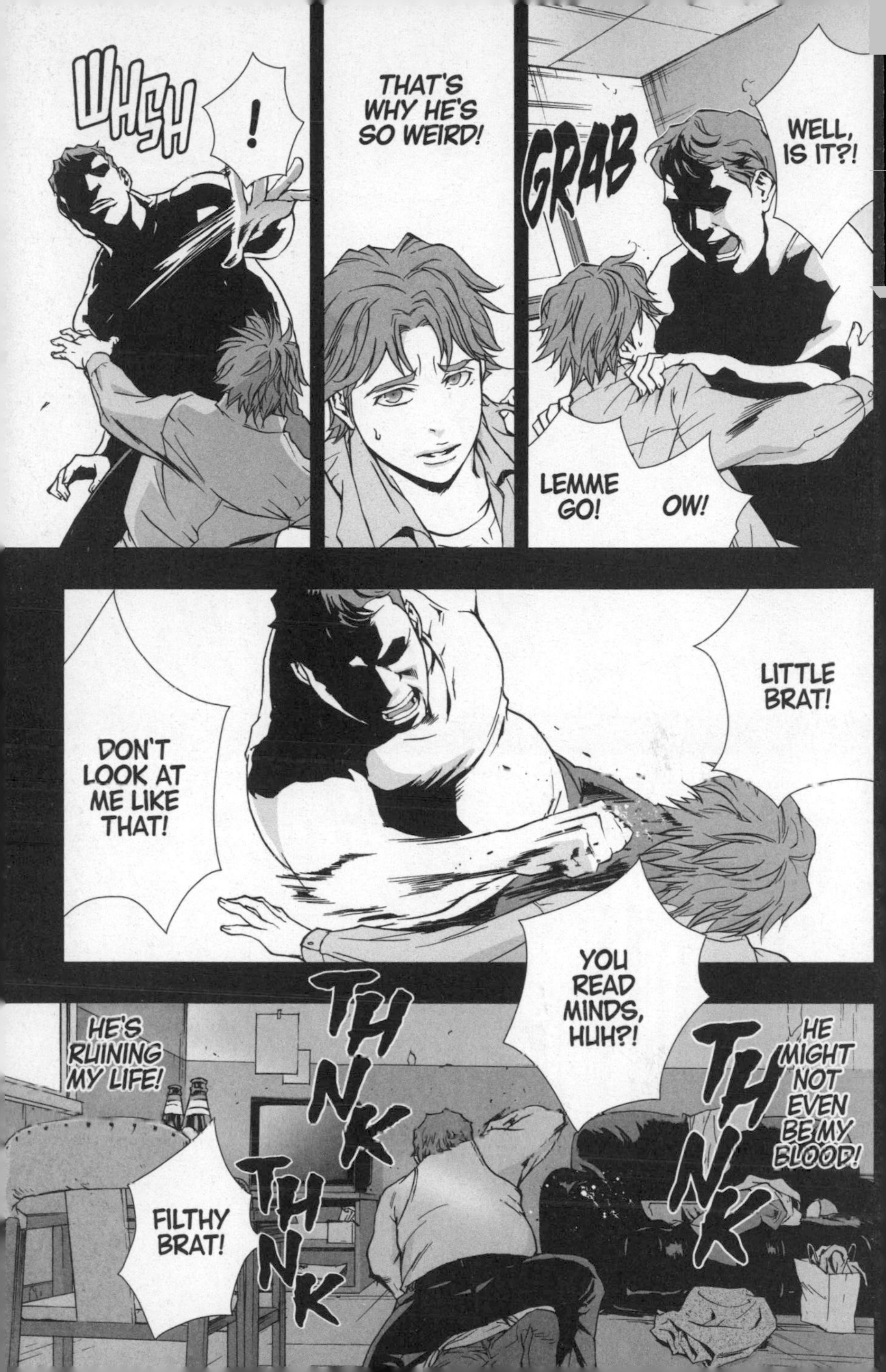
WELL, IS IT?!
GRAB
OW!
LEMME GO!
THAT'S WHY HE'S SO WEIRD!
!
WHSH
LITTLE BRAT!
DON'T LOOK AT ME LIKE THAT!
HE MIGHT NOT EVEN BE MY BLOOD!
THNK
YOU READ MINDS, HUH?!
THNK
HE'S RUINING MY LIFE!
THNK
FILTHY BRAT!

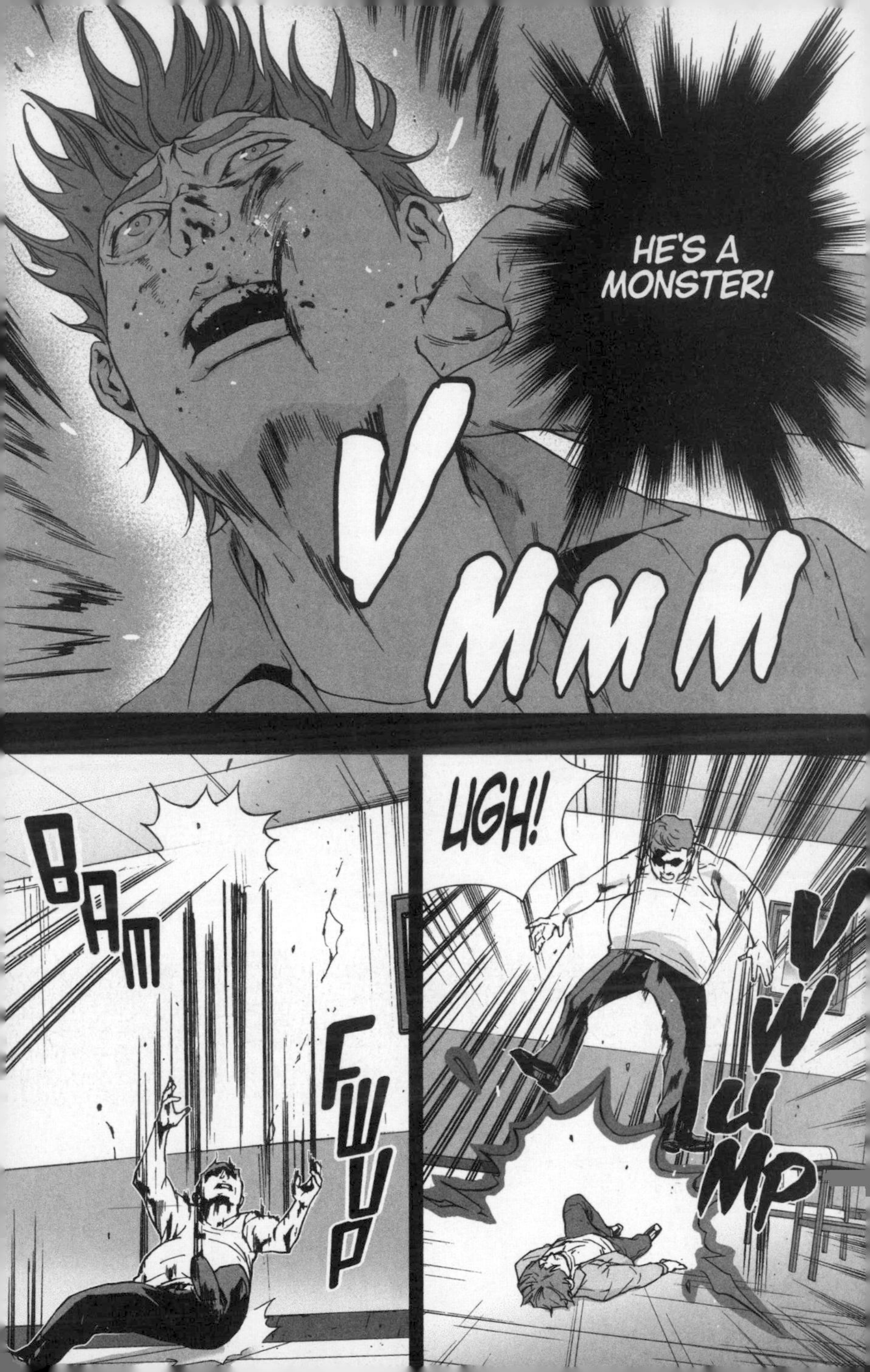
HE'S A MONSTER!
VMMM
UGH!
VWUMP
BAM
FWUP

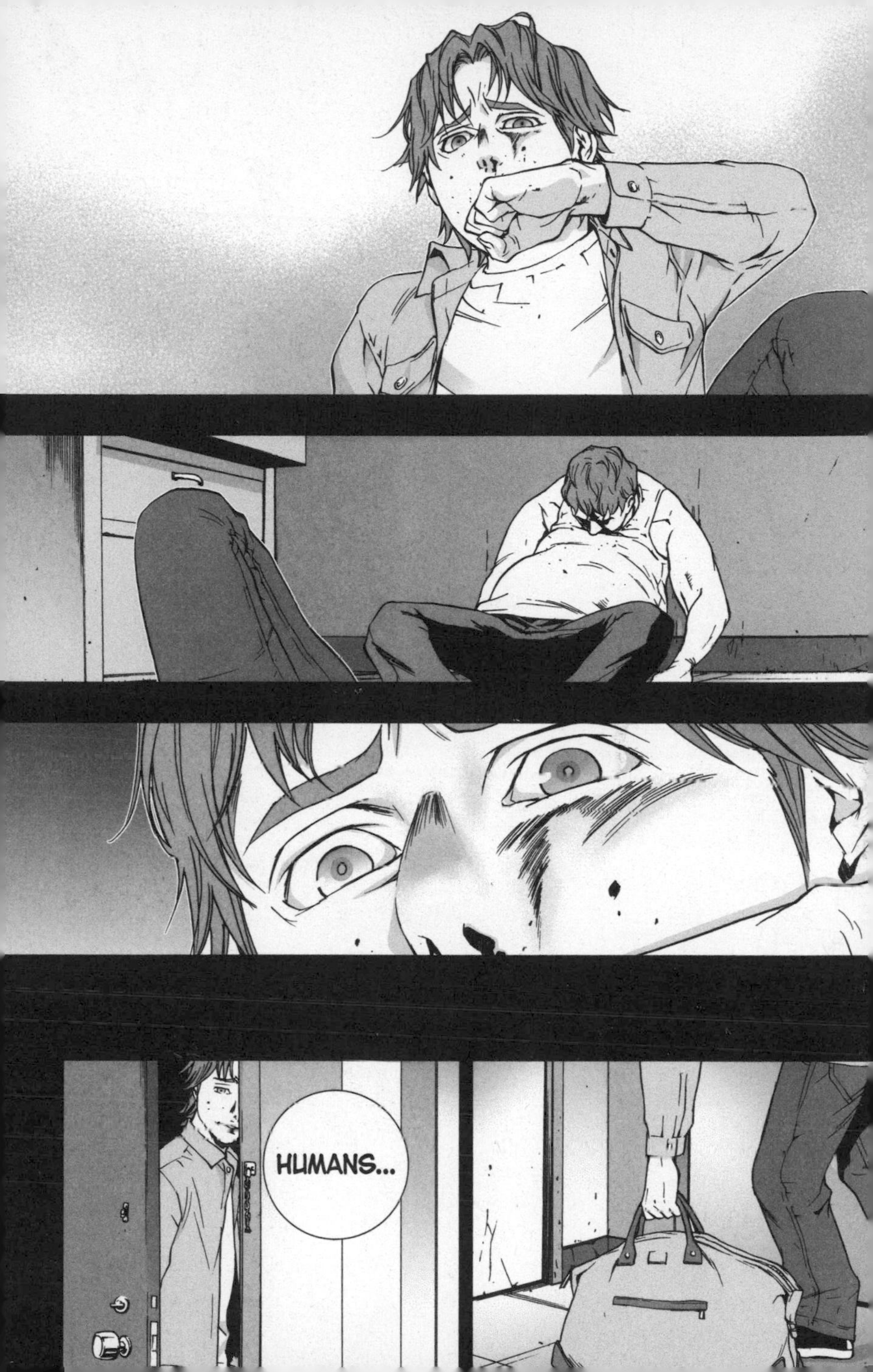
HUMANS...

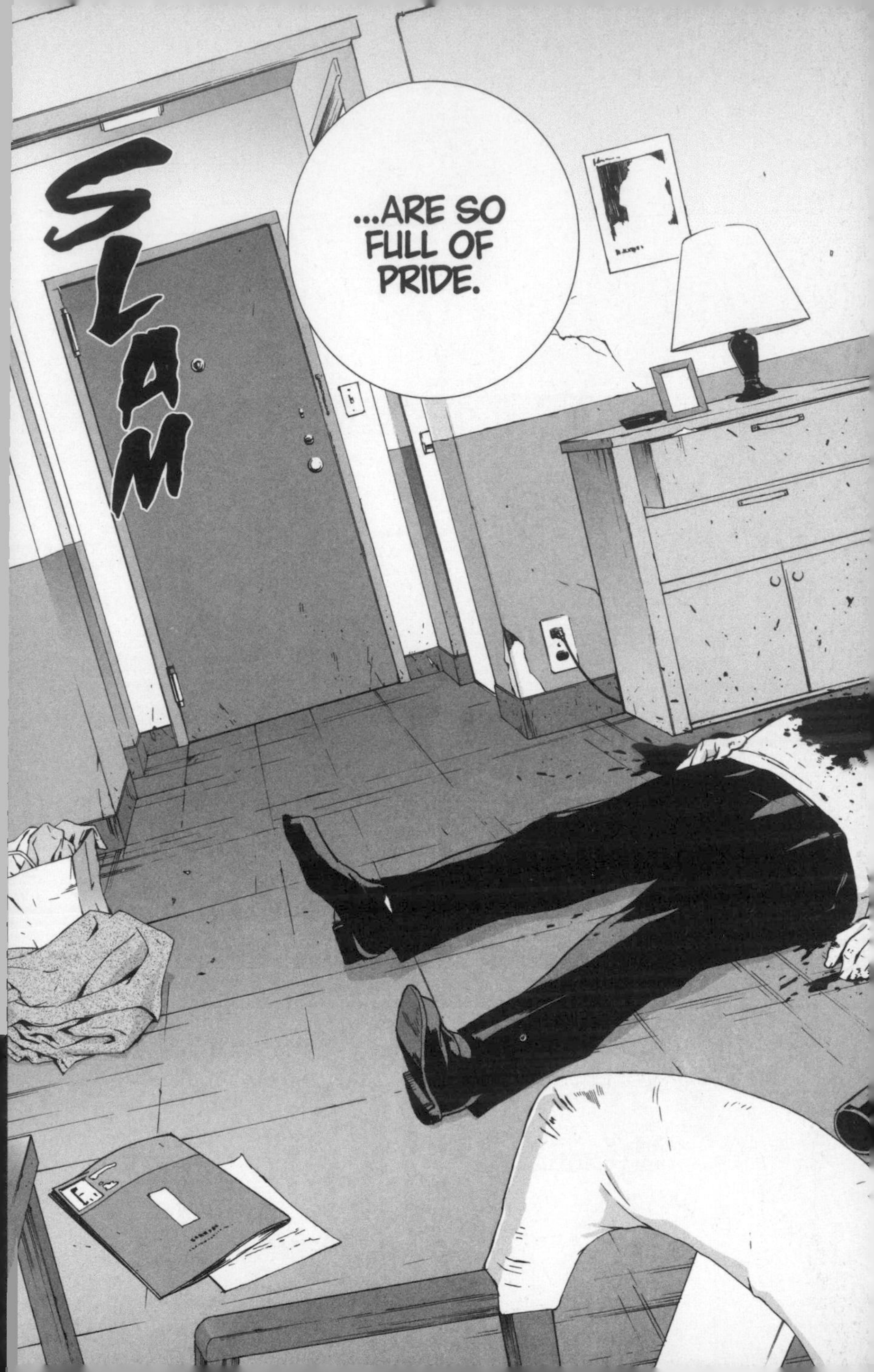
...ARE SO FULL OF PRIDE.
SLAM

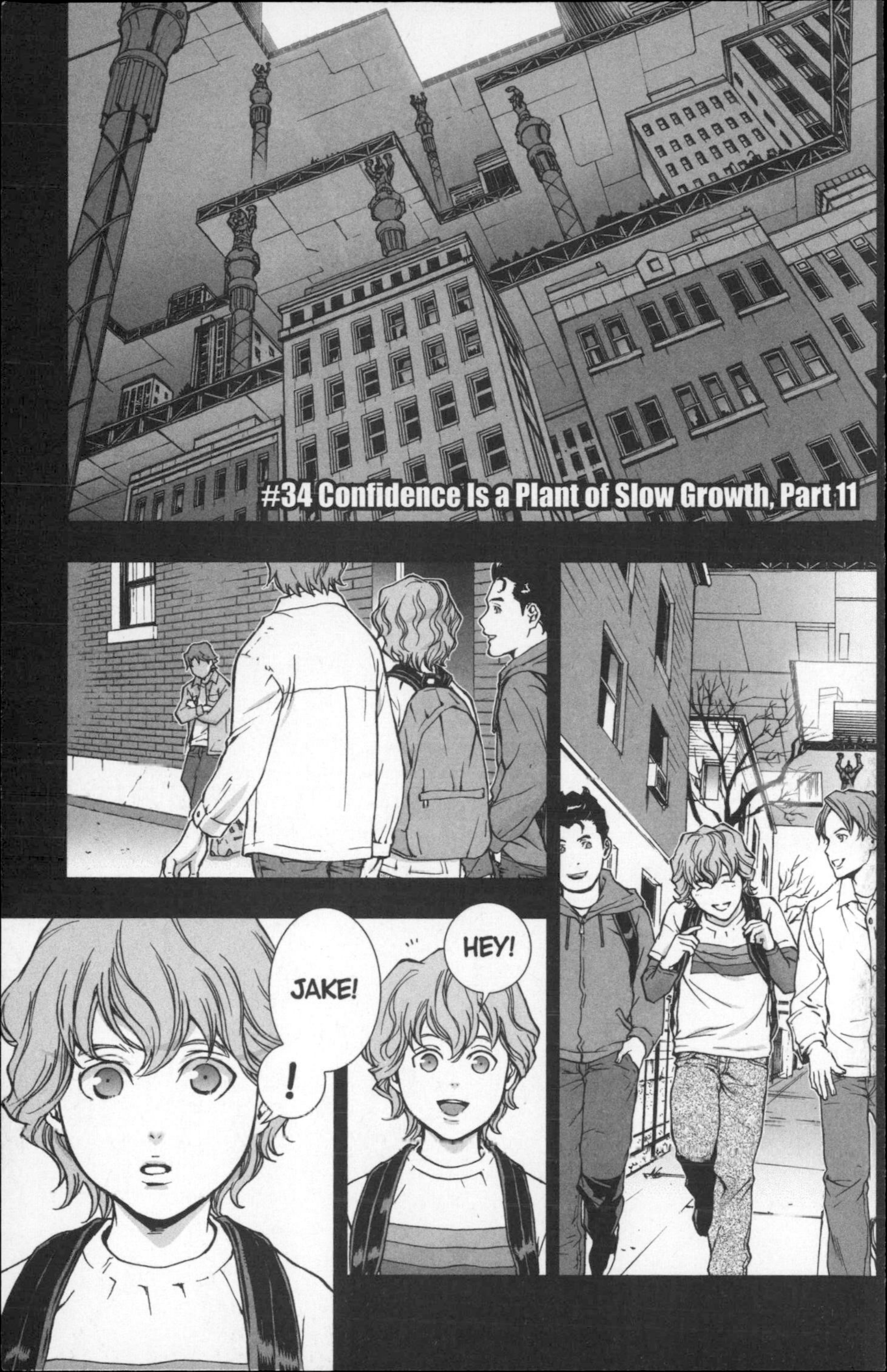
#34 Confidence Is a Plant of Slow Growth, Part 11
HEY!
JAKE!
!

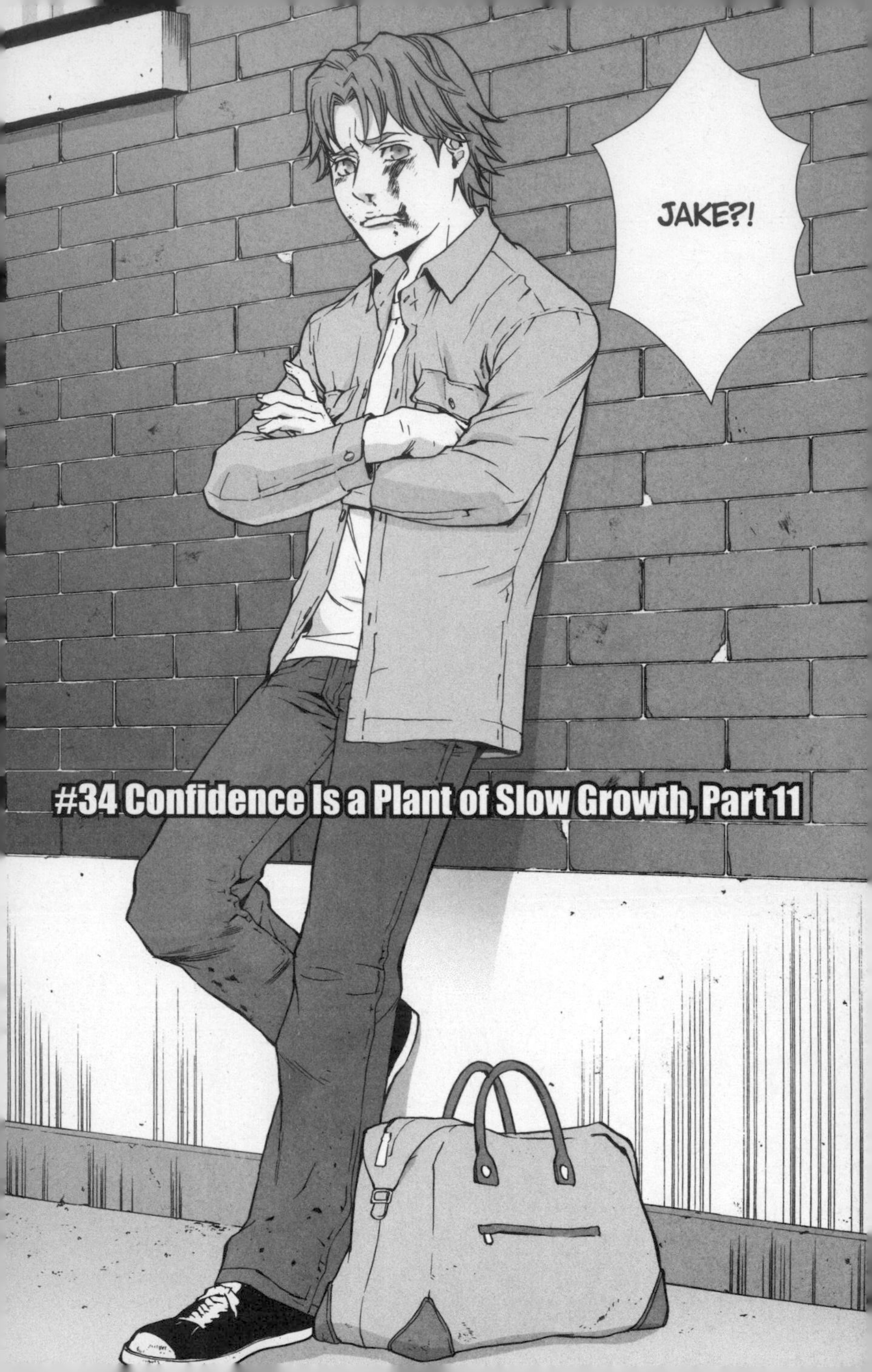
JAKE?!
#34 Confidence Is a Plant of Slow Growth, Part 11

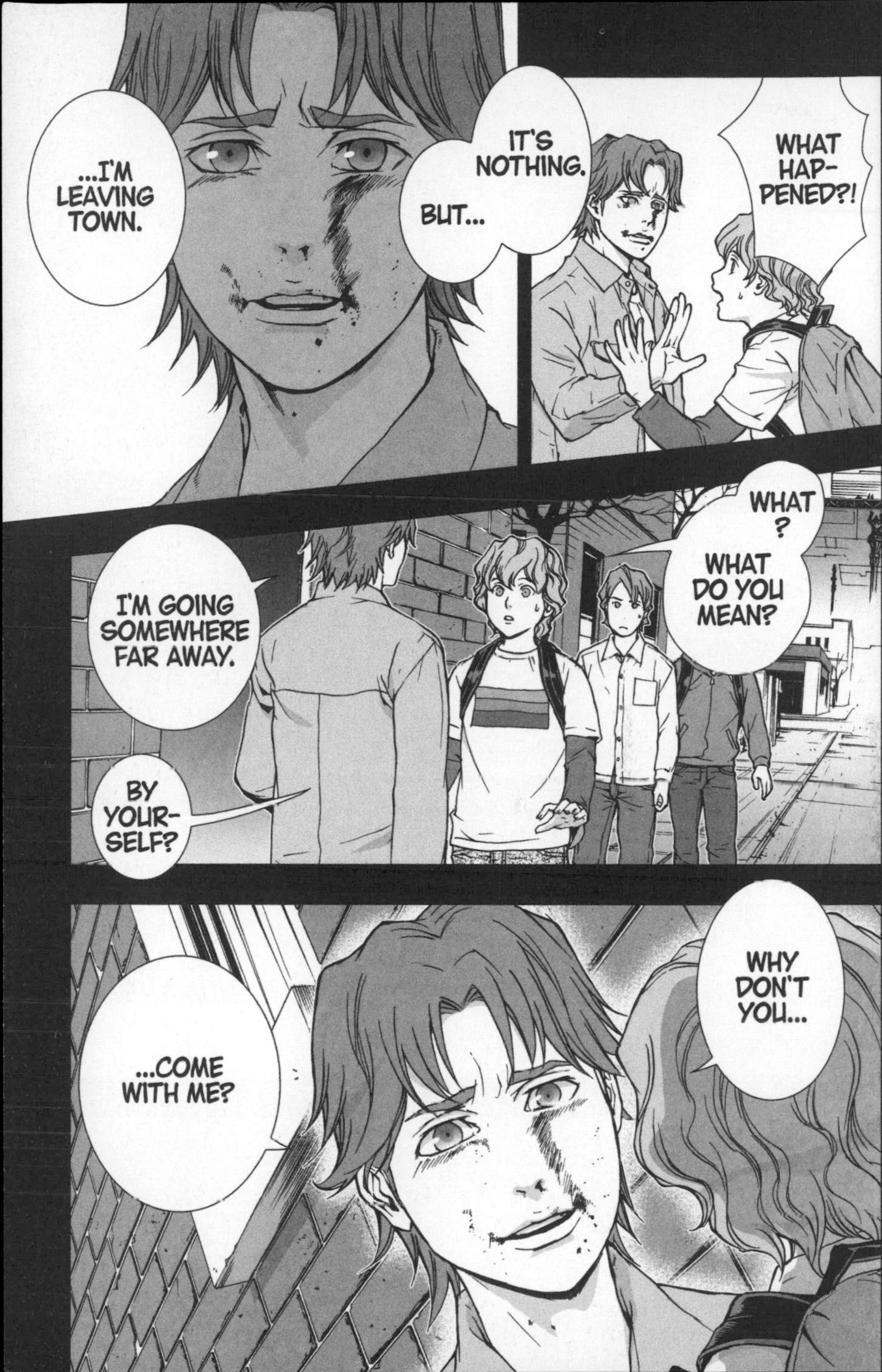
WHAT HAP-PENED?!
IT'S NOTHING.
BUT...
...I'M LEAVING TOWN.
WHAT? WHAT DO YOU MEAN?
I'M GOING SOMEWHERE FAR AWAY.
BY YOUR-SELF?
WHY DON'T YOU...
...COME WITH ME?

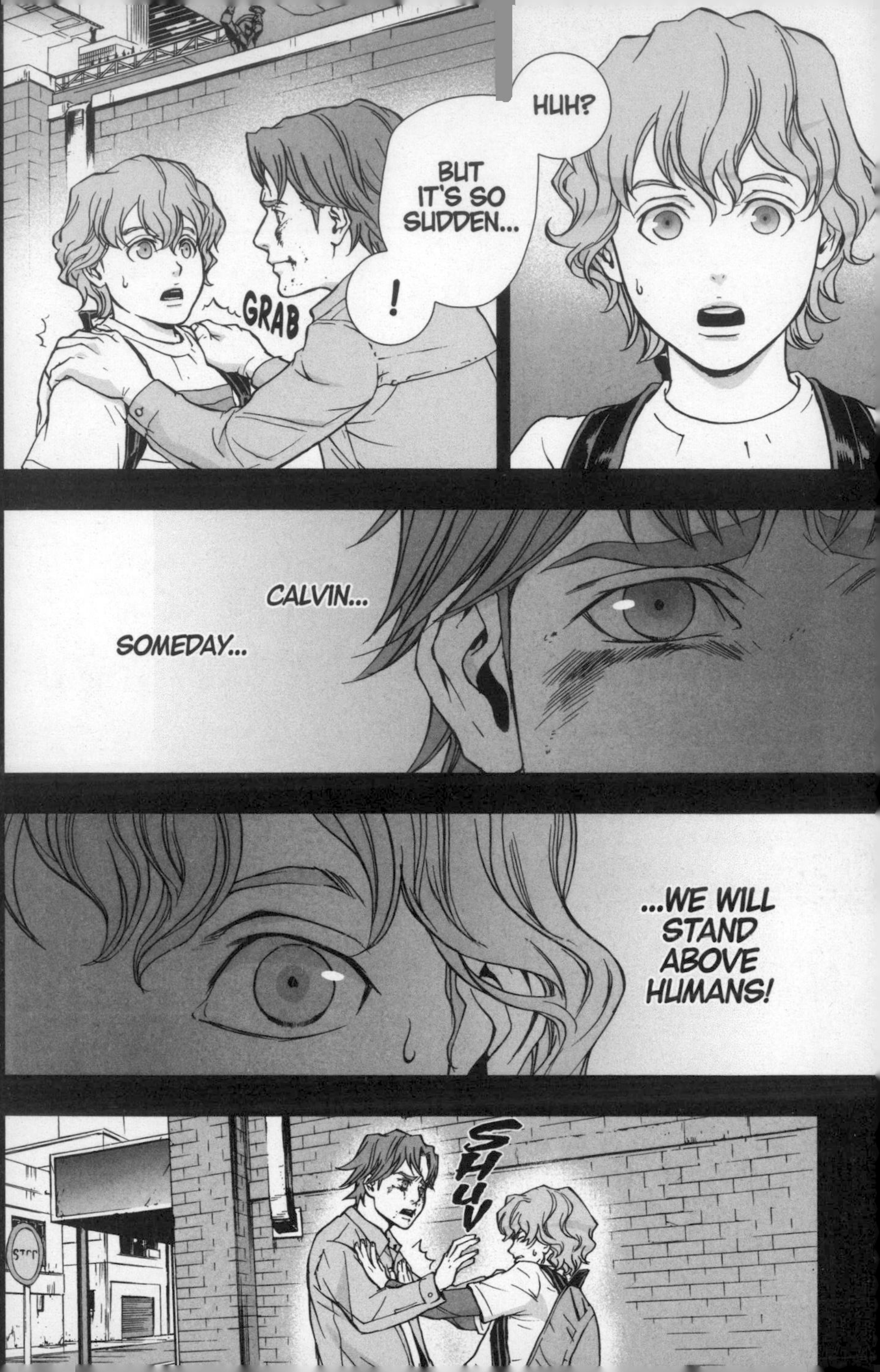
HUH?
BUT IT'S SO SUDDEN...
!
GRAB
CALVIN...
SOMEDAY...
...WE WILL STAND ABOVE HUMANS!
SHUV

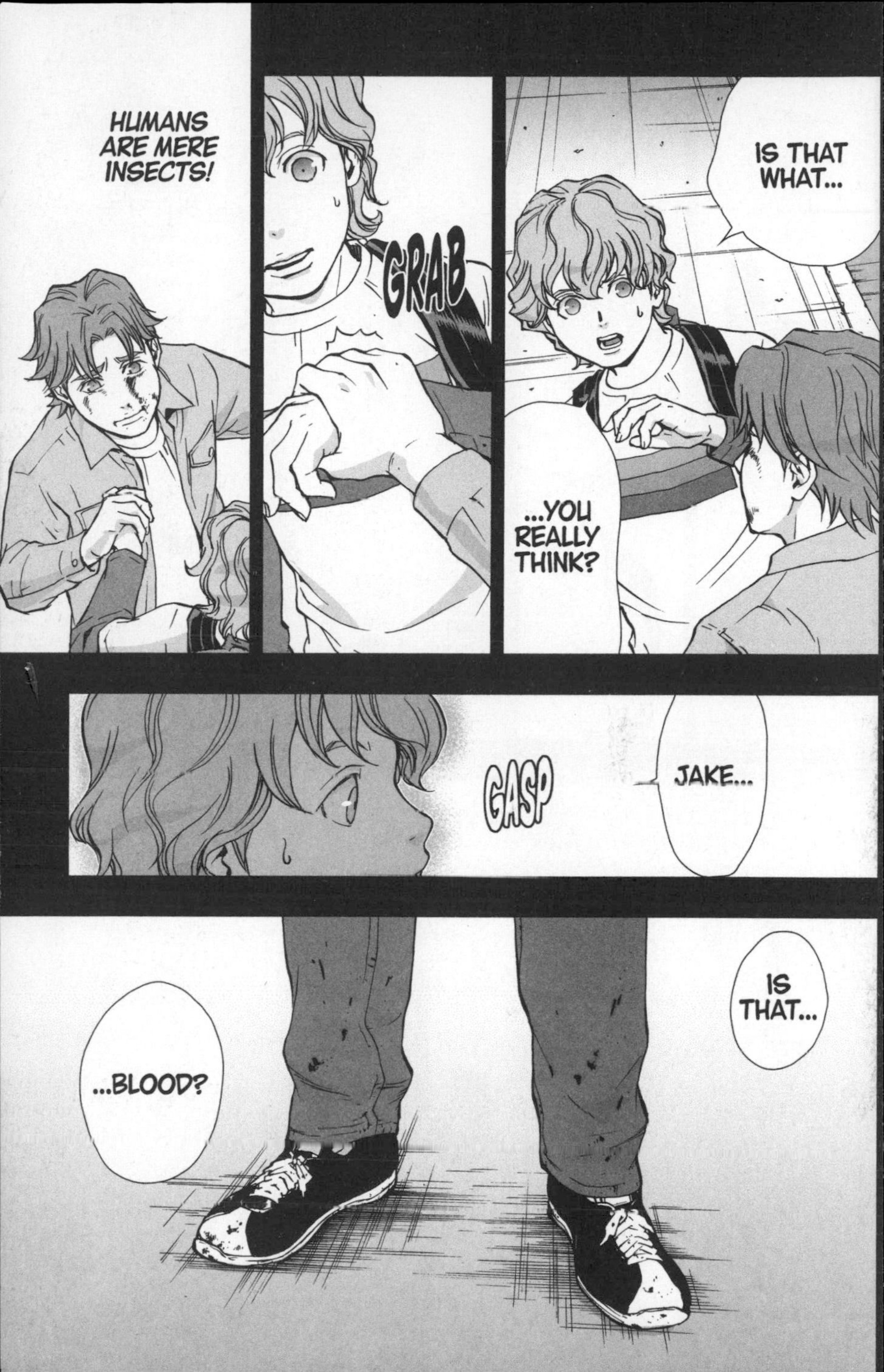
IS THAT WHAT...
...YOU REALLY THINK?
GRAB
HUMANS ARE MERE INSECTS!
JAKE...
GASP
IS THAT...
...BLOOD?

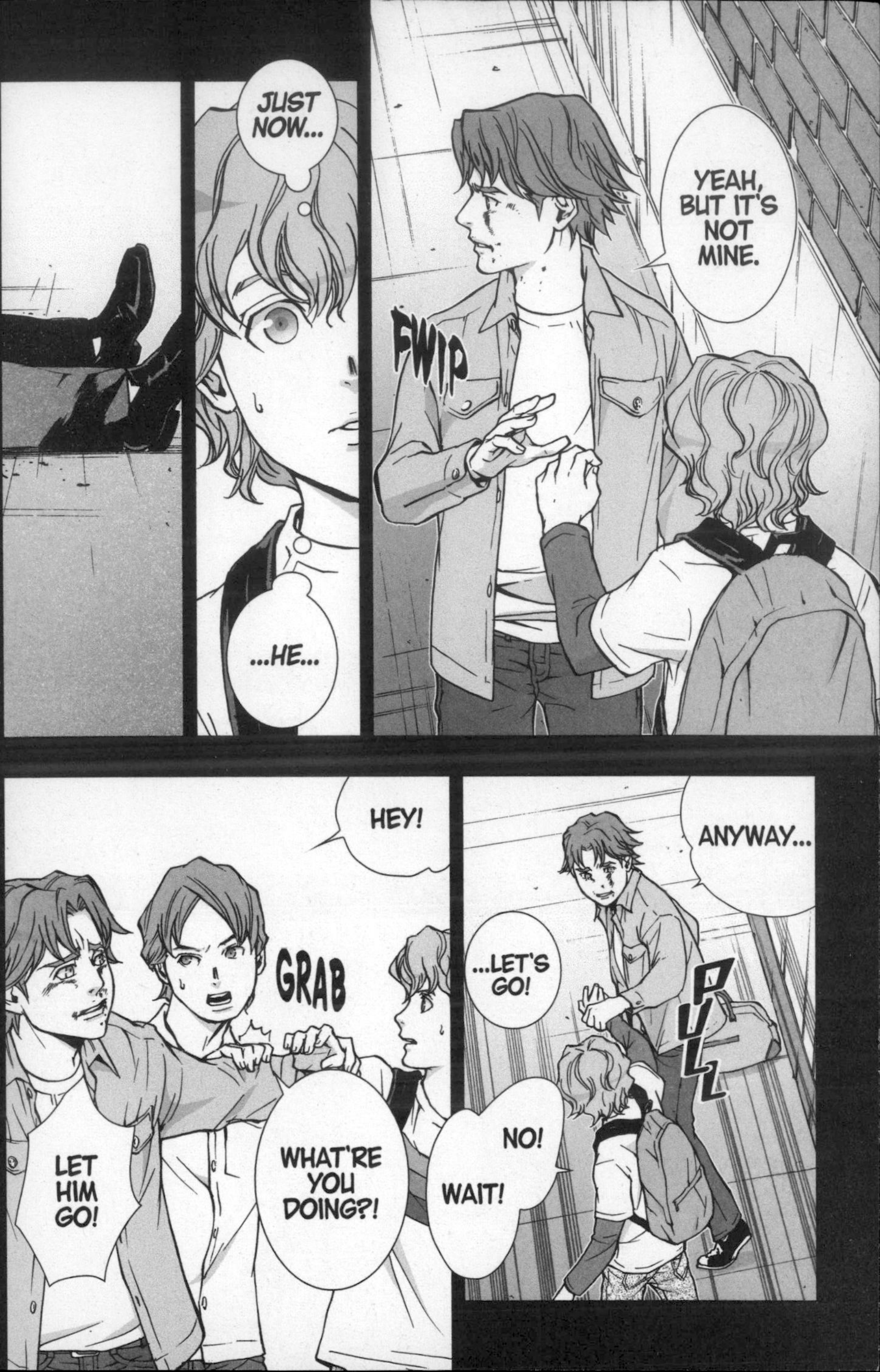
YEAH, BUT IT'S NOT MINE.
FWIP
JUST NOW...
...HE...
ANYWAY...
...LET'S GO!
PULL
NO!
WAIT!
HEY!
GRAB
WHAT'RE YOU DOING?!
LET HIM GO!

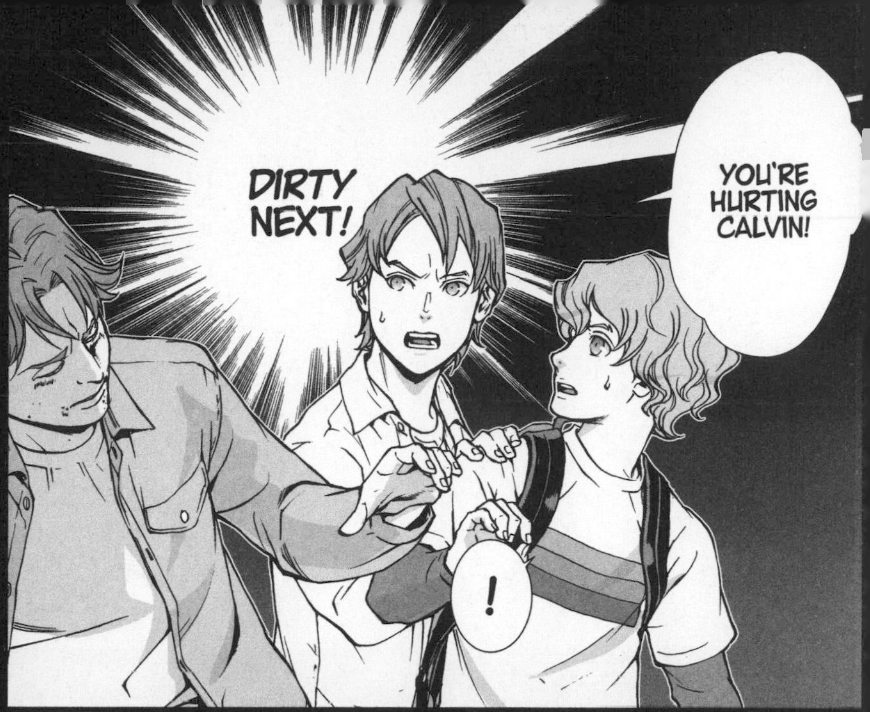
YOU'RE HURTING CALVIN!
DIRTY NEXT!
!

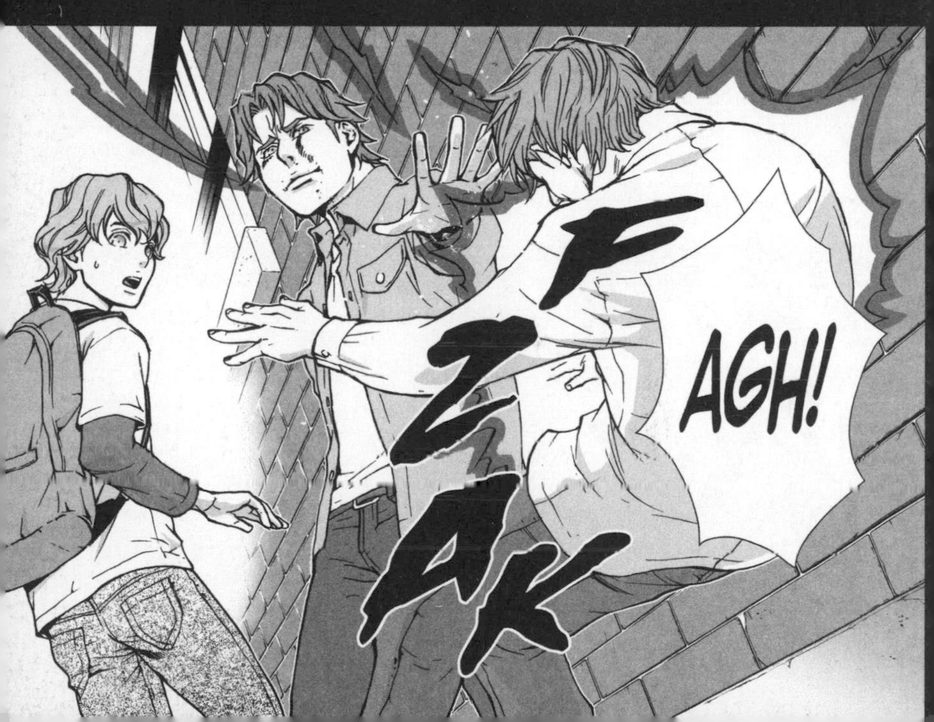
AGH!

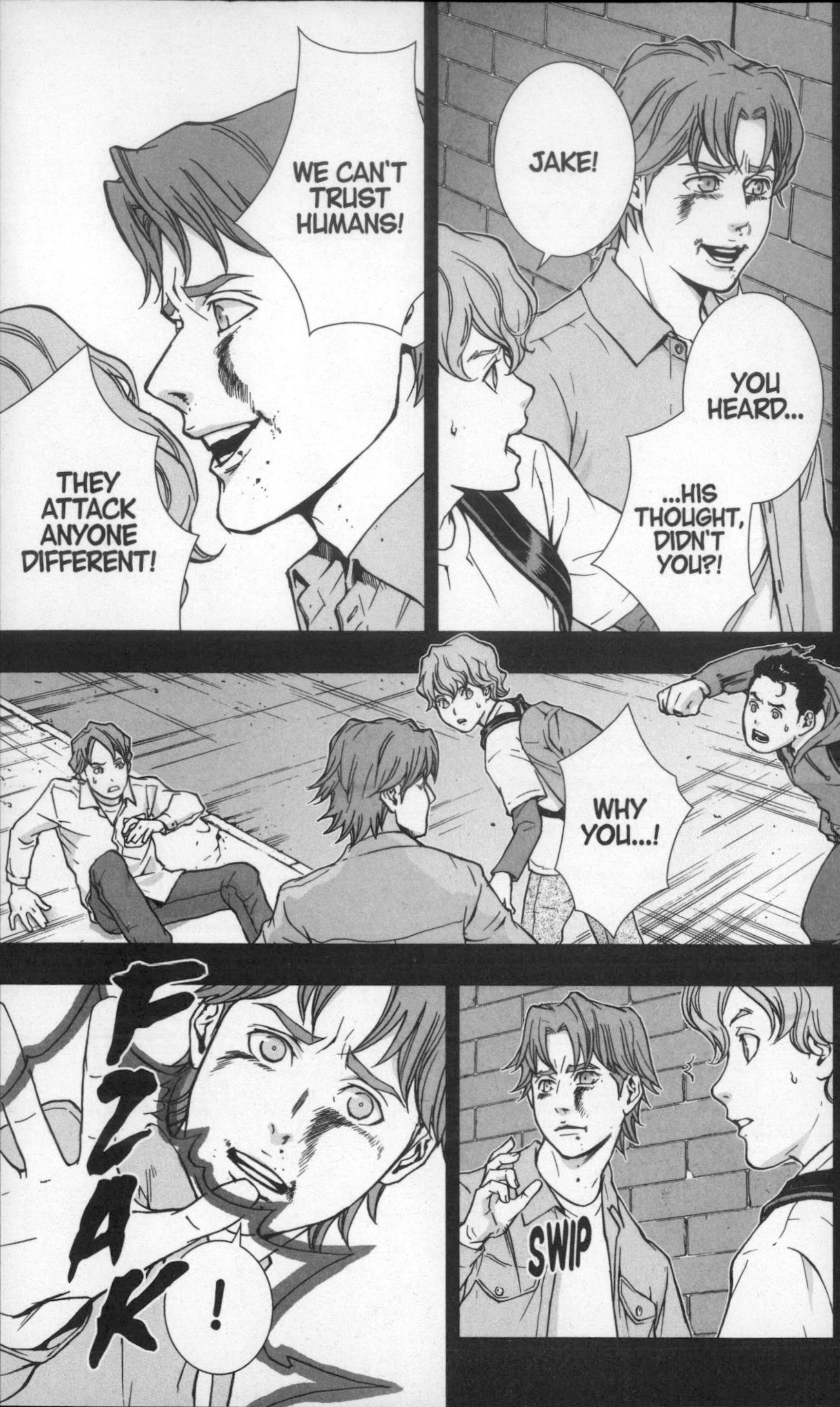
JAKE!
YOU HEARD...
...HIS THOUGHT, DIDN'T YOU?!
WE CAN'T TRUST HUMANS!
THEY ATTACK ANYONE DIFFERENT!
WHY YOU...!
SWIP
FZAK
!

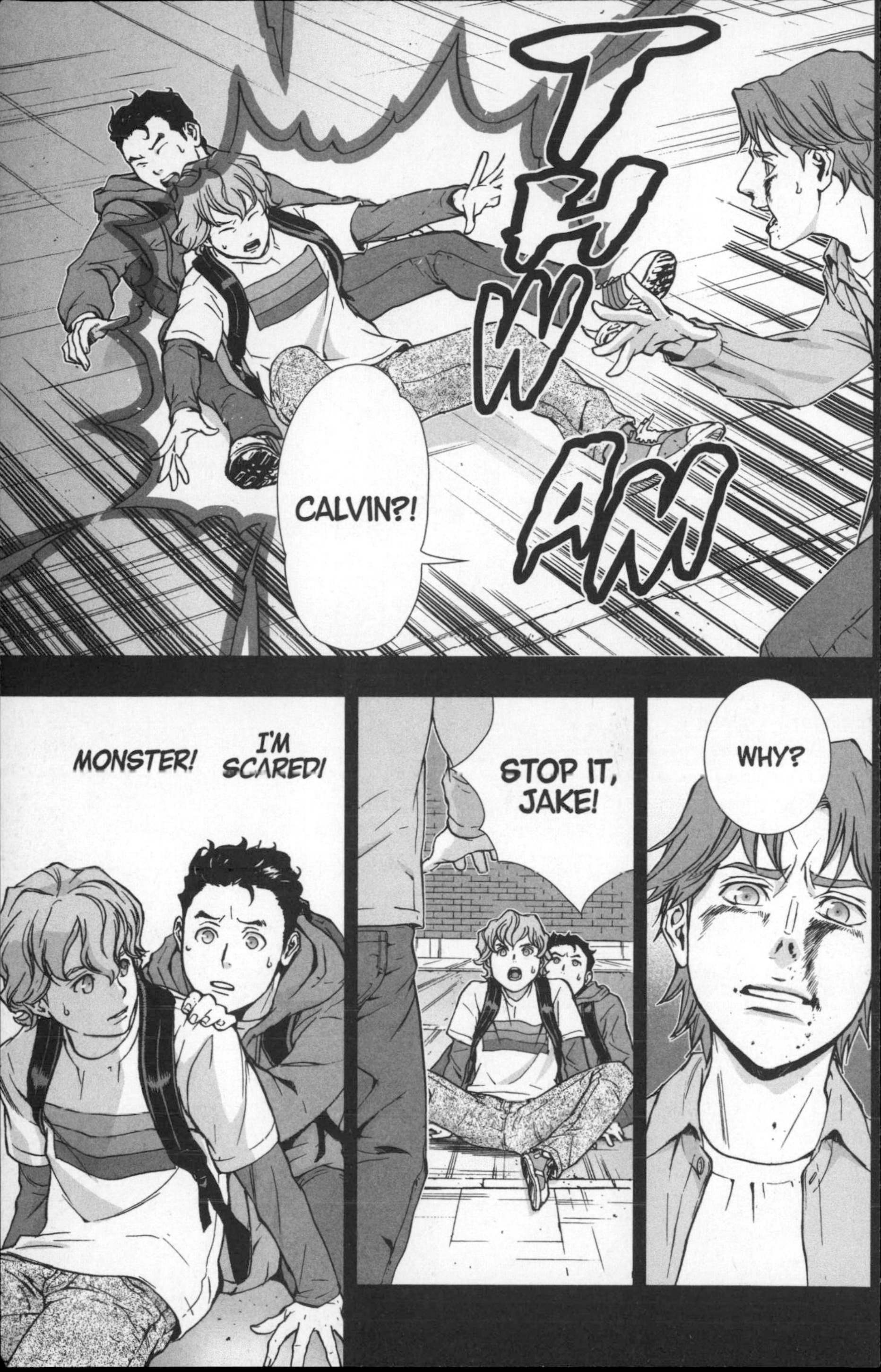
THWAM
CALVIN?!
WHY?
STOP IT, JAKE!
I'M SCARED!
MONSTER!

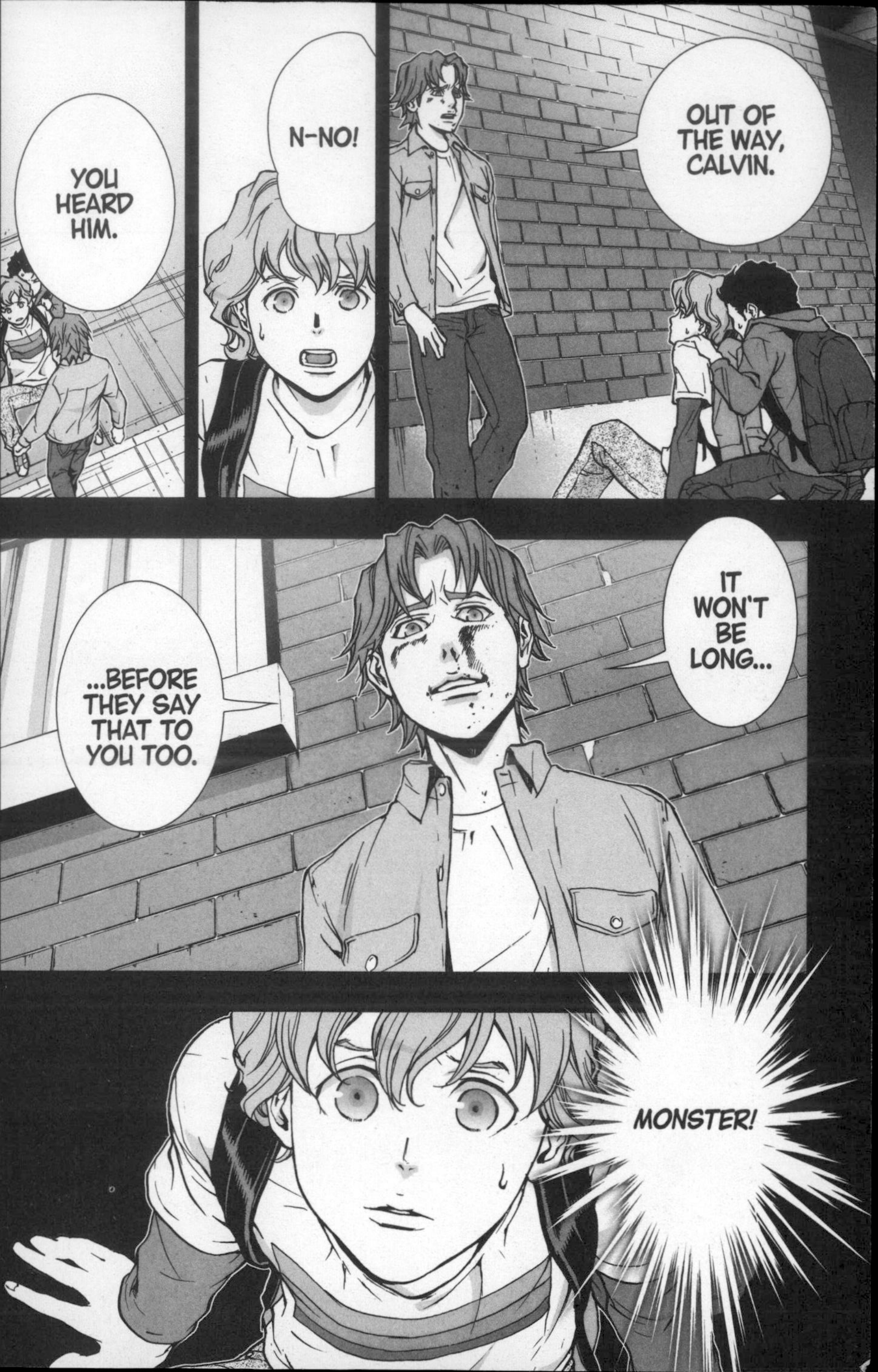
OUT OF THE WAY, CALVIN.
N-NO!
YOU HEARD HIM.
IT WON'T BE LONG...
...BEFORE THEY SAY THAT TO YOU TOO.
MONSTER!

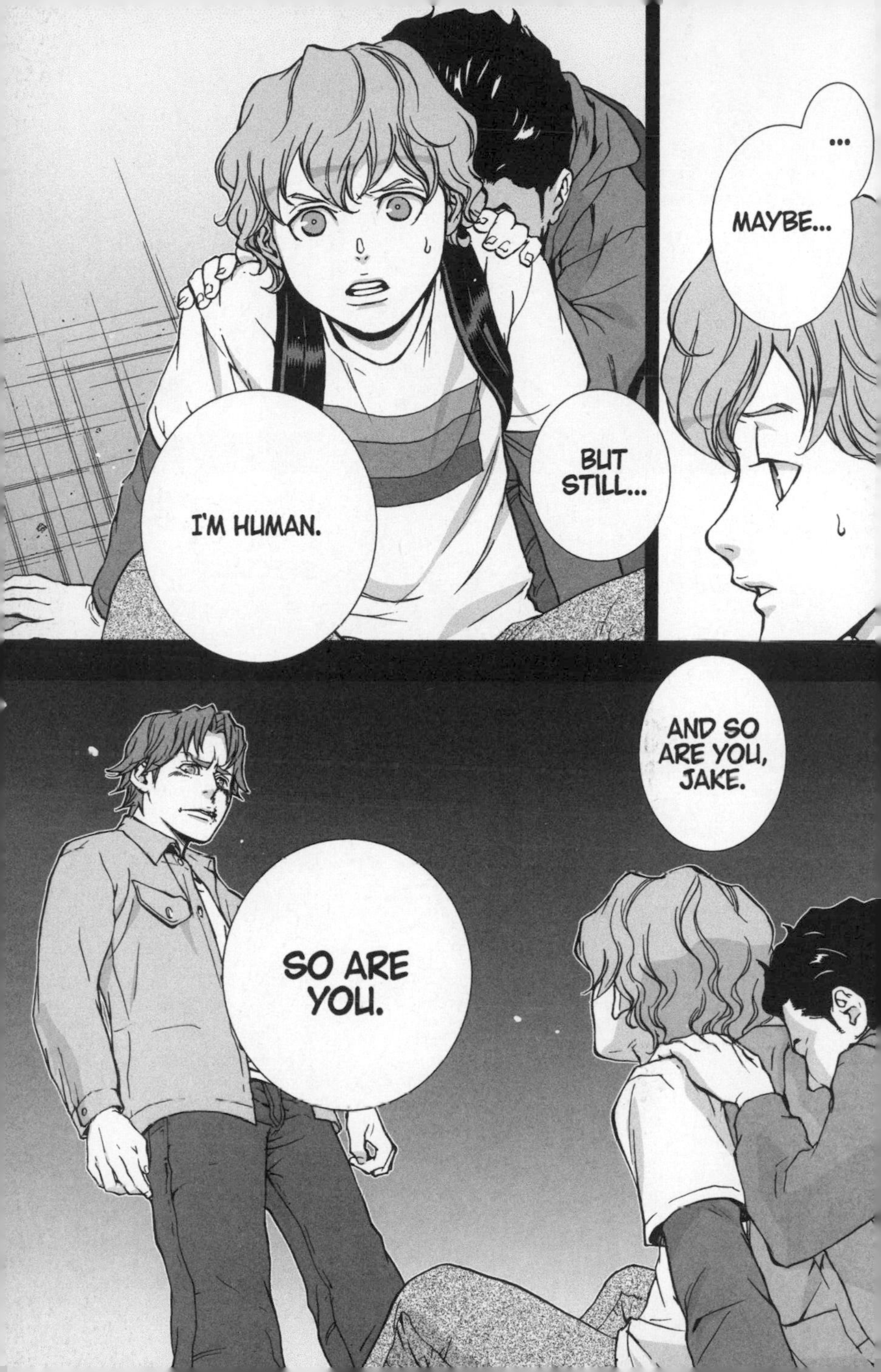
...
MAYBE...
BUT STILL...
I'M HUMAN.
AND SO ARE YOU, JAKE.
SO ARE YOU.

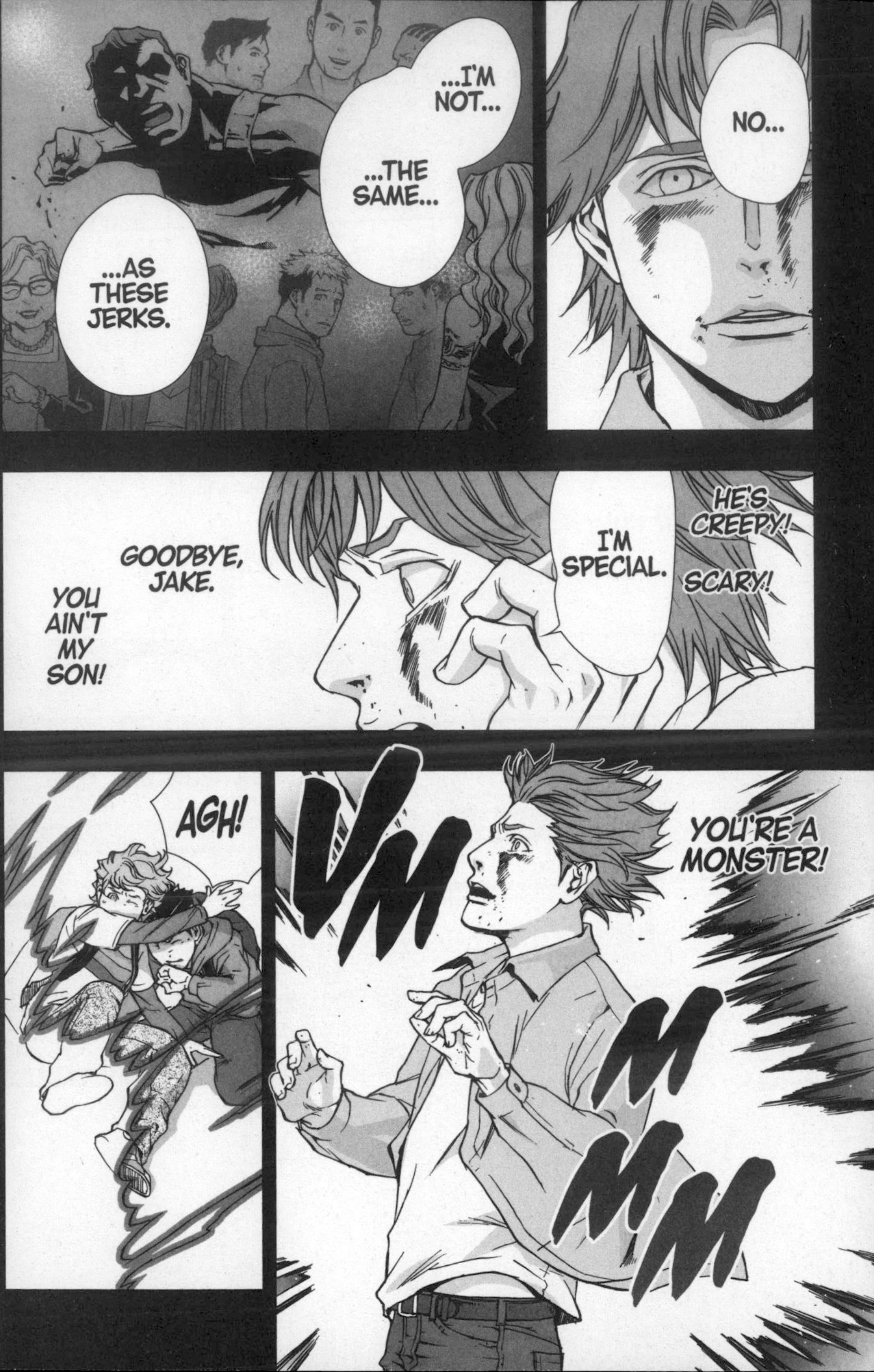
NO...
...I'M NOT...
...THE SAME...
...AS THESE JERKS.
HE'S CREEPY!
SCARY!
I'M SPECIAL.
GOODBYE, JAKE.
YOU AIN'T MY SON!
YOU'RE A MONSTER!
VM
MMMM
AGH!

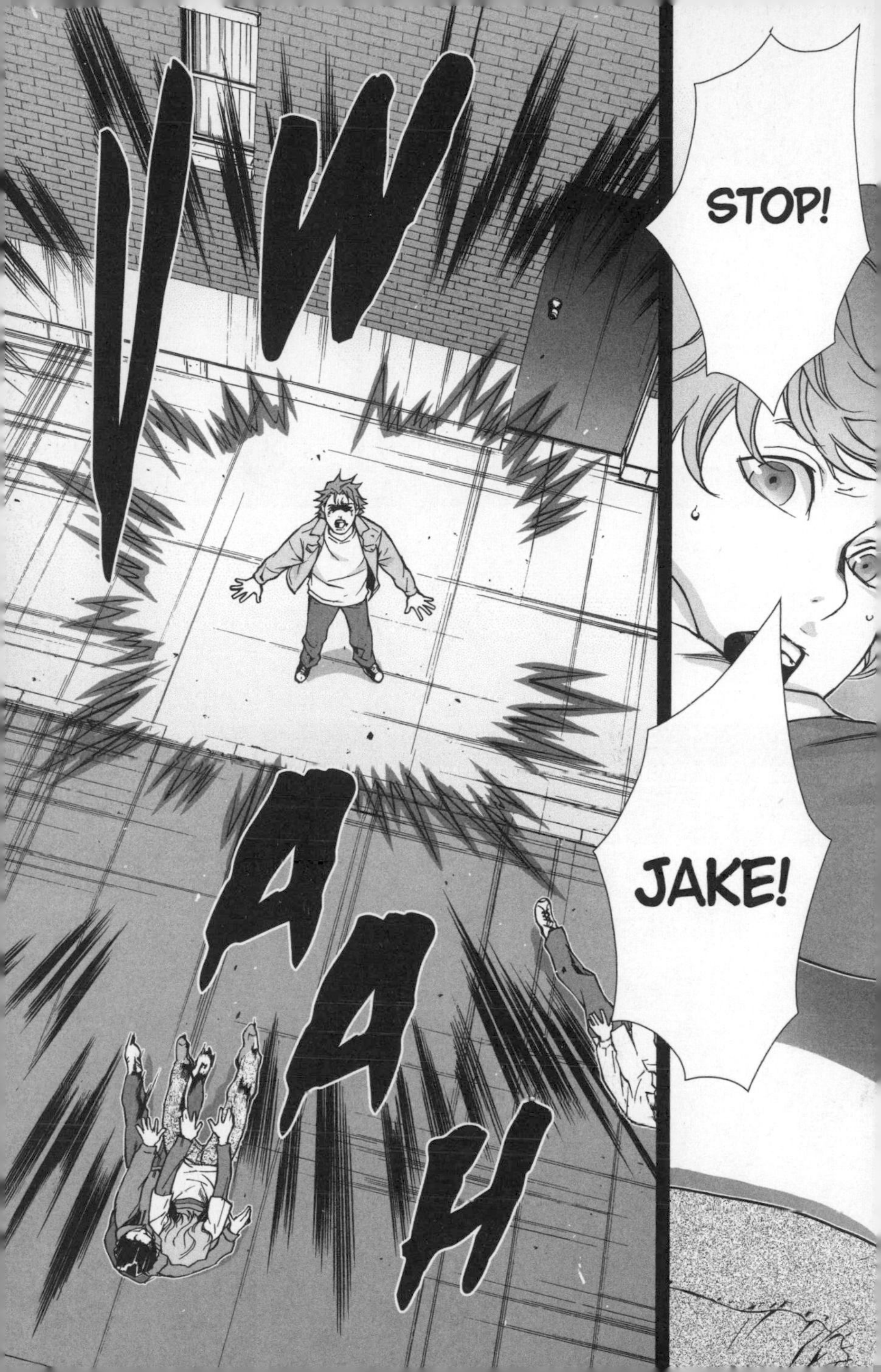
STOP!
JAKE!

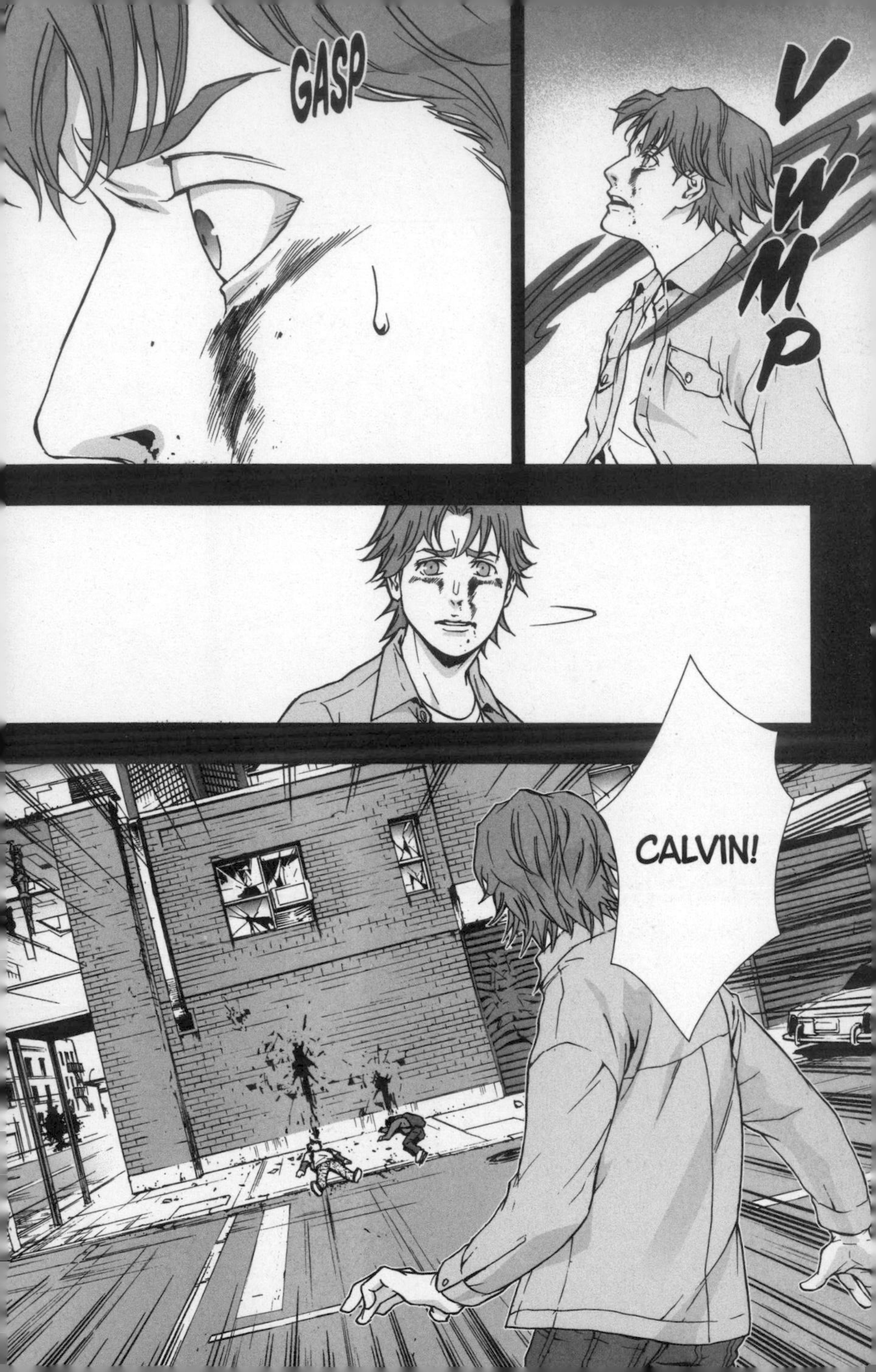
VWMP
GASP
CALVIN!

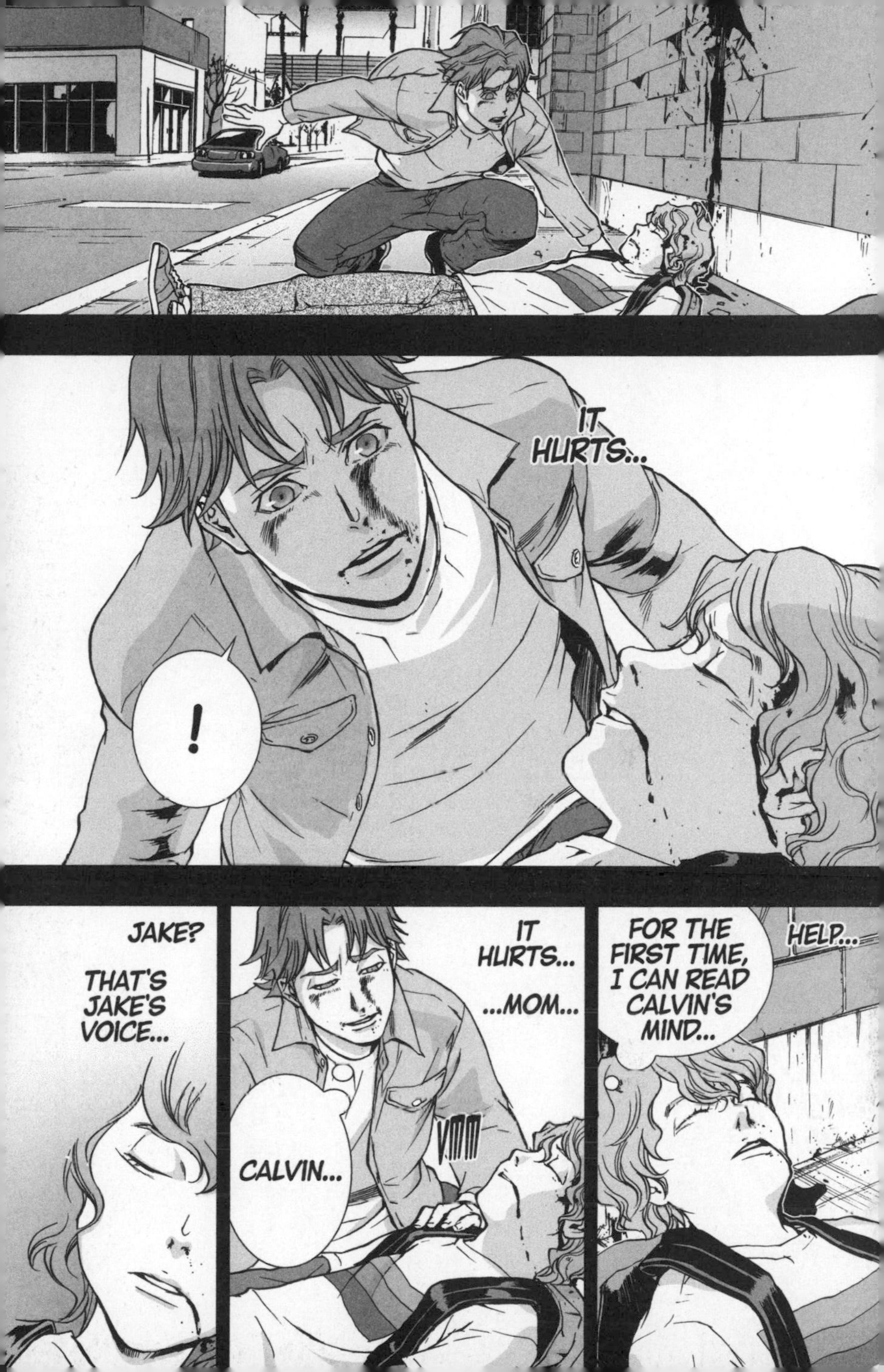
IT HURTS...
!
HELP...
FOR THE FIRST TIME, I CAN READ CALVIN'S MIND...
IT HURTS...
...MOM...
VMM
CALVIN...
JAKE?
THAT'S JAKE'S VOICE...

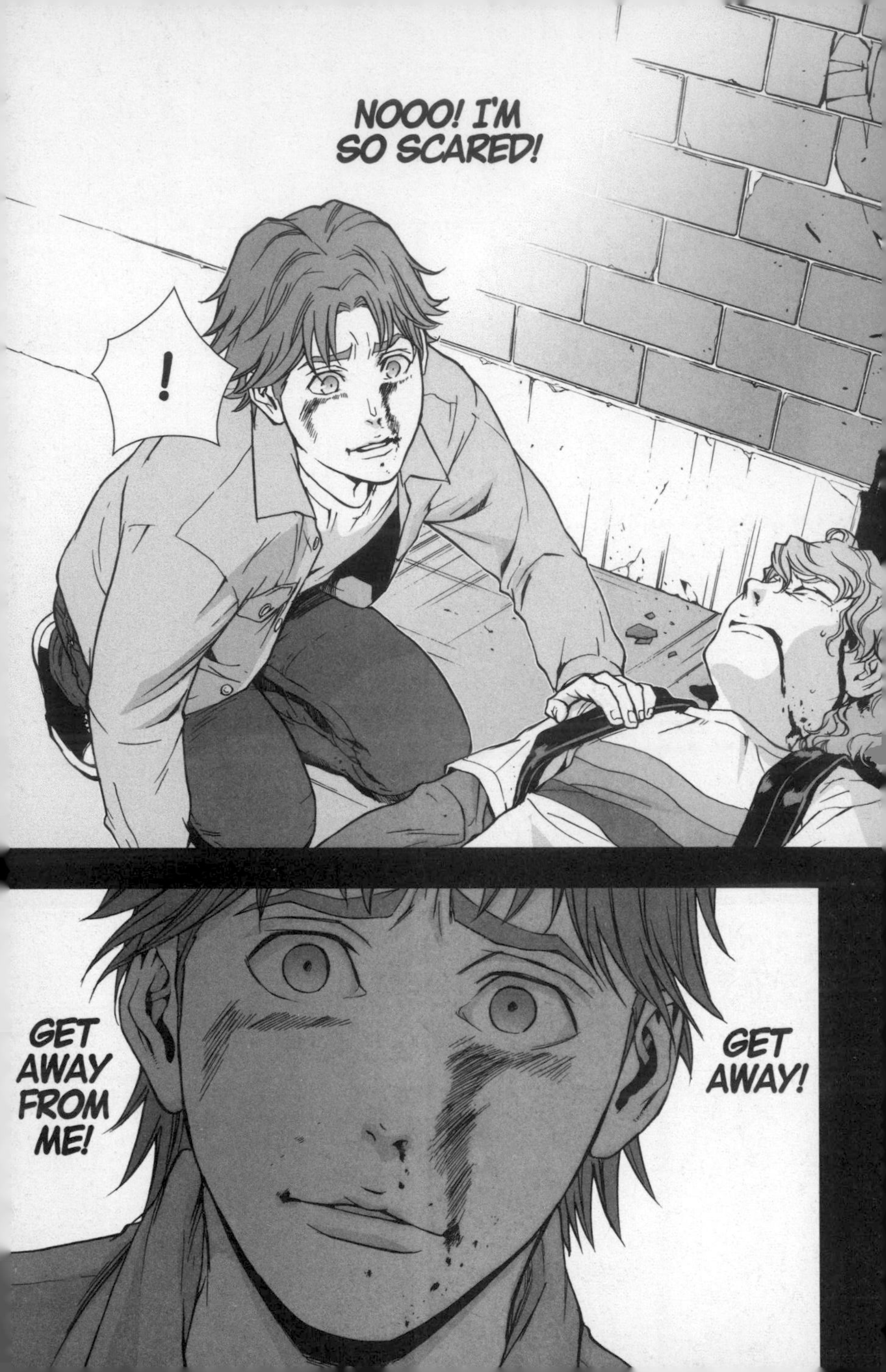
NOOO! I'M SO SCARED!
!
GET AWAY!
GET AWAY FROM ME!

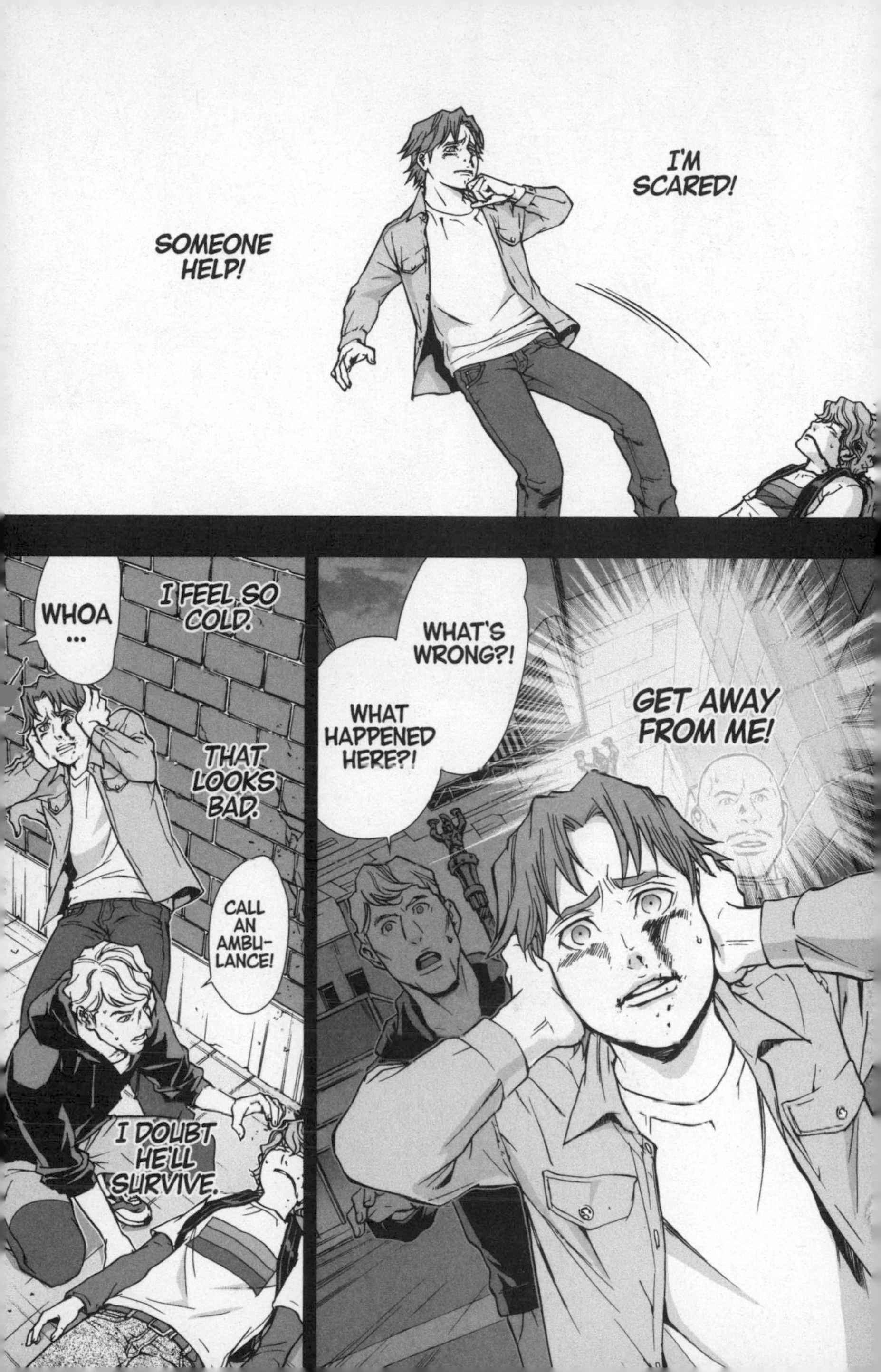
I'M SCARED!
SOMEONE HELP!
GET AWAY FROM ME!
WHAT'S WRONG?!
WHAT HAPPENED HERE?!
I FEEL SO COLD.
WHOA ...
THAT LOOKS BAD.
CALL AN AMBULANCE!
I DOUBT HE'LL SURVIVE.

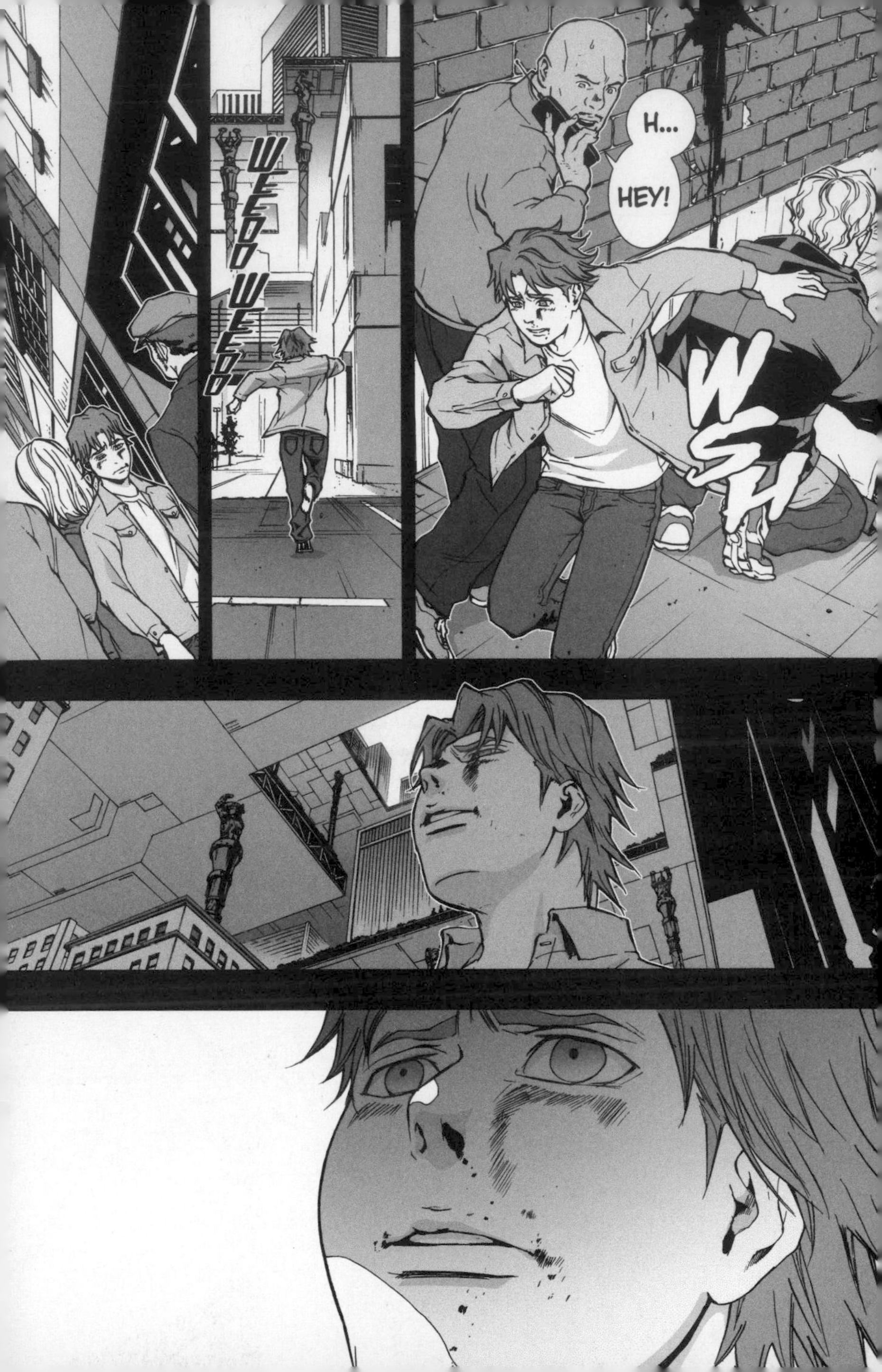
H...
HEY!
WSH
WEEDO WEEDO WEEDO

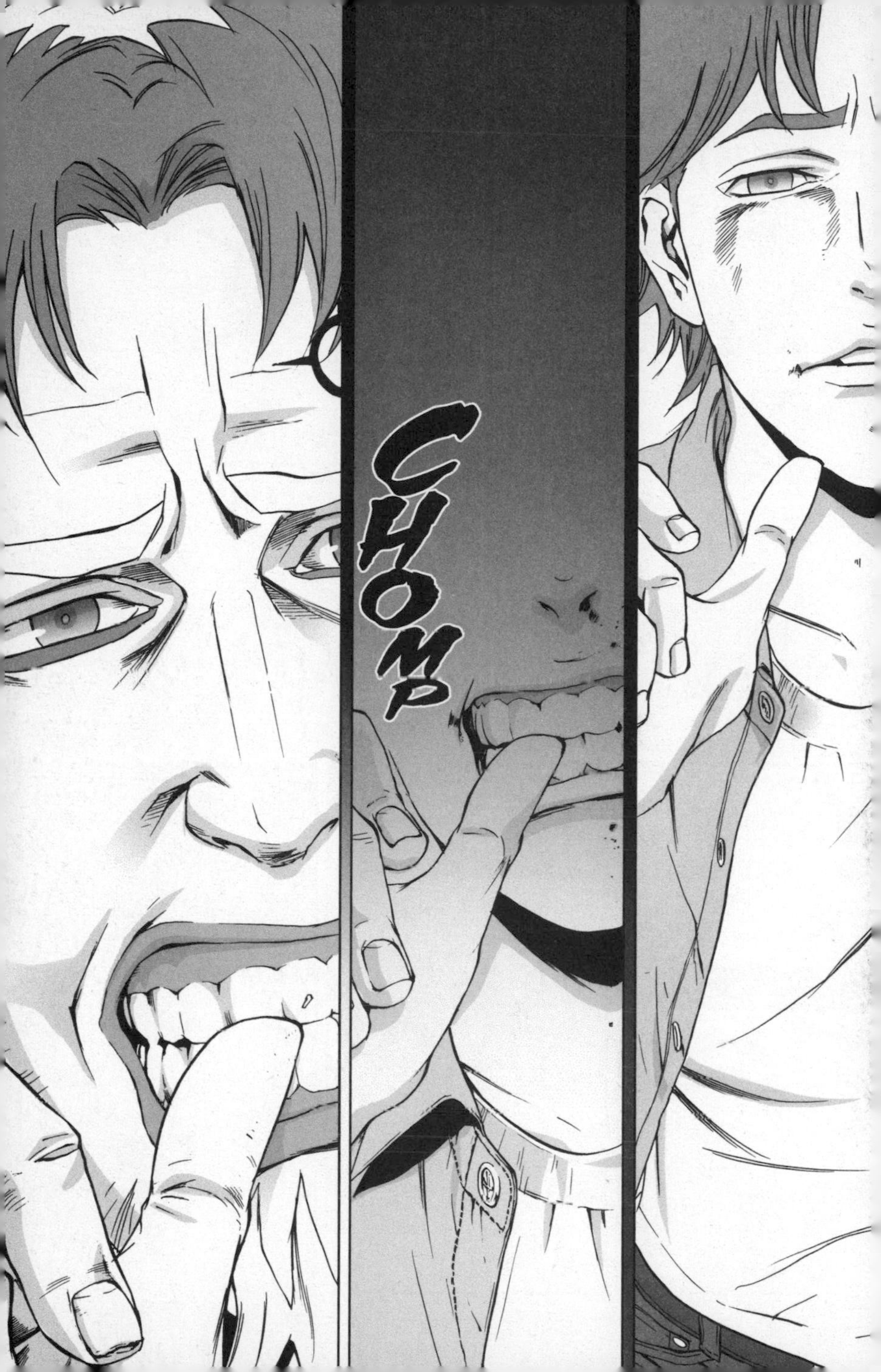
CHOMP

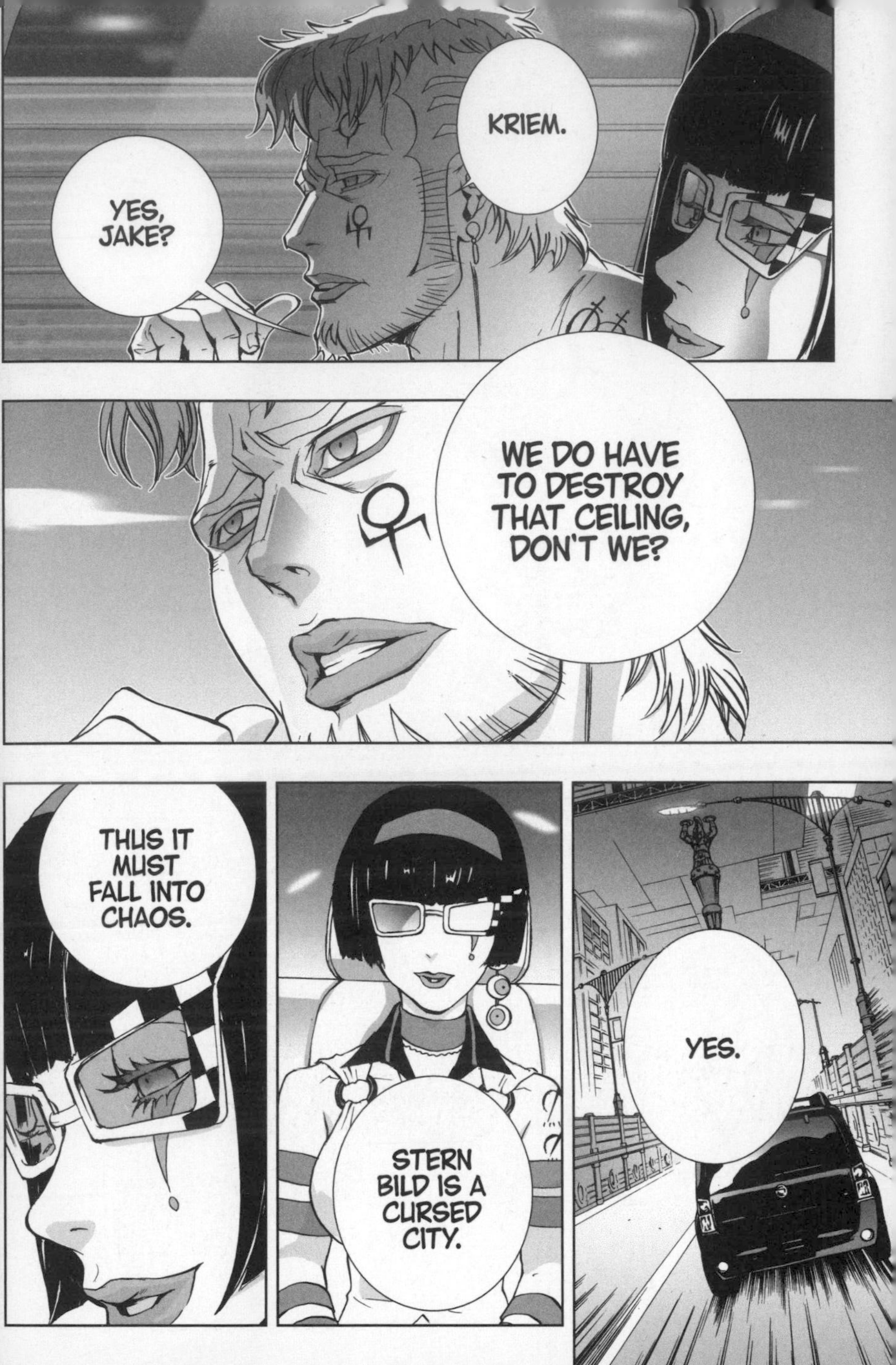
KRIEM.
YES, JAKE?
WE DO HAVE TO DESTROY THAT CEILING, DON'T WE?
YES.
STERN BILD IS A CURSED CITY.
THUS IT MUST FALL INTO CHAOS.

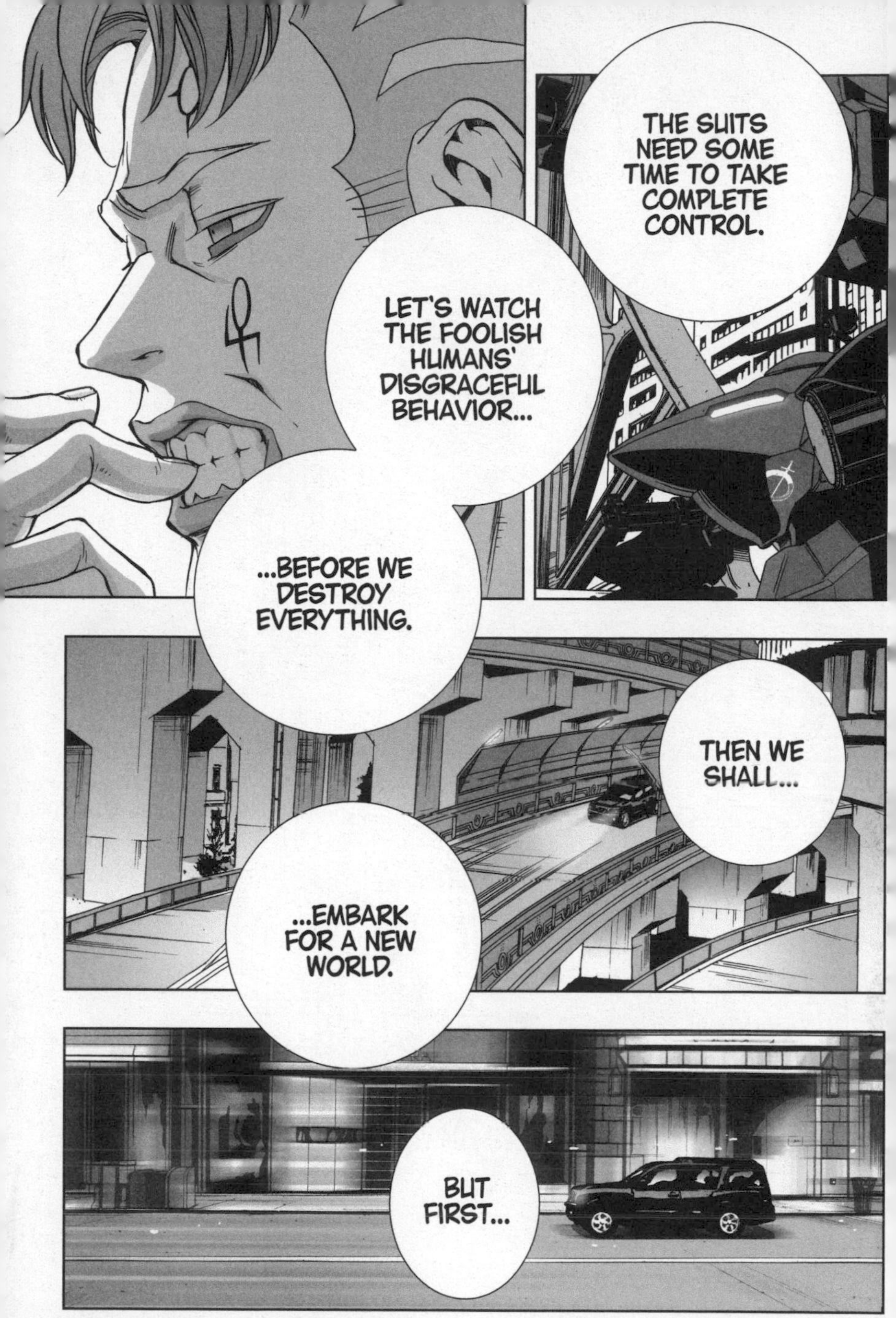
THE SUITS NEED SOME TIME TO TAKE COMPLETE CONTROL.
LET'S WATCH THE FOOLISH HUMANS' DISGRACEFUL BEHAVIOR...
...BEFORE WE DESTROY EVERYTHING.
THEN WE SHALL...
...EMBARK FOR A NEW WORLD.
BUT FIRST...

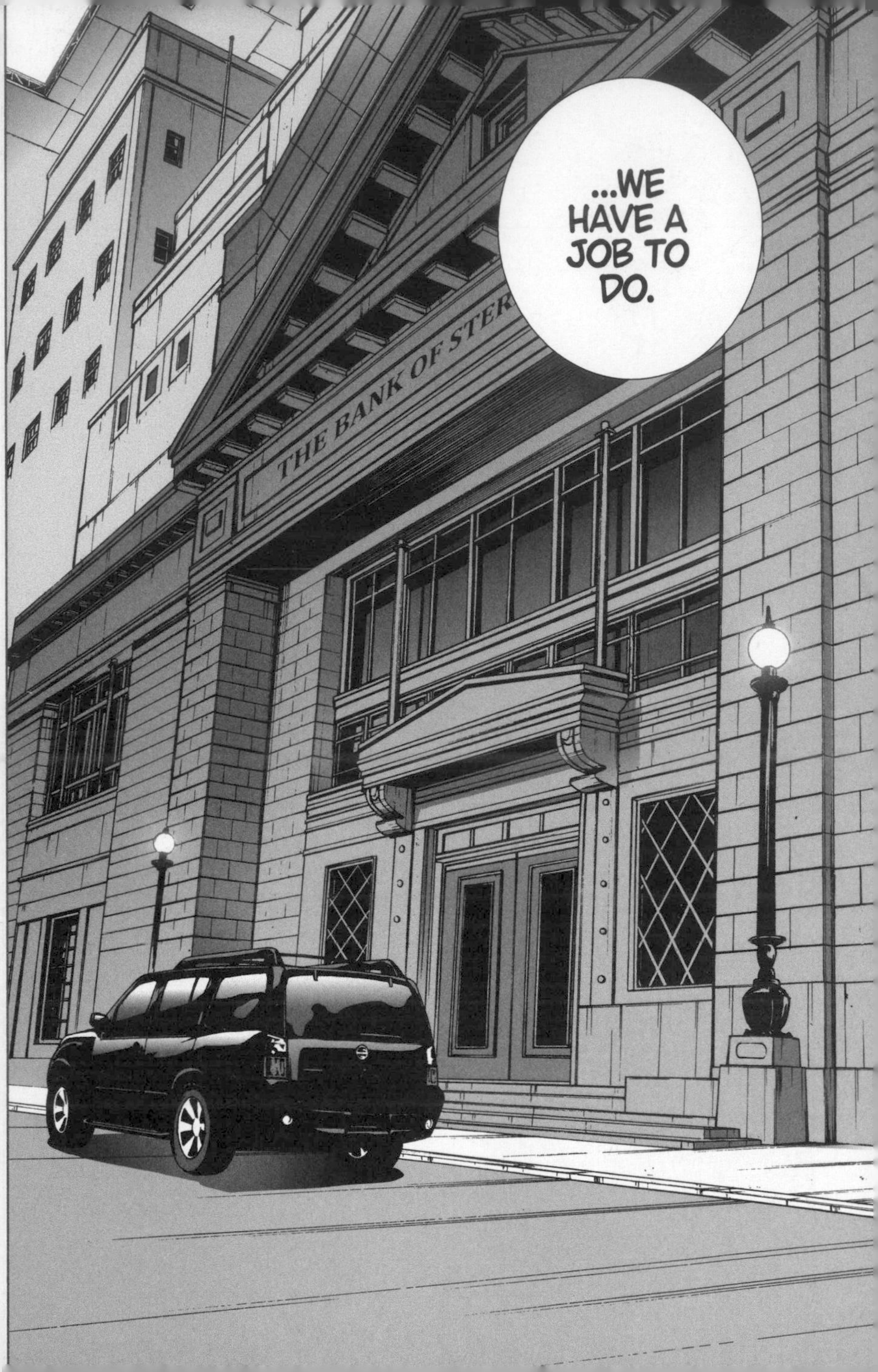
...WE HAVE A JOB TO DO.
THE BANK OF STER

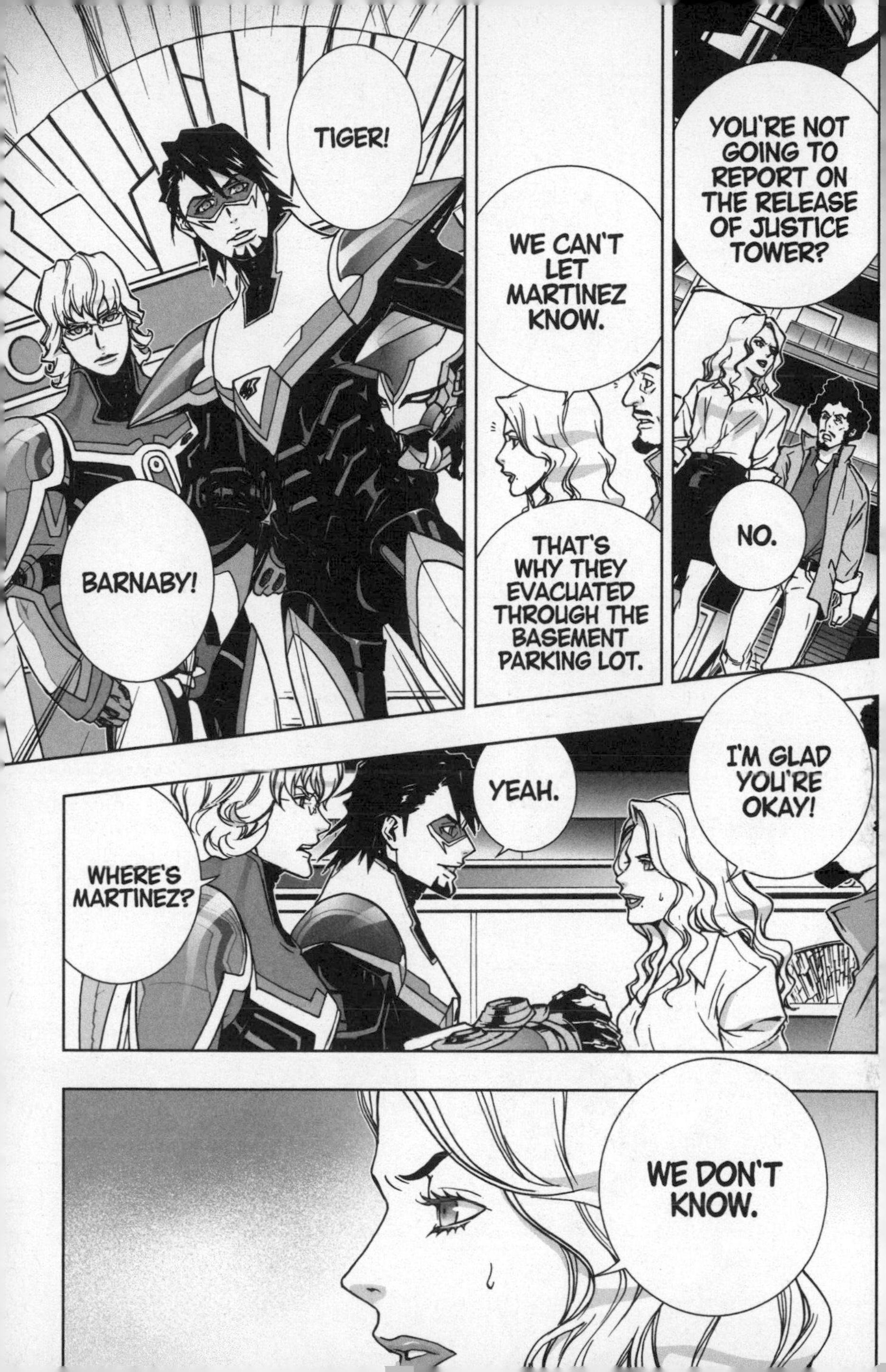
YOU'RE NOT GOING TO REPORT ON THE RELEASE OF JUSTICE TOWER?
NO.
WE CAN'T LET MARTINEZ KNOW.
THAT'S WHY THEY EVACUATED THROUGH THE BASEMENT PARKING LOT.
TIGER!
BARNABY!
I'M GLAD YOU'RE OKAY!
YEAH.
WHERE'S MARTINEZ?
WE DON'T KNOW.

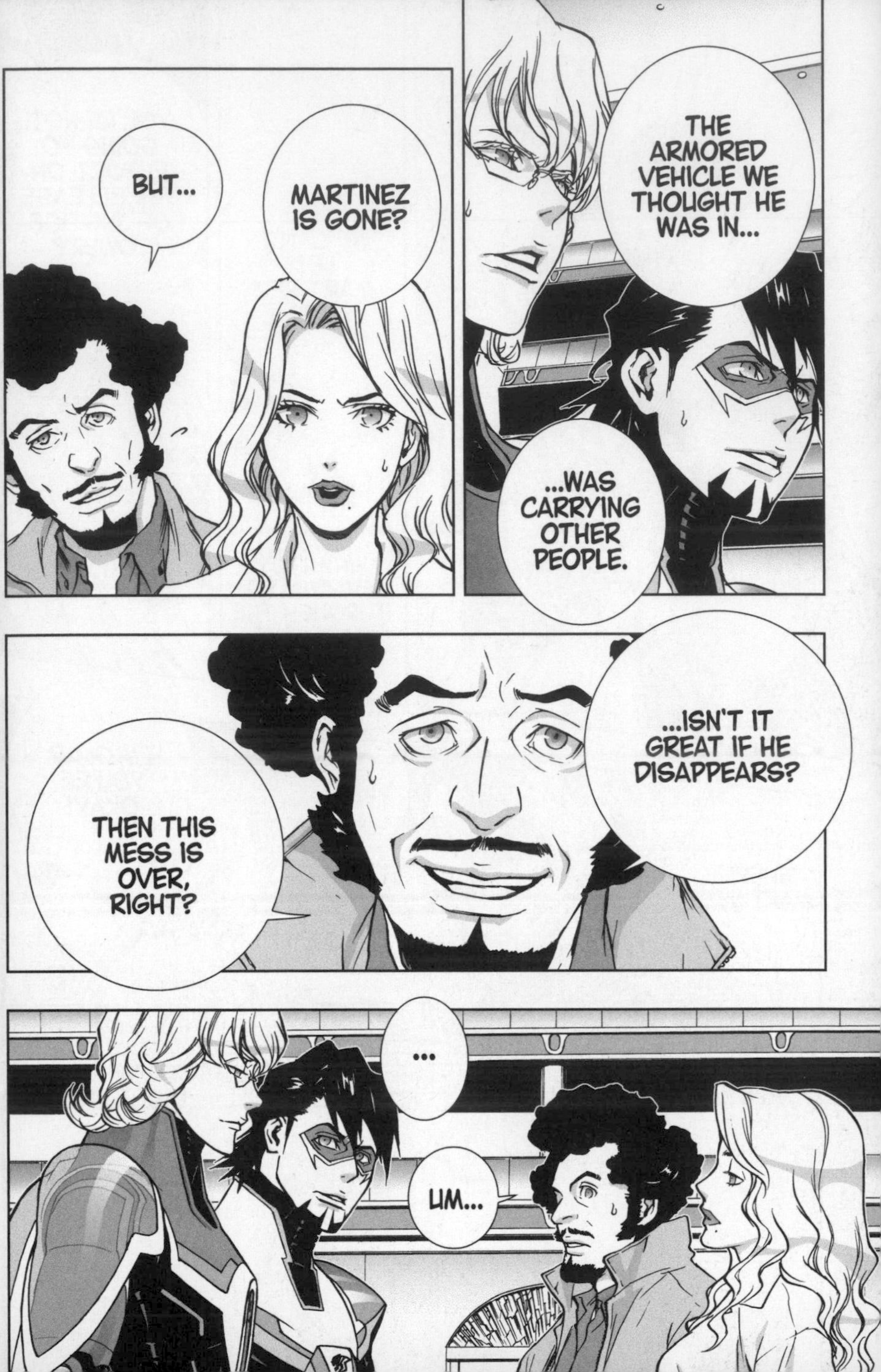
THE ARMORED VEHICLE WE THOUGHT HE WAS IN...
...WAS CARRYING OTHER PEOPLE.
MARTINEZ IS GONE?
BUT...
...ISN'T IT GREAT IF HE DISAPPEARS?
THEN THIS MESS IS OVER, RIGHT?
...
UM...

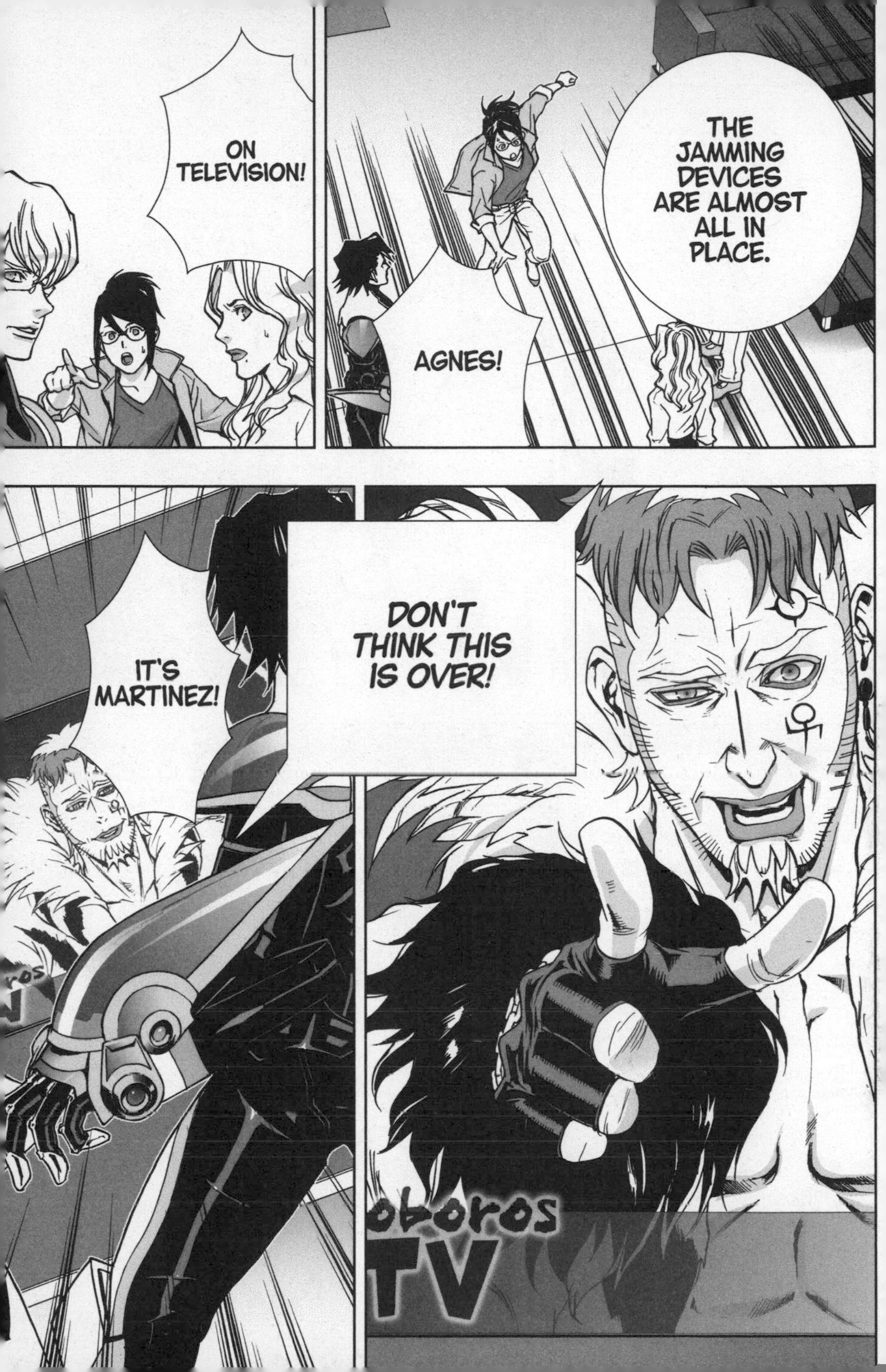
THE JAMMING DEVICES ARE ALMOST ALL IN PLACE.
AGNES!
ON TELEVISION!
TV
DON'T THINK THIS IS OVER!
IT'S MARTINEZ!

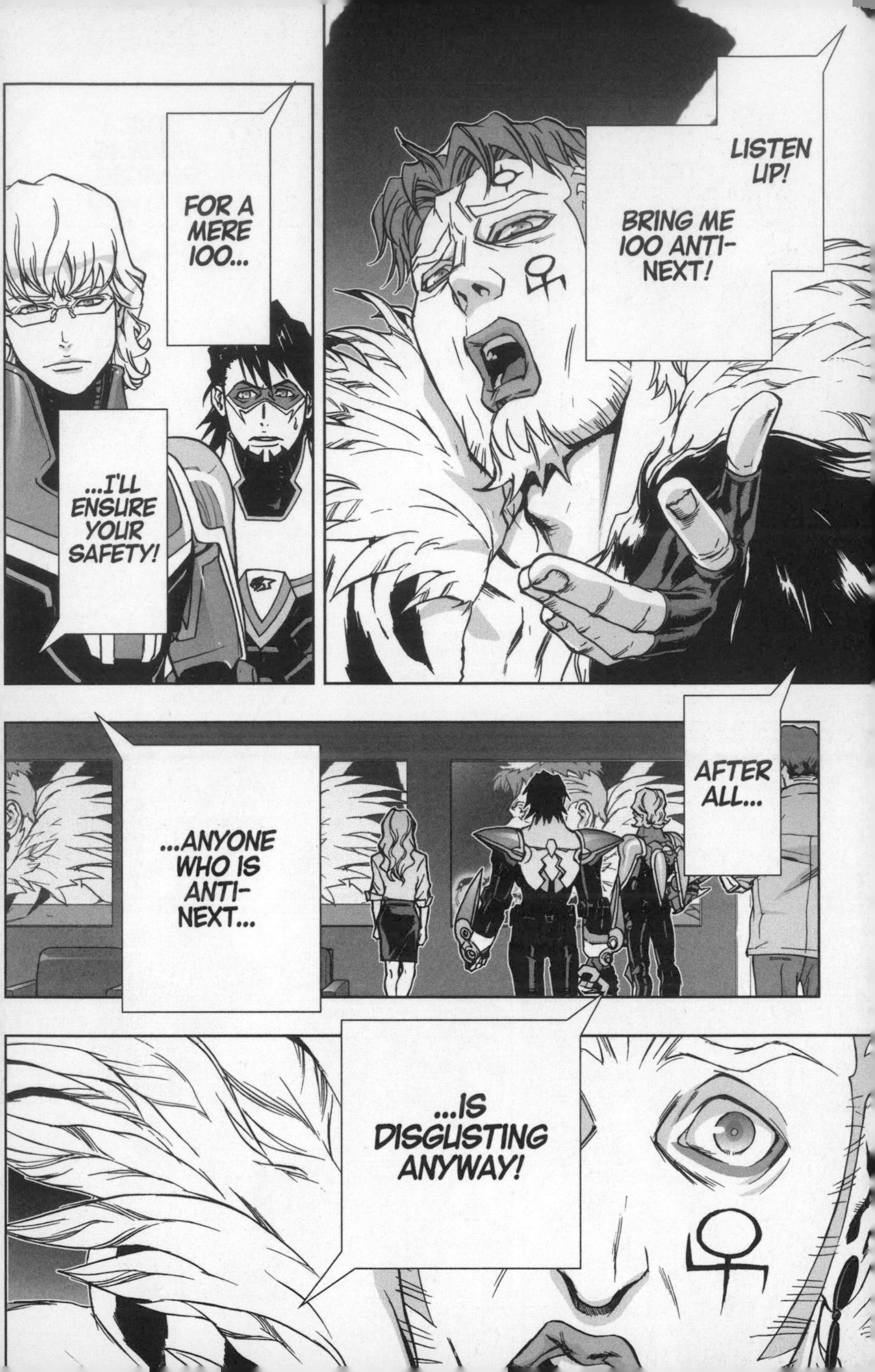
LISTEN UP!
BRING ME 100 ANTI-NEXT!
FOR A MERE 100...
...I'LL ENSURE YOUR SAFETY!
AFTER ALL...
...ANYONE WHO IS ANTI-NEXT...
...IS DISGUSTING ANYWAY!

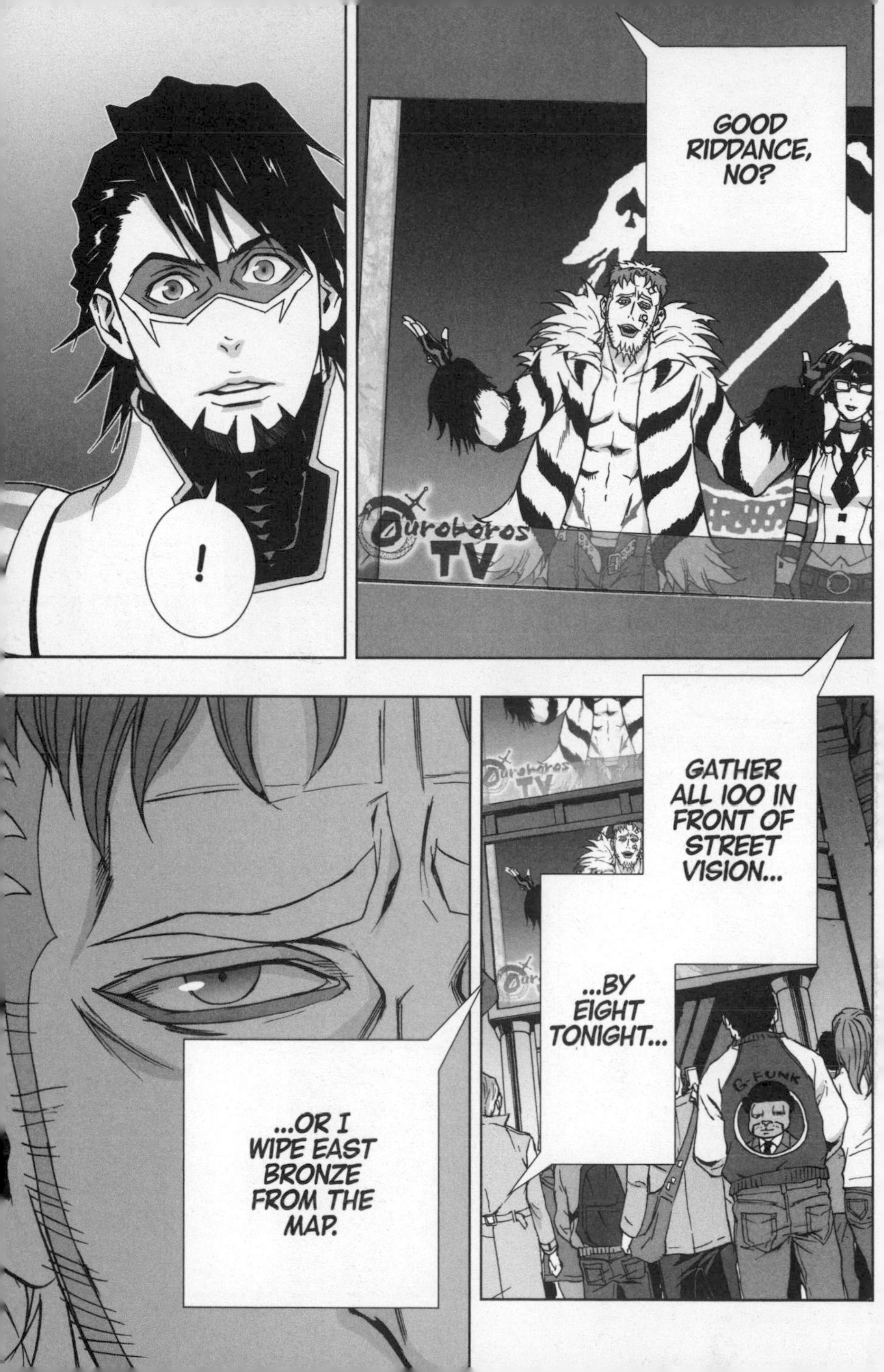
GOOD RIDDANCE, NO?
Ouroboros TV
!
GATHER ALL 100 IN FRONT OF STREET VISION...
...BY EIGHT TONIGHT...
G-FUNK
...OR I WIPE EAST BRONZE FROM THE MAP.

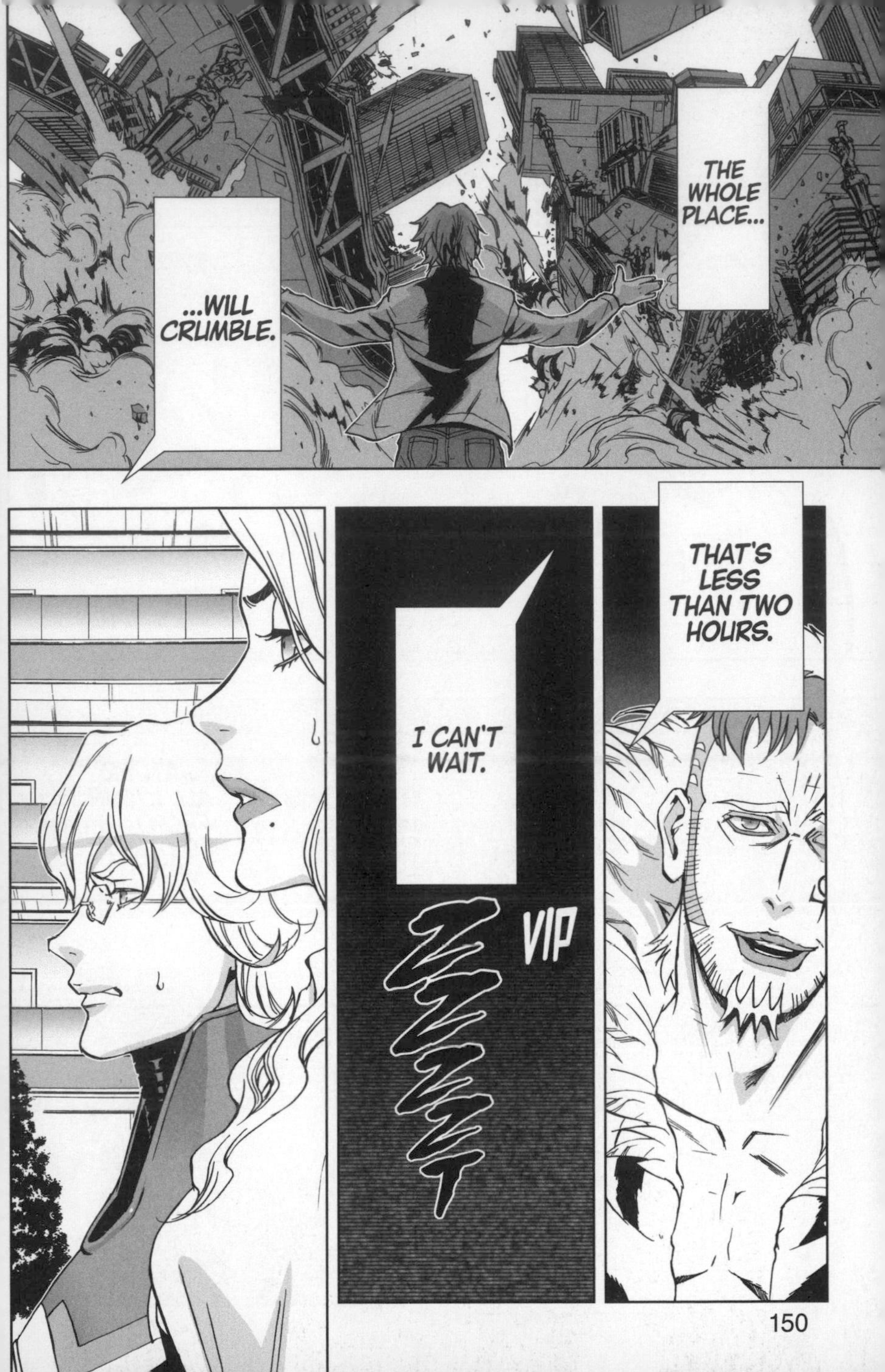
THE WHOLE PLACE...
...WILL CRUMBLE.
THAT'S LESS THAN TWO HOURS.
I CAN'T WAIT.
VIP

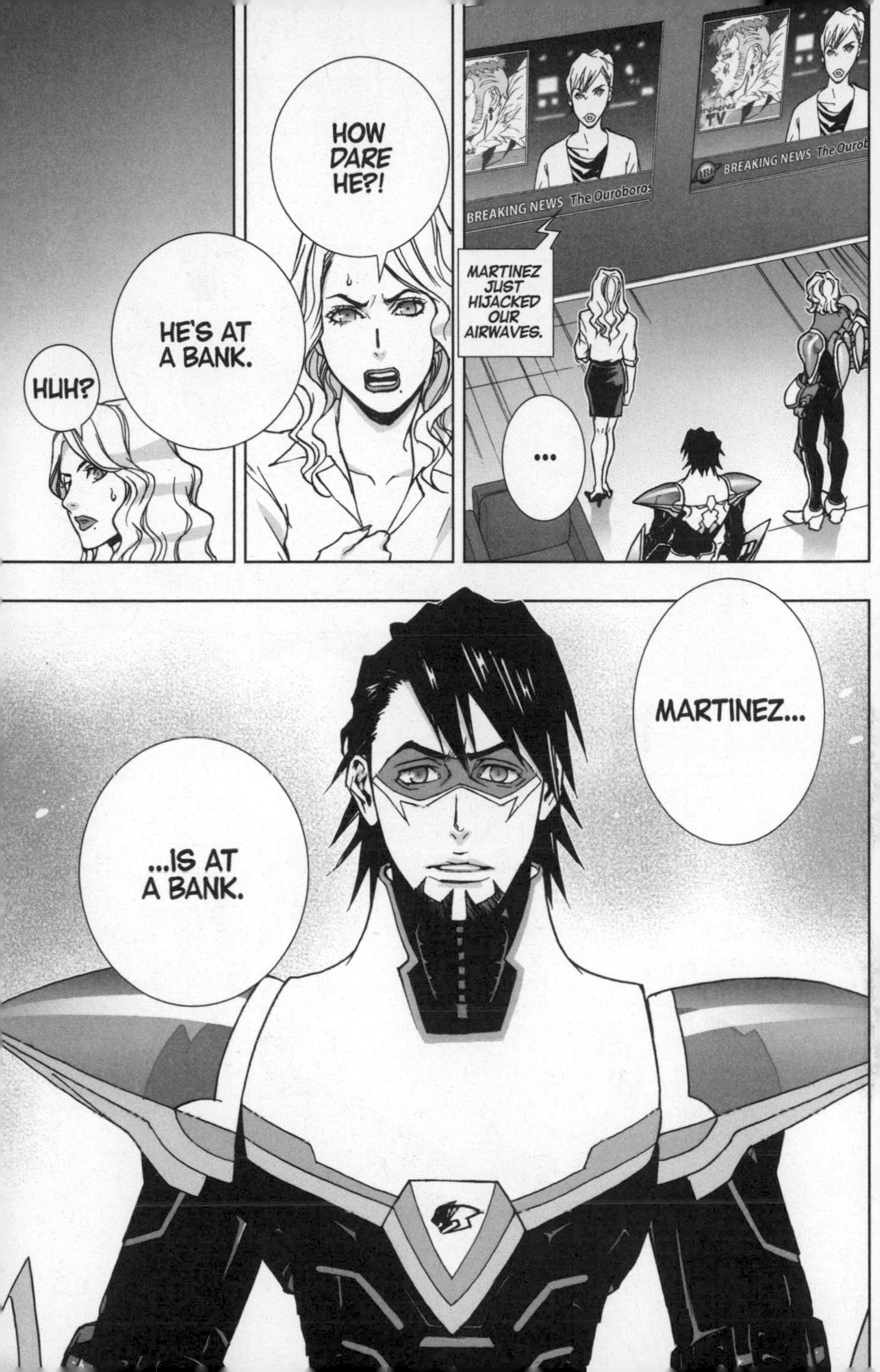
BREAKING NEWS The Ourob
BREAKING NEWS The Ouroboros
MARTINEZ JUST HIJACKED OUR AIRWAVES.
...
HOW DARE HE?!
HE'S AT A BANK.
HUH?
MARTINEZ...
...IS AT A BANK.

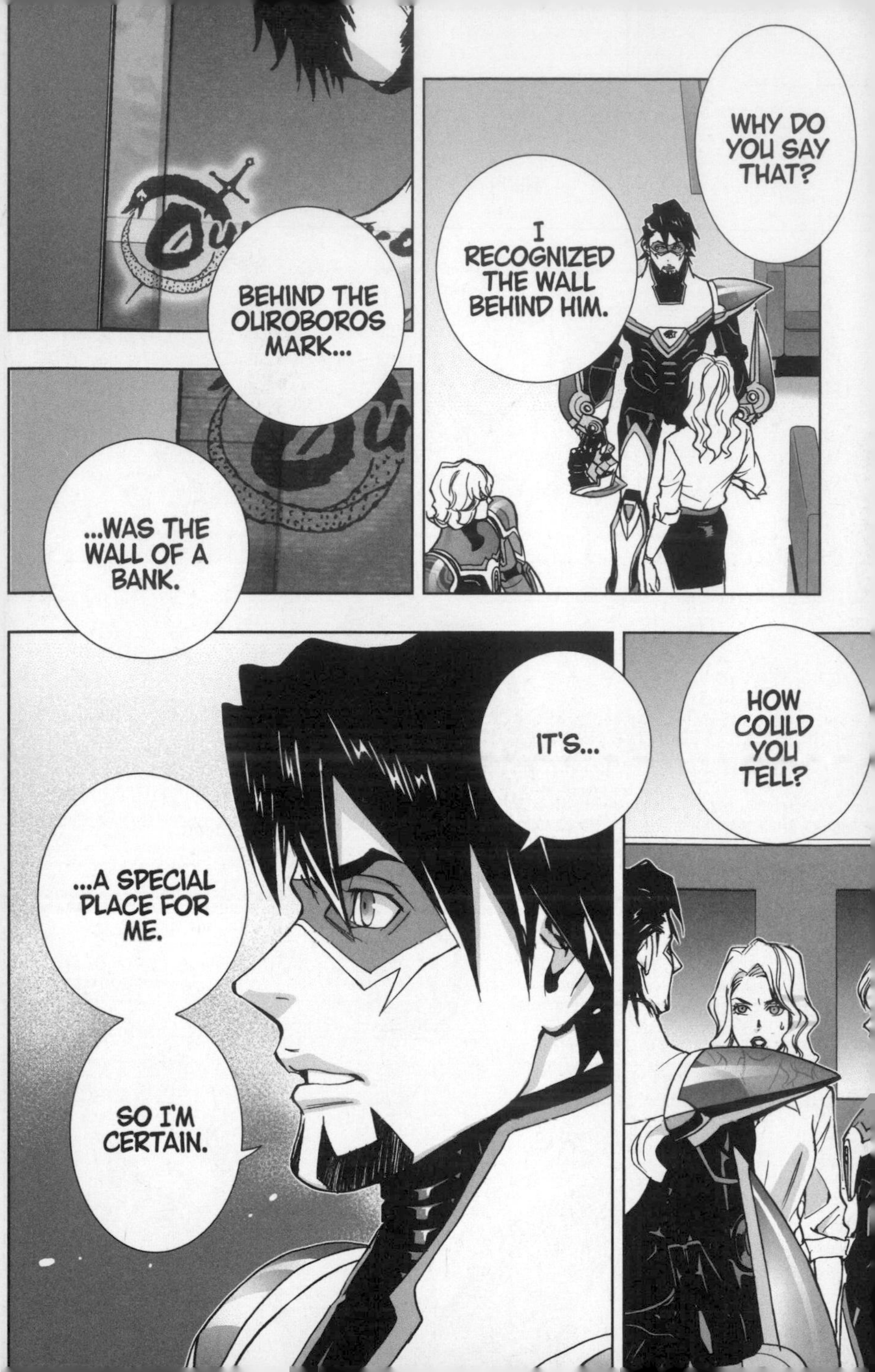
WHY DO YOU SAY THAT?
I RECOGNIZED THE WALL BEHIND HIM.
BEHIND THE OUROBOROS MARK...
...WAS THE WALL OF A BANK.
HOW COULD YOU TELL?
IT'S...
...A SPECIAL PLACE FOR ME.
SO I'M CERTAIN.

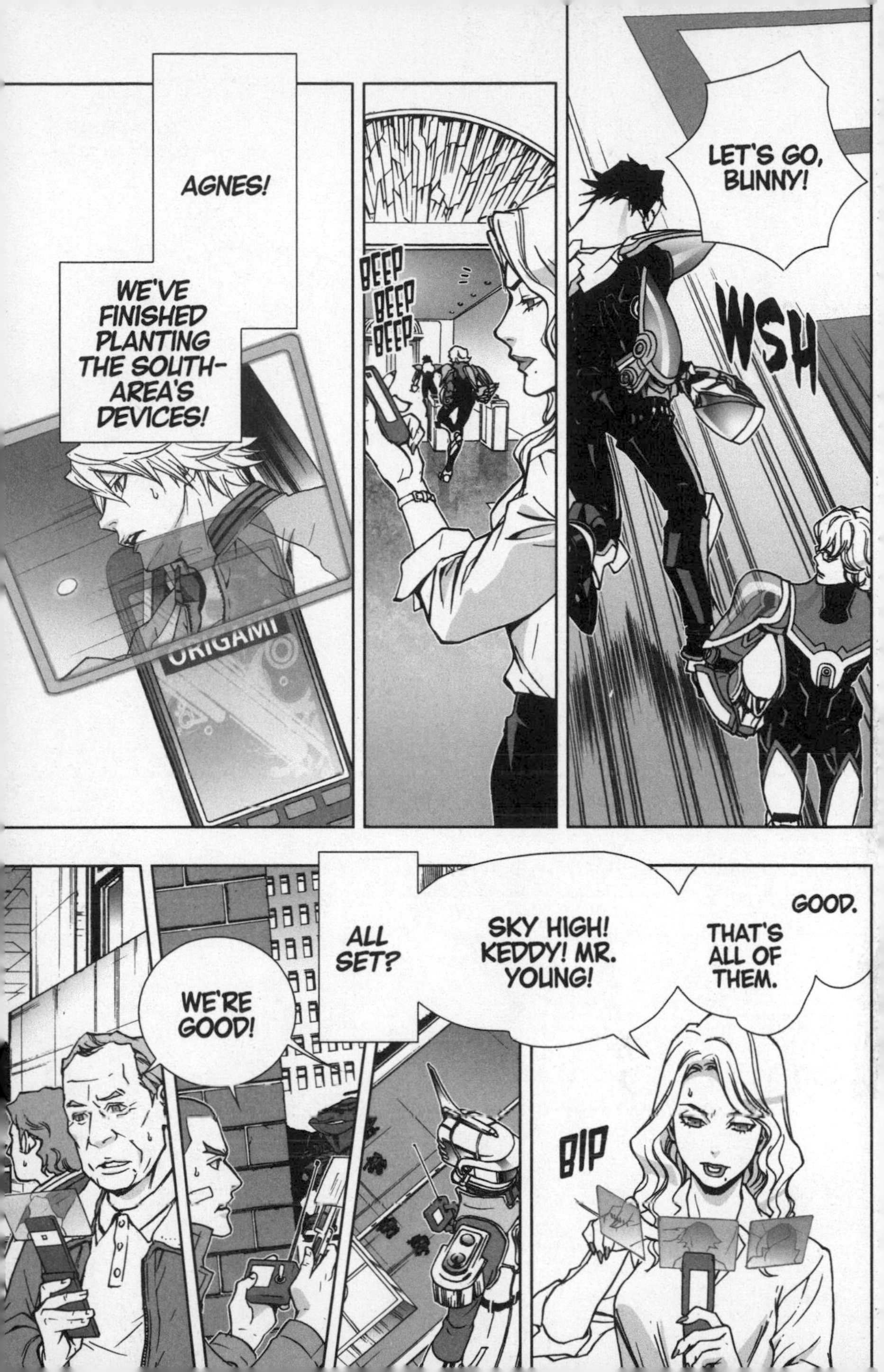
LET'S GO, BUNNY!
WSH
BEEP BEEP BEEP
AGNES!
WE'VE FINISHED PLANTING THE SOUTH-AREA'S DEVICES!
ORIGAMI
GOOD.
THAT'S ALL OF THEM.
BIP
SKY HIGH! KEDDY! MR. YOUNG!
ALL SET?
WE'RE GOOD!

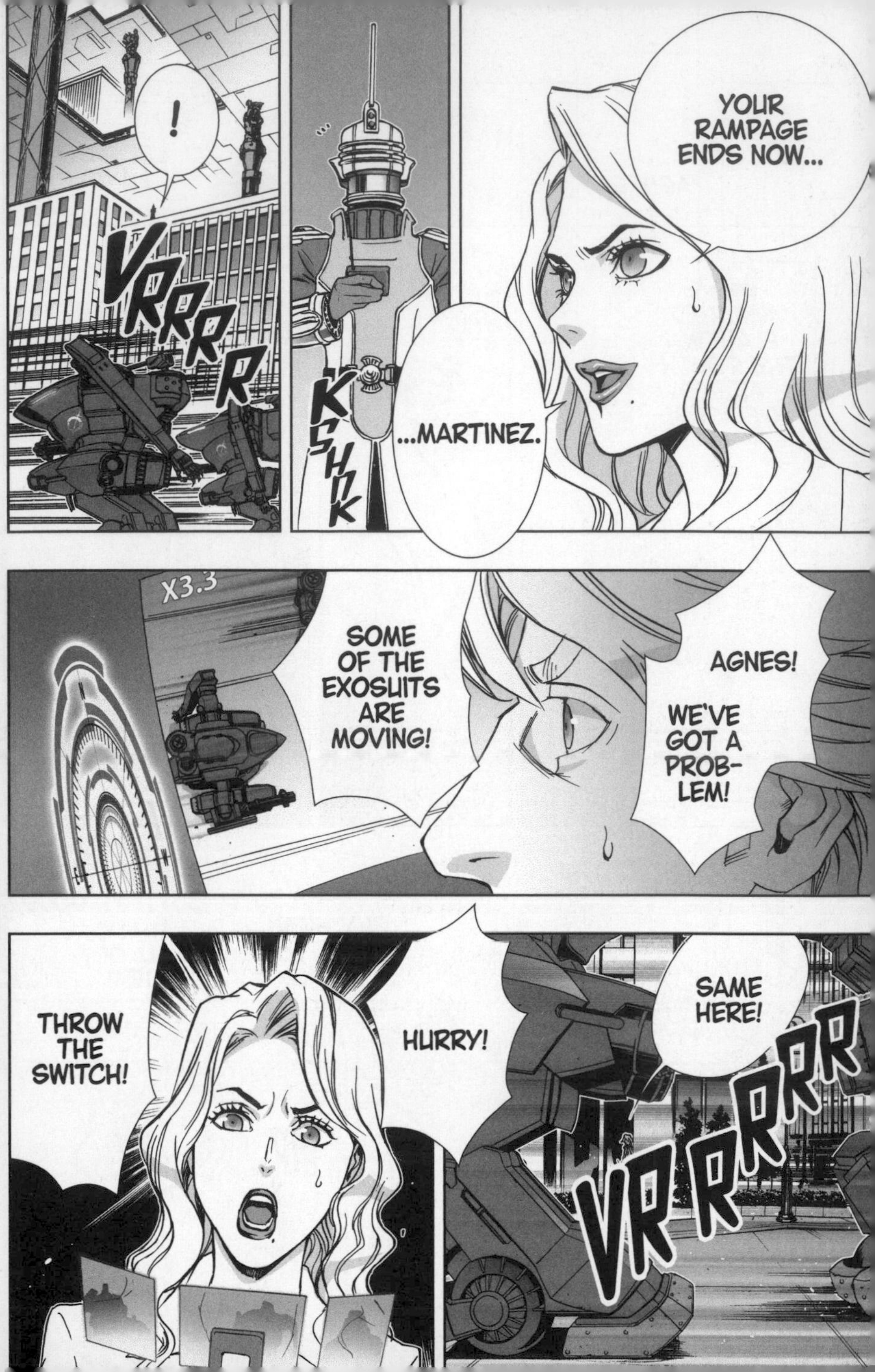
YOUR RAMPAGE ENDS NOW...
...MARTINEZ.
KSHNK
...
!
VRRRRR
AGNES!
WE'VE GOT A PROB-LEM!
SOME OF THE EXOSUITS ARE MOVING!
X3.3
SAME HERE!
VRRRRRR
HURRY!
THROW THE SWITCH!

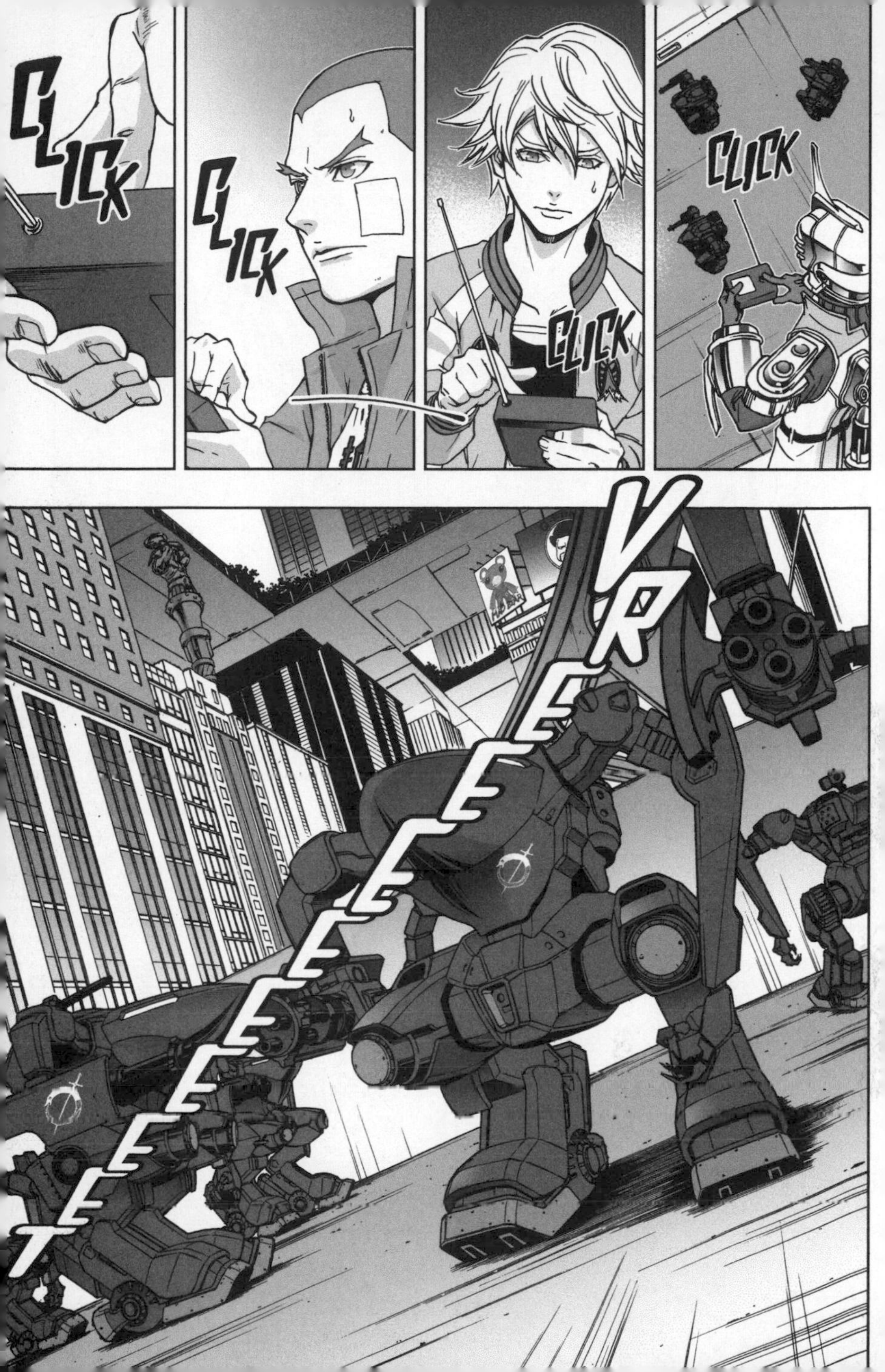
CLICK
CLICK
CLICK
CLICK
VREEEEEEEEEEEEEEET

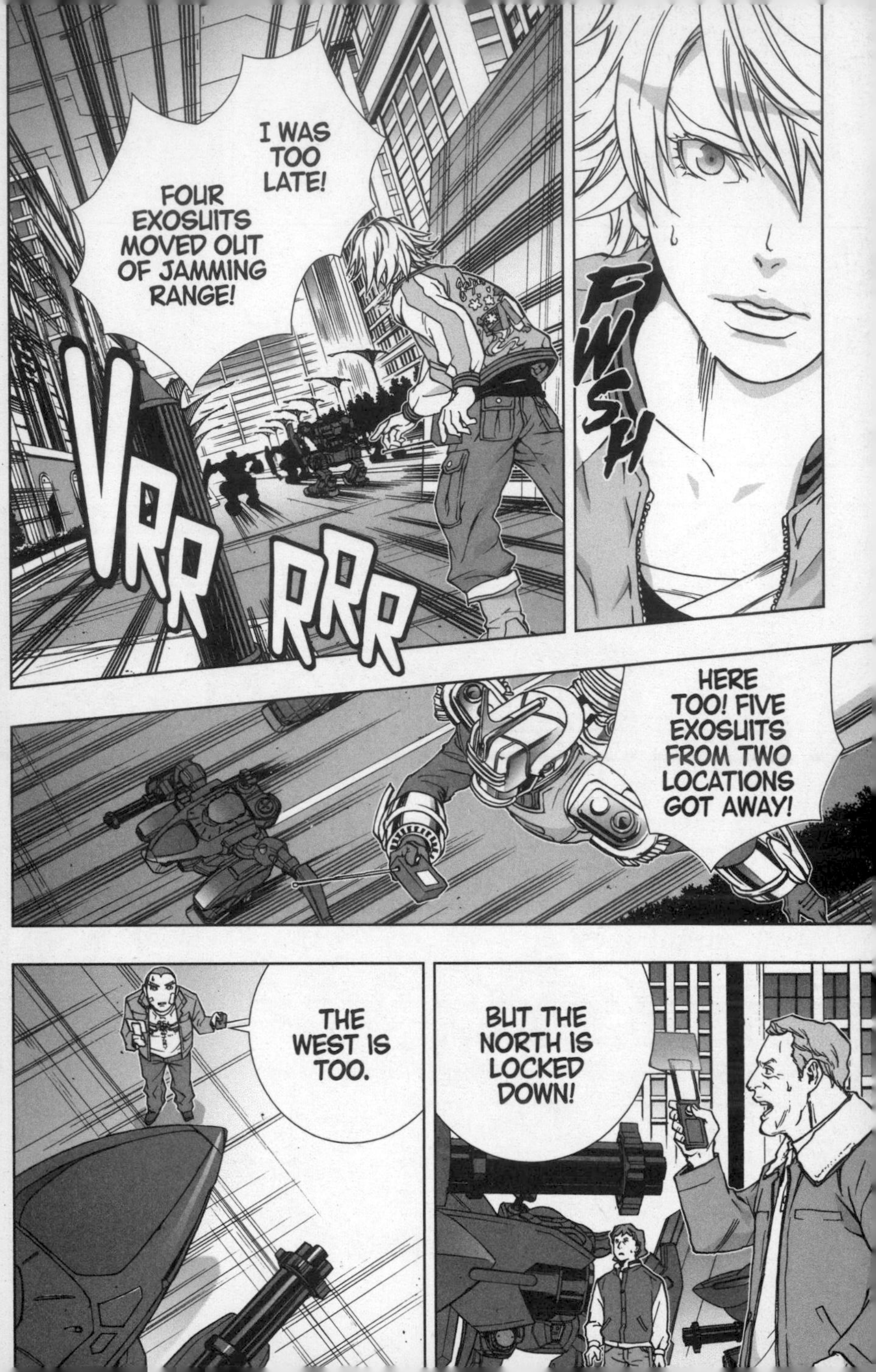
FWSH
I WAS TOO LATE!
FOUR EXOSUITS MOVED OUT OF JAMMING RANGE!
VRR RRR
HERE TOO! FIVE EXOSUITS FROM TWO LOCATIONS GOT AWAY!
BUT THE NORTH IS LOCKED DOWN!
THE WEST IS TOO.

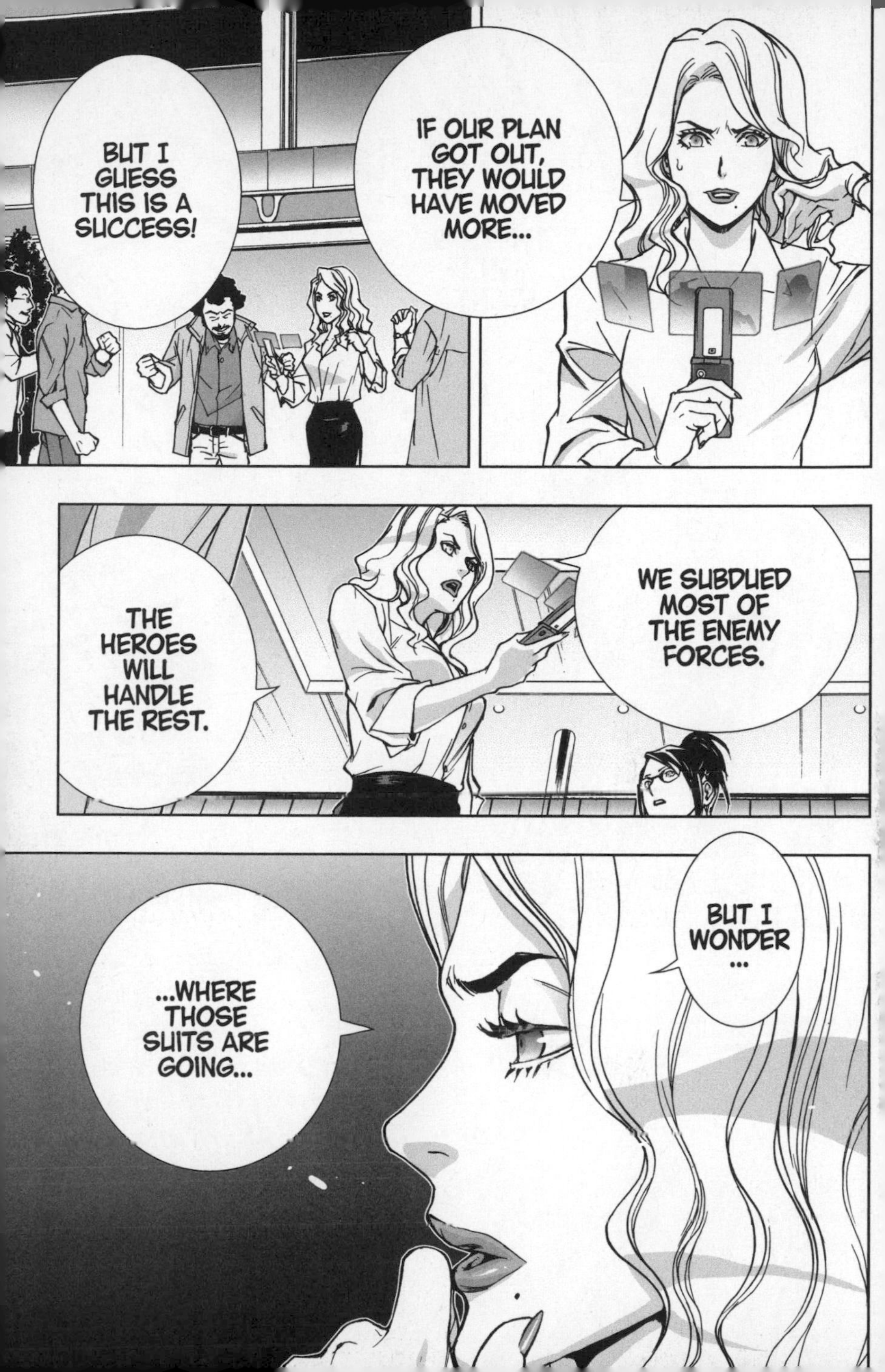
IF OUR PLAN GOT OUT, THEY WOULD HAVE MOVED MORE...
BUT I GUESS THIS IS A SUCCESS!
WE SUBDUED MOST OF THE ENEMY FORCES.
THE HEROES WILL HANDLE THE REST.
BUT I WONDER...
...WHERE THOSE SUITS ARE GOING...

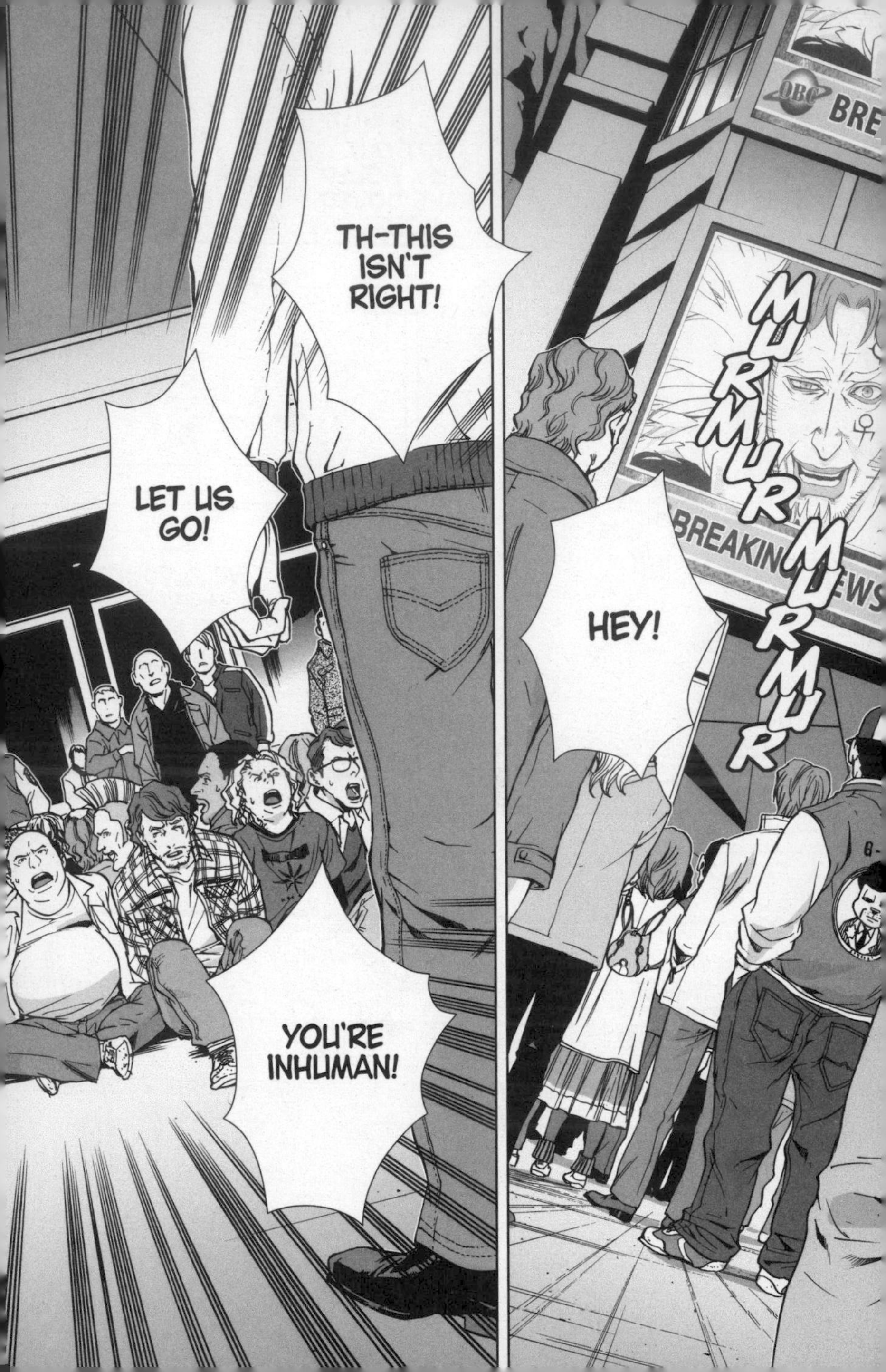
OBC
MURMUR
MURMUR
HEY!
TH-THIS ISN'T RIGHT!
LET US GO!
YOU'RE INHUMAN!

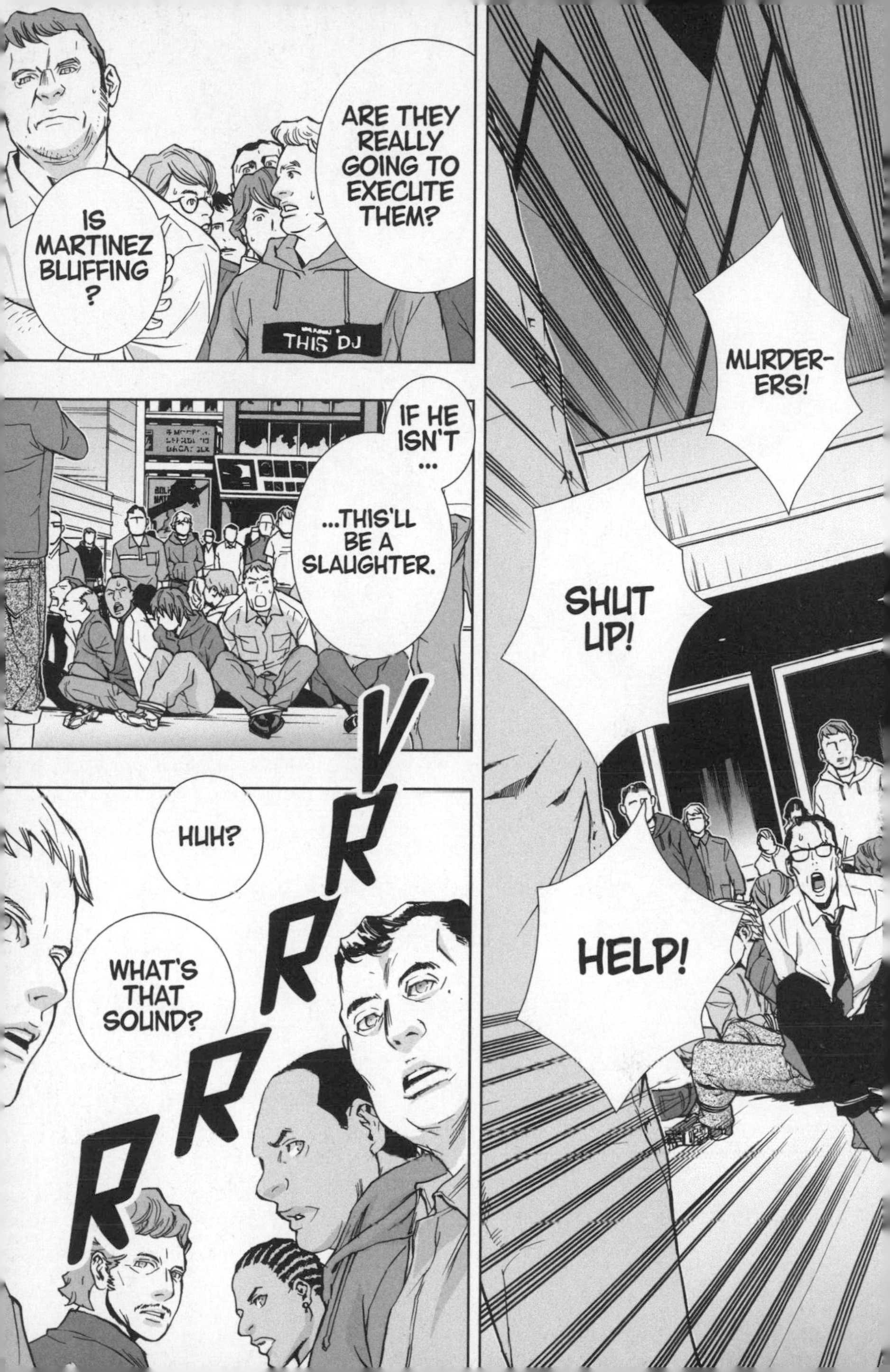
MURDERERS!
SHUT UP!
HELP!
ARE THEY REALLY GOING TO EXECUTE THEM?
IS MARTINEZ BLUFFING?
THIS DJ
IF HE ISN'T...
...THIS'LL BE A SLAUGHTER.
VRRRRR
HUH?
WHAT'S THAT SOUND?

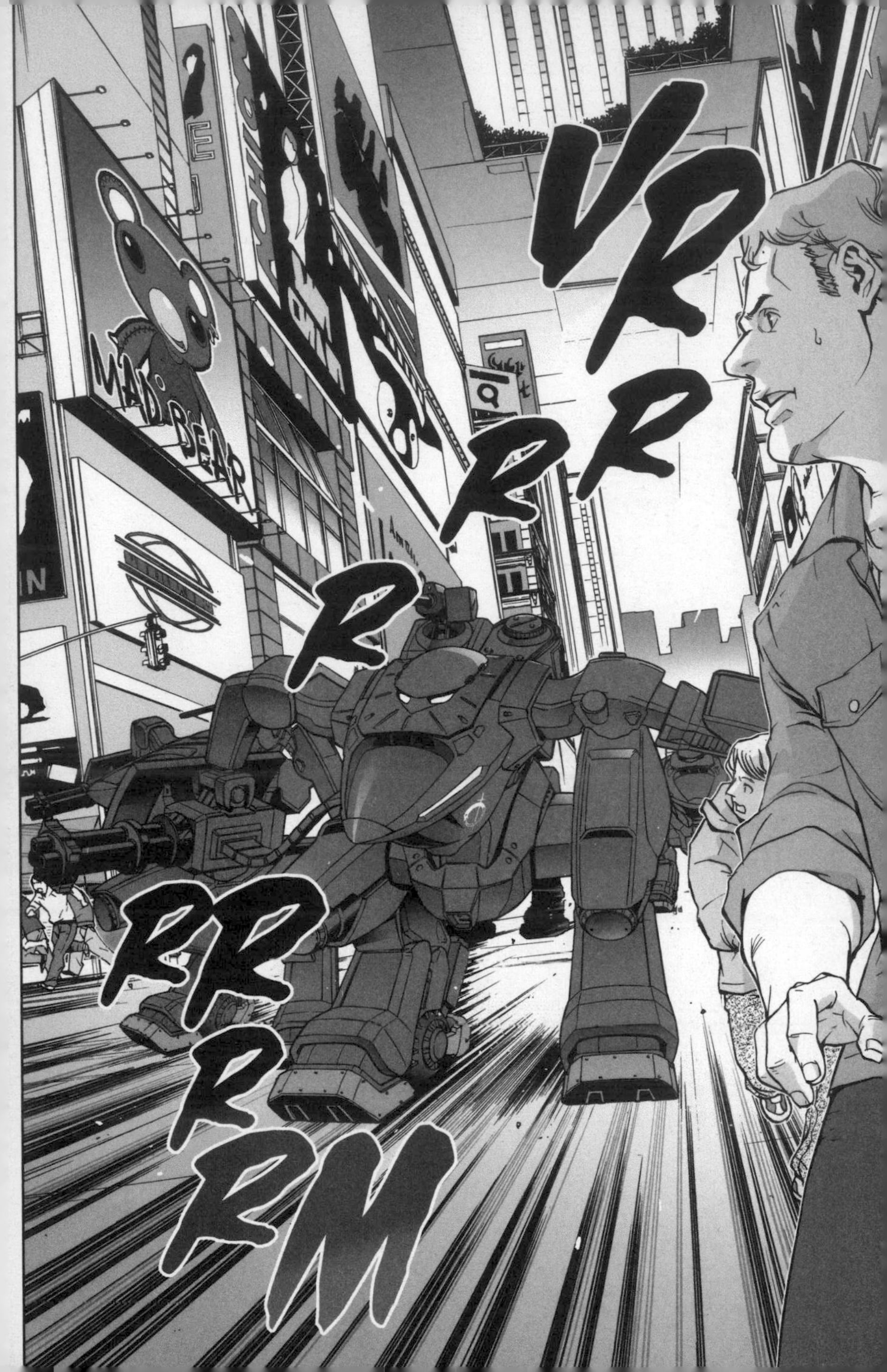
VRRRRRRRRM
MAD BEAR

TIGER&BUNNY
To Be Continued

Mizuki Sakakibara

Assistants
Ayako Mayuzumi
Beth
Eri Saito
Sachiko Ito
Fuku

MIZUKI SAKAKIBARA

Mizuki Sakakibara's American comics debut was Marvel's *Exile* in 2002. Currently, *TIGER & BUNNY* is serialized in *Newtype Ace* magazine by Kadokawa Shoten.

MASAFUMI NISHIDA

Story director. *TIGER & BUNNY* was his first work as a TV animation scriptwriter. He is well known for the movie *Gachi☆Boy* and the Japanese TV dramas *Maoh*, *Kaibutsu-kun*, and *Youkai Ningen Bem*.

MASAKAZU KATSURA

Original character designer. Masakazu Katsura is well known for the manga series *WING MAN*, *Denei Shojo* (*Video Girl Ai*), *I"s*, and *ZETMAN*. Katsura's works have been translated into several languages, including Chinese and French, as well as English.

TIGER&BUNNY 8

VIZ Media Edition

Art **MIZUKI SAKAKIBARA**
Planning / Original Story **SUNRISE**
Original Script **MASAFUMI NISHIDA**
Original Character and Hero Design **MASAKAZU KATSURA**

TIGER & BUNNY Volume 8
© Mizuki SAKAKIBARA 2014
© BNP/T&B PARTNERS, MBS
Edited by KADOKAWA SHOTEN
First published in Japan in 2014 by KADOKAWA CORPORATION, Tokyo.
English translation rights arranged with KADOKAWA CORPORATION, Tokyo.

Translation & English Adaptation **LABAAMEN & JOHN WERRY, HC LANGUAGE SOLUTIONS**
Touch-up Art & Lettering **STEPHEN DUTRO**
Design **FAWN LAU**
Editor **JENNIFER LEBLANC**

Printed in the U.S.A.

Published by VIZ Media, LLC
P.O. Box 77010
San Francisco, CA 94107

10 9 8 7 6 5 4 3 2 1
First printing, November 2015

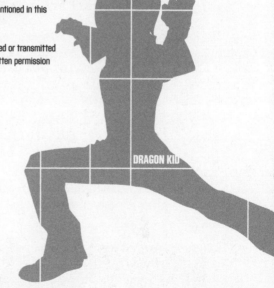

DRAGON KID

PARENTAL ADVISORY
TIGER & BUNNY is rated T for Teen and is recommended for ages 13 and up.
ratings.viz.com

www.viz.com

SEE INTO THE SOUL
OF *BLEACH*
WITH THE MANGA,
PROFILES AND ART BOOKS

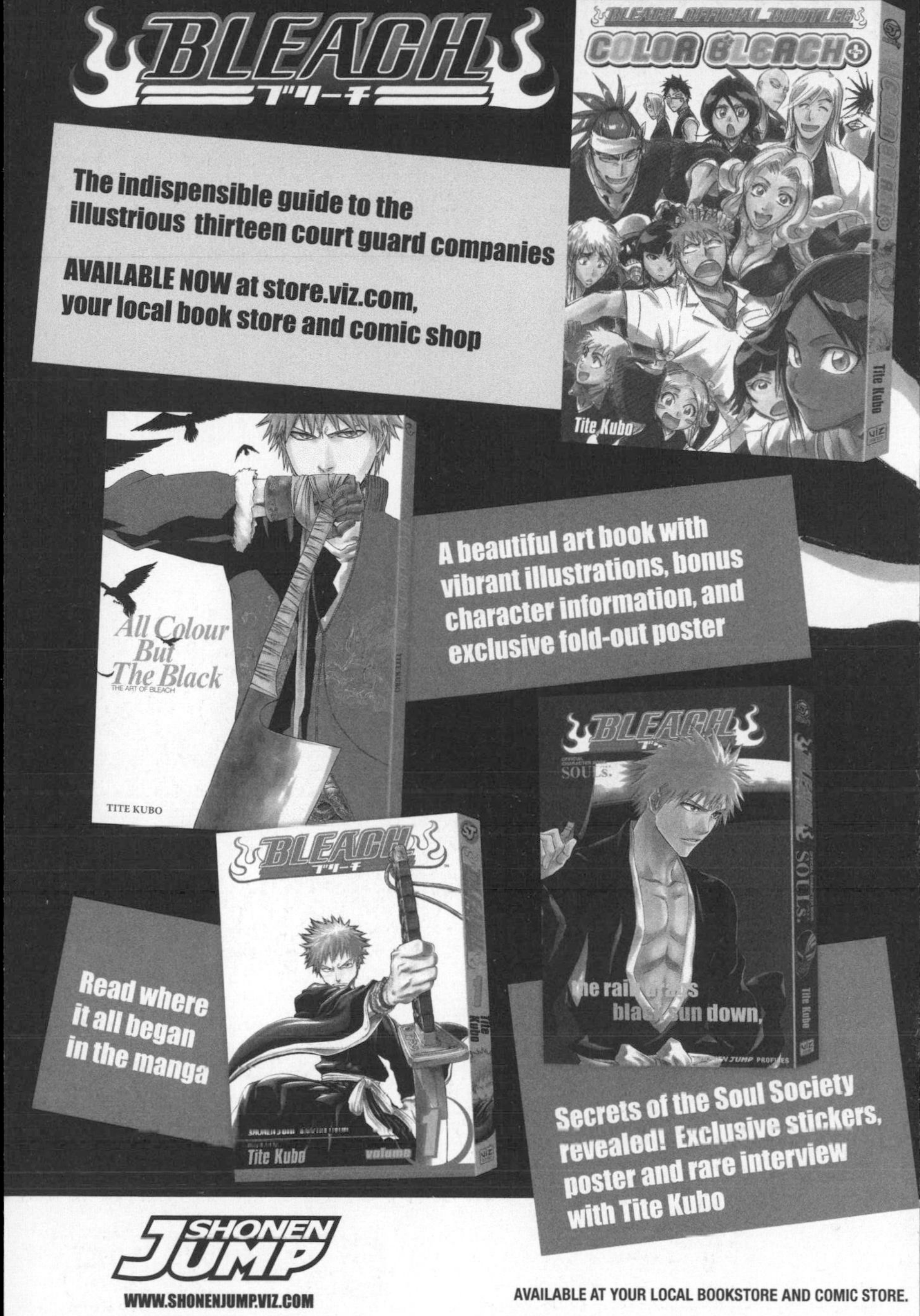
BLEACH
ブリーチ
BLEACH OFFICIAL BOOTLEG
COLOR BLEACH+
Tite Kubo
The indispensible guide to the illustrious thirteen court guard companies
AVAILABLE NOW at store.viz.com, your local book store and comic shop
All Colour But The Black
THE ART OF BLEACH
TITE KUBO
A beautiful art book with vibrant illustrations, bonus character information, and exclusive fold-out poster
BLEACH
SOULS.
Tite Kubo
BLEACH
ブリーチ
Tite Kubo
volume 1
Read where it all began in the manga
Secrets of the Soul Society revealed! Exclusive stickers, poster and rare interview with Tite Kubo
SHONEN JUMP
WWW.SHONENJUMP.VIZ.COM
AVAILABLE AT YOUR LOCAL BOOKSTORE AND COMIC STORE.

A PREMIUM BOX SET OF THE FIRST TWO STORY ARCS OF ONE PIECE!

A PIRATE'S TREASURE FOR ANY MANGA FAN!

STORY AND ART BY EIICHIRO ODA

Comes with
EXCLUSIVE
POSTER
and the
ROMANCE
DAWN
mini-comic!

As a child, Monkey D. Luffy dreamed of becoming King of the Pirates. But his life changed when he accidentally gained the power to stretch like rubber...at the cost of never being able to swim again! Years later, Luffy sets off in search of the "One Picce," said to be the greatest treasure in the world...

This box set includes VOLUMES 1-23, which comprise the EAST BLUE and BAROQUE WORKS story arcs.

EXCLUSIVE PREMIUMS and GREAT SAVINGS
over buying the individual volumes!

YOU'RE READING THE
WRONG WAY!

Tiger & Bunny reads from right to left, starting in the upper-right corner. Japanese is read from right to left, meaning that action, sound effects, and word-balloon order are completely reversed from English order.

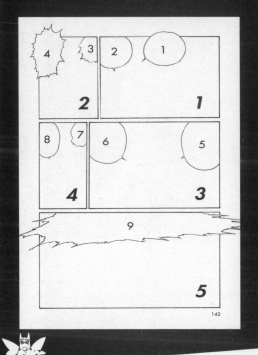